Essential Writings of
Friedrich Engels
Classics of Marxism and Socialism

Red and Black Publishers, St Petersburg, Florida

Library of Congress Cataloging-in-Publication Data

Engels, Friedrich, 1820-1895.
  [Selections. English. 2011]
  Essential writings of Friedrich Engels : classics of Marxism and socialism.
    p. cm.
  ISBN 978-1-61001-003-0
1. Socialism. 2. Communism. I. Title.
  HX39.E47 2011
  335.4--dc22

                                          2011000011

Red and Black Publishers, PO Box 7542, St Petersburg, Florida, 33734
Contact us at: info@RedandBlackPublishers.com
      Printed and manufactured in the United States of America

Contents

Socialism: Utopian and Scientific

General Introduction and the History of Materialism

The present little book is, originally, part of a larger whole. About 1875, Dr. E. Dühring, *privatdocent* (university lecturer who formerly received fees from his students rather than a wage) at Berlin University, suddenly and rather clamorously announced his conversion to Socialism, and presented the German public not only with an elaborate Socialist theory, but also with a complete practical plan for the reorganization of society. As a matter of course, he fell foul of his predecessors; above all, he honored Marx by pouring out upon him the full vials of his wrath.

This took place about the same time when the two sections of the Socialist party in Germany — Eisenachers and Lasselleans — had just effected their fusion (at the Gotha Unification Congress), and thus obtained not only an immense increase of strength, but, was what more, the faculty of employing the whole of this strength against the common enemy. The Socialist party in Germany was fast becoming a power. But, to make it a power, the first condition was that the newly-conquered unity should not be imperiled. And Dr. Dühring openly proceeded to form around himself a sect, the nucleus of a future separate party. It, thus, became necessary to take up the gauntlet thrown down to us, and to fight out the struggle, whether we liked it or not.

This, however, though it might not be an over-difficult, was evidently a long-winded business. As is well-known, we Germans are of a terribly ponderous *Grundlichkeit*, radical profundity or profound radicality, whatever you may like to call it. Whenever anyone of us expounds what he considers a new doctrine, he has first to elaborate it into an all-comprising system. He has to prove that both the first principles of logic and the fundamental laws of the universe had existed from all eternity for no other purpose than to ultimately lead to this newly-discovered, crowning theory. And Dr. Dühring, in this respect, was quite up to the national mark. Nothing less than a complete "System of Philosophy", mental, moral, natural, and historical; a complete "System of Political Economy and Socialism"; and, finally, a "Critical History of Political Economy" — three big volumes in octavo, heavy extrinsically and intrinsically, three army-corps of arguments mobilized against all previous philosophers and economists in general, and against Marx in particular — in fact, an attempt at a complete "revolution in science" — these were what I should have to tackle. I had to treat of all and every possible subject, from concepts of time and space to Bimetallism; from the eternity of matter and motion, to the perishable nature of moral ideas; from Darwin's natural selection to the education of youth in a future society. Anyhow, the systematic comprehensiveness of my opponent gave me the opportunity of developing, in opposition to him, and in a more connected form than had previously been done, the views held by Marx and myself on this great variety of subjects. And that was the principal reason which made me undertake this otherwise ungrateful task.

My reply was first published in a series of articles in the Leipzig *Vorwarts*, the chief organ of the Socialist party, and later on as a book: "*Herr Eugen Dührings Umwalzung der Wissenchaft*" (Mr. E. Dühring's "Revolution in Science"), a second edition of which appeared in Zurich, 1886.

At the request of my friend, Paul Lafargue, now representative of Lille in the French Chamber of Deputies, I arranged three chapters of this book as a pamphlet, which he translated and published in 1880, under the title: "*Socialisme utopique et Socialisme scientifique*". From this French text, a Polish and a Spanish edition were prepared. In 1883, our German friends brought out the pamphlet in the original language. Italian, Russian, Danish, Dutch, and Roumanian translations, based upon the German text, have since been published.

Thus, the present English edition, this little book circulates in 10 languages. I am not aware that any other Socialist work, not even our *Communist Manifesto* of 1848, or Marx's *Capital*, has been so often translated. In Germany, it has had four editions of about 20,000 copies in all.

The Appendix, "The Mark", was written with the intention of spreading among the German Socialist party some elementary knowledge of the history and development of landed property in Germany. This seemed all the more necessary at a time when the assimilation by that party of the working-people of the towns was in a fair way of completion, and when the agricultural laborers and peasant had to be taken in hand. This appendix has been included in the translation, as the original forms of tenure of land common to all Teutonic tribes, and the history of their decay, are even less known in England and in Germany. I have left the text as it stands in the original, without alluding to the hypothesis recently started by Maxim Kovalevsky, according to which the partition of the arable and meadow lands among the members of the Mark was preceded by their being cultivated for joint-account by a large patriarchal family community, embracing several generations (as exemplified by the still existing South Slavonian Zadruga), and that the partition, later on, took place when the community had increased, so as to become too unwieldy for joint-account management. Kovalevsky is probably quite right, but the matter is still *sub judice* (under consideration).

The economic terms used in this work, as afar as they are new, agree with those used in the English edition of Marx's *Capital*. We call "production of commodities" that economic phase where articles are produced not only for the use of the producers, but also for the purpose of exchange; that is, as commodities, not as use-values. This phase extends from the first beginnings of production for exchange down to our present time; it attains its full development under capitalist production only, that is, under conditions where the capitalist, the owner of the means of production, employs, for wages, laborers, people deprived of all means of production except their own labor-power, and pockets the excess of the selling price of the products over his outlay. We divide the history of industrial production since the Middle Ages into three periods:

-handicraft, small master craftsman with a few journeymen and apprentices, where each laborer produces a complete article;

-manufacture, where greater numbers of workmen, grouped in one large establishment, produce the complete article on the principle of division of labor, each workman performing only one partial operation, so that the product is complete only after having passed successively through the hands of all;

-modern industry, where the product is produced by machinery driven by power, and where the work of the laborer is limited to superintending and correcting the performance of the mechanical agent.

I am perfectly aware that the contents of this work will meet with objection from a considerable portion of the British public. But, if we Continentals had taken the slightest notice of the prejudices of British "respectability", we should be even worse off than we are. This book defends what we call "historical materialism", and the word *materialism* grates upon the ears of the immense majority of British readers. "Agnosticism" might be tolerated, but *materialism* is utterly inadmissible.

And, yet, the original home of all modern materialism, from the 17th century onwards, is England.

"Materialism is the natural-born son of Great Britain. Already the British schoolman, Duns Scotus, asked, 'whether it was impossible for the matter to think?'

"In order to effect this miracle, he took refuge in God's omnipotence — i.e., he made theology preach materialism. Moreover, he was a nominalist. Nominalism, the first form of materialism, is chiefly found among the English schoolmen.

"The real progenitor of English materialism is Bacon. To him, natural philosophy is the only true philosophy, and physics based upon the experience of the senses is the chiefest part of natural philosophy. Anaxagoras and his *homoiomeriae*, Democritus and his *atoms*, he often quotes as his authorities. According to him, the senses are infallible and the source of all knowledge. All science is based on experience, and consists in subjecting the data furnished by the senses to a rational method of investigation. Induction, analysis, comparison, observation, experiment, are the principal forms of such a rational method. Among the qualities inherent in matter, motion is the first and foremost, not only in the form of mechanical and mathematical motion, but chiefly in the form of an impulse, a vital spirit, a tension — or a 'qual', to use a term of Jakob Bohme's — of matter.

"In Bacon, its first creator, materialism still occludes within itself the germs of a many-sided development. On the one hand, matter, surrounded by a sensuous, poetic glamor, seems to attract man's whole entity by winning smiles. On the other, the aphoristically formulated doctrine pullulates with inconsistencies imported from theology.

"In its further evolution, materialism becomes one-sided. Hobbes is the man who systematizes Baconian materialism. Knowledge based upon the senses loses its poetic blossom, it passes into the abstract experience of the mathematician; geometry is proclaimed as the queen of sciences. Materialism takes to misanthropy. If it is to overcome its opponent, misanthropic, flashless spiritualism, and that on the latter's own ground, materialism has to chastise its own flesh and turn ascetic. Thus, from a sensual, it passes into an intellectual, entity; but thus, too, it evolves all the consistency, regardless of consequences, characteristic of the intellect.

"Hobbes, as Bacon's continuator, argues thus: if all human knowledge is furnished by the senses, then our concepts and ideas are but the phantoms, divested of their sensual forms, of the real world. Philosophy can but give names to these phantoms. One name may be applied to more than one of them. There may even be names of names. It would imply a contradiction if, on the one hand, we maintained that all ideas had their origin in the world of sensation, and, on the other, that a word was more than a word; that, besides the beings known to us by our senses, beings which are one and all individuals, there existed also beings of a general, not individual, nature. An unbodily substance is the same absurdity as an unbodily body. Body, being, substance, are but different terms for the same reality. It is impossible to separate thought from matter that thinks. This matter is the substratum of all changes going on in the world. The word infinite is meaningless, unless it states that our mind is capable of performing an endless process of addition. Only material things being perceptible to us, we cannot know anything about the existence of God. My own existence alone is certain. Every human passion is a mechanical movement, which has a beginning and an end. The objects of impulse are what we call good. Man is subject to the same laws as nature. Power and freedom are identical.

"Hobbes had systematized Bacon, without, however, furnishing a proof for Bacon's fundamental principle, the origin of all human knowledge from the world of sensation. It was Locke who, in his Essay on the Human Understanding, supplied this proof.

"Hobbes had shattered the theistic prejudices of Baconian materialism; Collins, Dodwell, Coward, Hartley, Priestley, similarly shattered the last theological bars that still hemmed in Locke's sensationalism. At all events, for practical materialists, Deism is but an easy-going way of getting rid of religion."

-Karl Marx
The Holy Family

Thus Karl Marx wrote about the British origin of modern materialism. If Englishmen nowadays do not exactly relish the compliment he paid their ancestors, more's the pity. It is none the less undeniable that Bacon, Hobbes, and Locke are the fathers of that brilliant school of French materialism which made the 18th century, in spite of all battles on land and sea won over Frenchmen by Germans and Englishmen, a pre-eminently French century, even before that crowning French Revolution, the results of which we outsiders, in England as well as Germany, are still trying to acclimatize.

There is no denying it. About the middle of this century, what struck every cultivated foreigner who set up his residence in England, was what he was then bound to consider the religious bigotry and stupidity of the English respectable middle-class. We, at that time, were all materialists, or, at least, very advanced free-thinkers, and to us it appeared inconceivable that almost all educated people in England should believe in all sorts of impossible miracles, and that even geologists like Buckland and Mantell should contort the facts of their science so as not to clash too much with the myths of the book of Genesis; while, in order to find people who dared to use their own intellectual faculties with regard to religious matters, you had to go amongst the uneducated, the "great unwashed", as they were then called, the working people, especially the Owenite Socialists.

But England has been "civilized" since then. The exhibition of 1851 sounded the knell of English insular exclusiveness. England became gradually internationalized, in diet, in manners, in ideas; so much so that I begin to wish that some English manners and customs had made as much headway on the Continent as other Continental habits have made here. Anyhow, the introduction and spread of salad-oil (before 1851 known only to the aristocracy) has been accompanied by a fatal spread of Continental scepticism in matters religious, and it has come to this, that agnosticism, though not yet considered "the thing" quite as much as the Church of England, is yet very nearly on a par, as far as respectability goes, with Baptism, and decidedly ranks above the Salvation Army. And I cannot help believing that under those circumstances it will be consoling to many who sincerely regret and condemn this progress of infidelity to learn that these "new-fangled notions" are not of foreign origin, are not "made in Germany", like so many other articles of daily use, but are undoubtedly Old English, and that their British originators 200 years ago went a good deal further than their descendants now dare to venture.

What, indeed, is agnosticism but, to use an expressive Lancashire term, "shamefaced" materialism? The agnostic's conception of Nature is materialistic throughout. The entire natural world is governed by law, and absolutely excludes the intervention of action from without. But, he adds, we have no means either of ascertaining or of disproving the existence of some Supreme Being beyond the known universe. Now, this might hold good at the time when Laplace, to Napoleon's question, why, in the great astronomer's *Treatise on Celestial Mechanics*, the Creator was not even mentioned, proudly replied, "I had no need of this hypothesis." But, nowadays, in our evolutionary conception of the universe, there is absolutely no room for either a Creator or a Ruler; and to talk of a Supreme Being shut out from the whole existing world, implies a contradiction in terms, and, as it seems to me, a gratuitous insult to the feelings of religious people.

Again, our agnostic admits that all our knowledge is based upon the information imparted to us by our senses. But, he adds, how do we know that our senses give us correct representations of the objects we perceive through them? And he proceeds to inform us that, whenever we speak of objects, or their qualities, of which he cannot know anything for certain, but merely the impressions which they have produced on his senses. Now, this line of reasoning seems undoubtedly hard to beat by mere argumentation. But before there was argumentation, there was action. *Im Anfang war die That* ("In the beginning was the deed"). And human action had solved the difficulty long before human ingenuity invented it. The proof of the pudding is in the eating. From the moment we turn to our own use these objects, according to the qualities we perceive in them, we put to an infallible test the correctness or otherwise of our sense-perception. If these perceptions have been wrong, then our estimate of the use to which an object can be turned must also be wrong, and our attempt must fail. But, if we succeed in accomplishing our aim, if we find that the object does agree with our idea of it, and does answer the purpose we intended it for, then that is proof positive that our perceptions of it and of its qualities, so far, agree with reality outside ourselves. And, whenever we find ourselves face-to-face with a failure, then we generally are not long in making out the cause that made us fail; we find that the perception upon which we acted was either incomplete and superficial, or combined with the results of other perceptions in a way not warranted by them — what we call defective reasoning. So long as we take care to train our senses properly, and to keep our action within the limits prescribed by perceptions properly made and properly used, so long as we shall find that the result of our action proves the conformity of our perceptions with the objective nature of the things perceived. Not in one single instance, so far, have we been led to the conclusion that our sense-perception, scientifically controlled, induce in our minds ideas respecting the outer world that are, by their very nature, at variance with reality, or that there is an inherent incompatibility between the outer world and our sense-perceptions of it.

But then come the Neo-Kantian agnostics and say: We may correctly perceive the qualities of a thing, but we cannot by any sensible or mental process grasp the thing-in-itself. This "thing-in-itself" is beyond our ken. To this Hegel, long since, has replied: If you know all the qualities of a thing, you know the thing itself; nothing remains but the fact that the said thing exists without us; and, when your senses have taught you that fact, you have grasped the last remnant of the thing-in-itself, Kant's celebrated unknowable *Ding an sich*. To which it may be added that in Kant's time our knowledge of natural objects was indeed so fragmentary that he might well suspect, behind the little we knew about each of them, a mysterious "thing-in-itself". But one after another these ungraspable things have been grasped, analyzed, and, what is more, reproduced by the giant progress of science; and what we can produce we certainly cannot consider as unknowable. To the chemistry of the first half of this century, organic substances were such mysterious objects; now we learn to build them up one after another from their chemical elements without the aid of organic processes. Modern chemists declare that as soon as the chemical constitution of no-matter-what body is known, it can be built up from its elements. We are still far from knowing the constitution of the highest organic substances, the albuminous bodies; but there is no reason why we should not, if only after centuries, arrive at the knowledge and, armed with it, produce artificial albumen. But, if we arrive at that, we shall at the same time have produced organic life, for life, from its lowest to its highest forms, is but the normal mode of existence of albuminous bodies.

As soon, however, as our agnostic has made these formal mental reservations, he talks and acts as the rank materialist he at bottom is. He may say that, as far as we know, matter and motion, or as it is now called, energy, can neither be created nor destroyed, but that we have no proof of their not having been created at some time or other. But if you try to use this admission against him in any particular case, he will quickly put you out of court. If he admits the possibility of spiritualism *in abstracto*, he will have none of it *in concreto*. As far as we know and can know, he will tell you there is no creator and no Ruler of the universe; as far as we are concerned, matter and energy can neither be created nor annihilated; for us, mind is a mode of energy, a function of the brain; all we know is that the material world is governed by immutable laws, and so forth. Thus, as far as he is a scientific man, as far as he knows anything, he is a materialist; outside his science, in spheres about which he knows nothing, he translates his ignorance into Greek and calls it agnosticism.

At all events, one thing seems clear: even if I was an agnostic, it is evident that I could not describe the conception of history sketched out in this little book as "historical agnosticism". Religious people would laugh at me, agnostics would indignantly ask, was I making fun of them? And, thus, I hope even British respectability will not be overshocked if I use, in English as well as in so many other languages, the term "historical materialism", to designate that view of the course of history which seeks the ultimate cause and the great moving power of all important historic events in the economic development of society, in the changes in the modes of production and exchange, in the consequent division of society into distinct classes, and in the struggles of these classes against one another.

This indulgence will, perhaps, be accorded to me all the sooner if I show that historical materialism may be of advantage even to British respectability. I have mentioned the fact that, about 40 or 50 years ago, any cultivated foreigner settling in England was struck by what he was then bound to consider the religious bigotry and stupidity of the English respectable middle-class. I am now going to prove that the respectable English middle-class of that time was not quite as stupid as it looked to the intelligent foreigner. Its religious leanings can be explained.

1892 English Edition Introduction
(History (the role of Religion) in the English middle-class)
When Europe emerged from the Middle Ages, the rising middle-class of the towns constituted its revolutionary element. It had conquered a recognized position within mediaeval feudal organization, but this position, also, had become too narrow for its expansive power. The development of the middle-class, the bourgeoisie, became incompatible with the maintenance of the feudal system; the feudal system, therefore, had to fall.

But the great international centre of feudalism was the Roman Catholic Church. It united the whole of feudalized Western Europe, in spite of all internal wars, into one grand political system, opposed as much to the schismatic Greeks as to the Mohammedan countries. It had organized its own hierarchy on the feudal model, and, lastly, it was itself by far the most powerful feudal lord, holding, as it did, fully 1/3rd of the soil of the Catholic world. Before profane feudalism could be successfully attacked in each country and in detail, this, its sacred central organization, had to be destroyed.

Moreover, parallel with the rise of the middle-class went on the great revival of science; astronomy, mechanics, physics, anatomy, physiology were again cultivated. And the bourgeoisie, for the development of its industrial production, required a science which ascertained the physical properties of natural objects and the modes of action of the forces of Nature. Now up to then science had but been the humble handmaid of the Church, had not been allowed to overlap the limits set by faith, and for that reason had been no science at all. Science rebelled against the Church; the bourgeoisie could not do without science, and, therefore, had to join in the rebellion.

The above, though touching but two of the points where the rising middle-class was bound to come into collision with the established religion, will be sufficient to show, first, that the class most directly interested in the struggle against the pretensions of the Roman Church was the bourgeoisie; and second, that every struggle against feudalism, at that time, had to take on a religious disguise, had to be directed against the Church in the first instance. But if the universities and the traders of the cities started the cry, it was sure to find, and did find, a strong echo in the masses of the country people, the peasants, who everywhere had to struggle for their very existence with their feudal lords, spiritual and temporal.

The long fight of the bourgeoisie against feudalism culminated in three great, decisive battles.

The first was what is called the Protestant Reformation in Germany. The war cry raised against the Church, by Luther, was responded to by two insurrections of a political nature; first, that of the lower nobility under Franz von Sickingen (1523), then the great Peasants' War, 1525. Both were defeated, chiefly in consequence of the indecision of the parties most interested, the burghers of the towns – an indecision into the causes of which we cannot here enter. From that moment, the struggle degenerated into a fight between the local princes and the central power, and ended by blotting out Germany, for 200 years, from the politically active nations of Europe. The Lutheran Reformation produced a new creed indeed, a religion adapted to absolute monarchy. No sooner were the peasant of Northeast Germany converted to Lutheranism than they were from freemen reduced to serfs.

But where Luther failed, Calvin won the day. Calvin's creed was one fit for the boldest of the bourgeoisie of his time. His predestination doctrine was the religious expression of the fact that in the commercial world of competition success or failure does not depend upon a man's activity or cleverness, but upon circumstances uncontrollable by him. It is not of him that willeth or of him that runneth, but of the mercy of unknown superior economic powers; and this was especially true at a period of economic revolution, when all old commercial routes and centres were replaced by new ones, when India and America were opened to the world, and when even the most sacred economic articles of faith – the value of gold and silver – began to totter and to break down. Calvin's church constitution of God was republicanized, could the kingdoms of this world remains subject to monarchs, bishops, and lords? While German Lutheranism became a willing tool in the hands of princes, Calvinism founded a republic in Holland, and active republican parties in England, and, above all, Scotland.

In Calvinism, the second great bourgeois upheaval found its doctrine ready cut and dried. This upheaval took place in England. The middle-class of the towns brought it on, and the yeomanry of the country districts fought it out. Curiously enough, in all the three great bourgeois risings, the peasantry furnishes the army that has to do the fighting; and the peasantry is just the class that, the victory once gained, is most surely ruined by the economic consequences of that victory. A hundred years after Cromwell, the yeomanry of England had almost disappeared. Anyhow, had it not been for that yeomanry and for the plebian element in the towns, the bourgeoisie alone would never have fought the matter out to the bitter end, and would never have brought Charles I to the scaffold. In order to secure even those conquests of the bourgeoisie that were ripe for gathering at the time, the revolution had to be carried considerably further – exactly as in 1793 in France and 1848 in Germany. This seems, in fact, to be one of the laws of evolution of bourgeois society.

Well, upon this excess of revolutionary activity there necessarily followed the inevitable reaction which, in its turn, went beyond the point where it might have maintained itself. After a series of oscillations, the new centre of gravity was at last attained and became a new starting-point. The grand period of English history, known to respectability under the name of "the Great Rebellion", and the struggles succeeding it, were brought to a close by the comparatively puny events entitled by Liberal historians "the Glorious Revolution".

The new starting-point was a compromise between the rising middle-class and the ex-feudal landowners. The latter, though called, as now, the aristocracy, had been long since on the way which led them to become what Louis Philippe in France became at a much later period: "The first bourgeois of the kingdom". Fortunately for England, the old feudal barons had killed one another during the War of the Roses. Their successors, though mostly scions of the old families, had been so much out of the direct line of descent that they constituted quite a new body, with habits and tendencies far more bourgeois than feudal. They fully understood the value of money, and at once began to increase their rents by turning hundreds of small farmers out and replacing them with sheep. Henry VIII, while squandering the Church lands, created fresh bourgeois landlords by wholesale; the innumerable confiscation of estates, regranted to absolute or relative upstarts, and continued during the whole of the 17th century, had the same result. Consequently, ever since Henry VII, the English "aristocracy", far from counteracting the development of industrial production, had, on the contrary, sought to indirectly profit thereby; and there had always been a section of the great landowners willing, from economical or political reasons, to cooperate with the leading men of the financial and industrial bourgeoisie. The compromise of 1689 was, therefore, easily accomplished. The political spoils of "pelf and place" were left to the great landowning families, provided the economic interests of the financial, manufacturing, and commercial middle-class were sufficiently attended to. And these economic interests were at that time powerful enough to determine the general policy of the nation. There might be squabbles about matters of detail, but, on the whole, the aristocratic oligarchy knew too well that its own economic prosperity was irretrievably bound up with that of the industrial and commercial middle-class.

From that time, the bourgeoisie was a humble, but still a recognized, component of the ruling classes of England. With the rest of them, it had a common interest in keeping in subjection the great working mass of the nation. The merchant or manufacturer himself stood in the position of master, or, as it was until lately called, of "natural superior" to his clerks, his work-people, his domestic servants. His interest was to get as much and as good work out of them as he could; for this end, they had to be trained to proper submission. He was himself religious; his religion had supplied the standard under which he had fought the king and the lords; he was not long in discovering the opportunities this same religion offered him for working upon the minds of his natural inferiors, and making them submissive to the behests of the masters it had pleased God to place over them. In short, the English bourgeoisie now had to take a part in keeping down the "lower orders", the great producing mass of the nation, and one of the means employed for that purpose was the influence of religion.

There was another factor that contributed to strengthen the religious leanings of the bourgeoisie. That was the rise of materialism in England. This new doctrine not only shocked the pious feelings of the middle-class; it announced itself as a philosophy only fit for scholars and cultivated men of the world, in contrast to religion, which was good enough for the uneducated masses, including the bourgeoisie. With Hobbes, it stepped on the stage as a defender of royal prerogative and omnipotence; it called upon absolute monarchy to keep down that *puer robustus sed malitiosus* ("Robust but malicious boy") – to wit, the people. Similarly, with the successors of Hobbes, with Bolingbroke, Shaftesbury, etc., the new deistic form of materialism remained an aristocratic, esoteric doctrine, and, therefore, hateful to the middle-class both for its religious heresy and for its anti-bourgeois political connections. Accordingly, in opposition to the materialism and deism of the aristocracy, those Protestant sects which had furnished the flag and the fighting contingent against the Stuarts continued to furnish the main strength of the progressive middle-class, and form even today the backbone of "the Great Liberal Party".

In the meantime, materialism passed from England to France, where it met and coalesced with another materialistic school of philosophers, a branch of Cartesianism. In France, too, it remained at first an exclusively aristocratic doctrine. But, soon, its revolutionary character asserted itself. The French materialists did not limit their criticism to matters of religious belief; they extended it to whatever scientific tradition or political institution they met with; and to prove the claim of their doctrine to universal application, they took the shortest cut, and boldly applied it to all subjects of knowledge in the giant work after which they were named – the Encyclopaedia. Thus, in one or the other of its two forms – avowed materialism or deism – it became the creed of the whole cultured youth of France; so much so that, when the Great Revolution broke out, the doctrine hatched by English Royalists gave a theoretical flag to French Republicans and Terrorists, and furnished the text for the Declaration of the Rights of Man. The Great French Revolution was the third uprising of the bourgeoisie, but the first that had entirely cast off the religious cloak, and was fought out on undisguised political lines; it was the first, too, that was really fought out up to the destruction of one of the combatants, the aristocracy, and the complete triumph of the other, the bourgeoisie. In England, the continuity of pre-revolutionary and post-revolutionary institutions, and the compromise between landlords and capitalists, found its expression in the continuity of judicial precedents and in the religious preservation of the feudal forms of the law. In France, the Revolution constituted a complete breach with the traditions of the past; it cleared out the very last vestiges of feudalism, and created in the Code Civil a masterly adaptation of the old Roman law – that almost perfect expression of the juridical relations corresponding to the economic stage called by Marx the production of commodities – to modern capitalist conditions; so masterly that this French revolutionary code still serves as a model for reforms of the law of property in all other countries, not excepting England. Let us, however, not forget that if English law continues to express the economic relations of capitalist society in that barbarous feudal language which corresponds to the thing expressed, just as English spelling corresponds to English pronunciation – *vous ecrivez Londres et vous prononcez Constantinople*, said a Frenchman – that same English law is the only one which has preserved through ages, and transmitted to America and the Colonies, the best part of that old Germanic personal freedom, local self-government, and independence from all interference (but that of the law courts), which on the Continent has been lost during the period of absolute monarchy, and has nowhere been as yet fully recovered.

To return to our British bourgeois. The French Revolution gave him a splendid opportunity, with the help of the Continental monarchies, to destroy French maritime commerce, to annex French colonies, and to crush the last French pretensions to maritime rivalry. That was one reason why he fought it. Another was that the ways of this revolution went very much against his grain. Not only its "execrable" terrorism, but the very attempt to carry bourgeois rule to extremes. What should the British bourgeois do without his aristocracy, that taught him manners, such as they were, and invented fashions for him – that furnished officers for the army, which kept order at home, and the navy, which conquered colonial possessions and new markets aboard? There was, indeed, a progressive minority of the bourgeoisie, that minority whose interests were not so well attended to under the compromise; this section, composed chiefly of the less wealthy middle-class, did sympathize with the Revolution, but it was powerless in Parliament.

Thus, if materialism became the creed of the French Revolution, the God-fearing English bourgeois held all the faster to his religion. Had not the reign of terror in Paris proved what was the upshot, if the religious instincts of the masses were lost? The more materialism spread from France to neighboring countries, and was reinforced by similar doctrinal currents, notably by German philosophy, the more, in fact, materialism and free thought generally became, on the Continent, the necessary qualifications of a cultivated man, the more stubbornly the English middle-class stuck to its manifold religious creeds. These creeds might differ from one another, but they were, all of them, distinctly religious, Christian creeds.

While the Revolution ensured the political triumph of the bourgeoisie in France, in England Watt, Arkwright, Cartwright, and others, initiated an industrial revolution, which completely shifted the centre of gravity of economic power. The wealth of the bourgeoisie increased considerably faster than that of the landed aristocracy. Within the bourgeoisie itself, the financial aristocracy, the bankers, etc., were more and more pushed into the background by the manufacturers. The compromise of 1689, even after the gradual changes it had undergone in favor of the bourgeoisie, no longer corresponded to the relative position of the parties to it. The character of these parties, too, had changed; the bourgeoisie of 1830 was very different from that of the preceding century. The political power still left to the aristocracy, and used by them to resist the pretensions of the new industrial bourgeoisie, became incompatible with the new economic interests. A fresh struggle with the aristocracy was necessary; it could end only in a victory of the new economic power. First, the Reform Act was pushed through, in spite of all resistance, under the impulse of the French Revolution of 1830. It gave to the bourgeoisie a recognized and powerful place in Parliament. Then the Repeal of the Corn Laws (a move toward free-trade), which settled, once and for all, the supremacy of the bourgeoisie, and especially of its most active portion, the manufacturers, over the landed aristocracy. This was the greatest victory of the bourgeoisie; it was, however, also the last it gained in its own exclusive interest. Whatever triumphs it obtained later on, it had to share with a new social power – first its ally, but soon its rival.

The industrial revolution had created a class of large manufacturing capitalists, but also a class – and a far more numerous one – of manufacturing work-people. This class gradually increased in numbers, in proportion as the industrial revolution seized upon one branch of manufacture after another, and in the same proportion it increased its power. This power it proved as early as 1824, by forcing a reluctant Parliament to repeal the acts forbidding combinations of workmen. During the Reform agitation, the workingmen constituted the Radical wing of the Reform party; the Act of 1832 having excluded them from the suffrage, the formulated their demands in the People's Charter, and constituted themselves, in opposition to the great bourgeois Anti-Corn Law party, into an independent party, the Chartists, the first working-men's party of modern times.

Then came the Continental revolutions of February and March 1848, in which the working people played such a prominent part, and, at least in Paris, put forward demands which were certainly inadmissible from the point of view of capitalist society. And then came the general reaction. First, the defeat of the Chartists on April 10, 1848; then the crushing of the Paris workingmen's insurrection in June of the same year; then the disasters of 1849 in Italy, Hungary, South Germany, and at last the victory of Louis Bonaparte over Paris, December 2, 1851. For a time, at least, the bugbear of working-class pretensions was put down, but at what cost! If the British bourgeois had been convinced before of the necessity of maintaining the common people in a religious mood, how much more must he feel that necessity after all these experiences? Regardless of the sneers of his Continental compeers, he continued to spend thousands and tens of thousands, year after year, upon the evangelization of the lower orders; not content with his own native religious machinery, he appealed to Brother Jonathan, the greatest organizer in existence of religion as a trade, and imported from America revivalism, Moody and Sankey, and the like; and, finally, he accepted the dangerous aid of the Salvation Army, which revives the propaganda of early Christianity, appeals to the poor as the elect, fights capitalism in a religious way, and thus fosters an element of early Christian class antagonism, which one day may become troublesome to the well-to-do people who now find the ready money for it.

It seems a law of historical development that the bourgeoisie can in no European country get hold of political power – at least for any length of time – in the same exclusive way in which the feudal aristocracy kept hold of it during the Middle Ages. Even in France, where feudalism was completely extinguished, the bourgeoisie as a whole has held full possession of the Government for very short periods only. During Louis Philippe's reign, 1830-48, a very small portion of the bourgeoisie ruled the kingdom; by far the larger part were excluded from the suffrage by the high qualification. Under the Second Republic, 1848-51, the whole bourgeoisie ruled but for three years only; their incapacity brought on the Second Empire. It is only now, in the Third Republic, that the bourgeoisie as a whole have kept possession of the helm for more than 20 years; and they are already showing lively signs of decadence. A durable reign of the bourgeoisie has been possible only in countries like America, where feudalism was unknown, and society at the very beginning started from a bourgeois basis. And even in France and America, the successors of the bourgeoisie, the working people, are already knocking at the door.

In England, the bourgeoisie never held undivided sway. Even the victory of 1832 left the landed aristocracy in almost exclusive possession of all the leading Government offices. The meekness with which the middle-class submitted to this remained inconceivable to me until the great Liberal manufacturer, Mr. W. A. Forster, in a public speech, implored the young men of Bradford to learn French, as a means to get on in the world, and quoted from his own experience how sheepish he looked when, as a Cabinet Minister, he had to move in society where French was, at least, as necessary as English! The fact was, the English middle-class of that time were, as a rule, quite uneducated upstarts, and could not help leaving to the aristocracy those superior Government places where other qualifications were required than mere insular narrowness and insular conceit, seasoned by business sharpness. Even now the endless newspaper debates about middle-class education show that the English middle-class does not yet consider itself good enough for the best education, and looks to something more modest. Thus, even after the repeal of the Corn Laws, it appeared a matter of course that the men who had carried the day – the Cobdens, Brights, Forsters, etc. – should remain excluded from a share in the official government of the country, until 20 years afterwards a new Reform Act opened to them the door of the Cabinet. The English bourgeoisie are, up to the present day, so deeply penetrated by a sense of their social inferiority that they keep up, at their own expense and that of the nation, an ornamental caste of drones to represent the nation worthily at all State functions; and they consider themselves highly honored whenever one of themselves is found worthy of admission into this select and privileged body, manufactured, after all, by themselves.

The industrial and commercial middle-class had, therefore, not yet succeeded in driving the landed aristocracy completely from political power when another competitor, the working-class, appeared on the stage. The reaction after the Chartist movement and the Continental revolutions, as well as the unparalleled extension of English trade from 1848-66 (ascribed vulgarly to Free Trade alone, but due far more to the colossal development of railways, ocean steamers, and means of intercourse generally), had again driven the working-class into the dependency of the Liberal party, of which they formed, as in pre-Chartist times, the Radical wing. Their claims to the franchise, however, gradually became irresistible; while the Whig leaders of the Liberals "funked", Disraeli showed his superiority by making the Tories seize the favorable moment and introduce household suffrage in the boroughs, along with a redistribution of seats. Then followed the ballot; then, in 1884, the extension of household suffrage to the counties and a fresh redistribution of seats, by which electoral districts were, to some extent, equalized. All these measures considerably increased the electoral power of the working-class, so much so that in at least 150 to 200 constituencies that class now furnished the majority of the voters. But parliamentary government is a capital school for teaching respect for tradition; if the middle-class look with awe and veneration upon what Lord John Manners playfully called "our old nobility", the mass of the working-people then looked up with respect and deference to what used to be designated as "their betters", the middle-class. Indeed, the British workman, some 15 years ago, was the model workman, whose respectful regard for the position of his master, and whose self-restraining modesty in claiming rights for himself, consoled our German economists of the Katheder-Socialist school for the incurable communistic and revolutionary tendencies of their own working-men at home.

But the English middle-class – good men of business as they are – saw farther than the German professors. They had shared their powers but reluctantly with the working-class. They had learnt, during the Chartist years, what that *puer robustus sed malitiosus*, the people, is capable of. And since that time, they had been compelled to incorporate the better part of the People's Charter in the Statutes of the United Kingdom. Now, if ever, the people must be kept in order by moral means, and the first and foremost of all moral means of action upon the masses is and remains – religion. Hence the parsons' majorities on the School Boards, hence the increasing self-taxation of the bourgeoisie for the support of all sorts of revivalism, from ritualism to the Salvation Army.

And now came the triumph of British respectability over the free thought and religious laxity of the Continental bourgeois. The workmen of France and Germany had become rebellious. They were thoroughly infected with Socialism, and, for very good reasons, were not at all particular as to the legality of the means by which to secure their own ascendancy. The *puer robustus*, here, turned from day-to-day more *malitiosus*. Nothing remained to the French and German bourgeoisie as a last resource but to silently drop their free thought, as a youngster, when sea-sickness creeps upon him, quietly drops the burning cigar he brought swaggeringly on board; one-by-one, the scoffers turned pious in outward behavior, spoke with respect of the

Church, its dogmas and rites, and even conformed with the latter as far as could not be helped. French bourgeois dined *maigre* on Fridays, and German ones say out long Protestant sermons in their pews on Sundays. They had come to grief with materialism. *"Die Religion muss dem Volk erhalten werden"* – religion must be kept alive for the people – that was the only and the last means to save society from utter ruin. Unfortunately for themselves, they did not find this out until they had done their level best to break up religion forever. And now it was the turn of the British bourgeoisie to sneer and to say: "Why, you fools, I could have told you that 200 years ago!"

However, I am afraid neither the religious stolidity of the British, nor the *post festum* conversion of the Continental bourgeois will stem the rising Proletarian tide. Tradition is a great retarding force, is the *vis inertiae* of history, but, being merely passive, is sure to be broken down; and thus religion will be no lasting safeguard to capitalist society. If our juridical, philosophical, and religious ideas are the more or less remote offshoots of the economical relations prevailing in a given society, such ideas cannot, in the long run, withstand the effects of a complete change in these relations. And, unless we believe in supernatural revelation, we must admit that no religious tenets will ever suffice to prop up a tottering society.

In fact, in England too, the working-people have begun to move again. They are, no doubt, shackled by traditions of various kinds. Bourgeois traditions, such as the widespread belief that there can be but two parties, Conservatives and Liberals, and that the working-class must work out its salvation by and through the great Liberal Party. Working-men's traditions, inherited from their first tentative efforts at independent action, such as the exclusion, from ever so many old Trade Unions, of all applicants who have not gone through a regular apprenticeship; which means the breeding, by every such union, of its own blacklegs. But, for all that, the English working-class is moving, as even Professor Brentano has sorrowfully had to report to his brother Katheder-Socialists. It moves, like all things in England, with a slow and measured step, with hesitation here, with more or less unfruitful, tentative attempts there; it moves now and then with an over-cautious mistrust of the name of Socialism, while it gradually absorbs the substance; and the movement spreads and seizes one layer of the workers after another. It has now shaken out of their torpor the unskilled laborers of the East End of London, and we all know what a splendid impulse these fresh forces have given it in return. And if the pace of the movement is not up to the impatience of some people, let them not forget that it is the working-class which keeps alive the finest qualities of the English character, and that, if a step in advance is once gained in England, it is, as a rule, never lost afterwards. If the sons of the old Chartists, for reasons unexplained above, were not quite up to the mark, the grandsons bid fair to be worthy of their forefathers.

But the triumph of the European working-class does not depend upon England alone. It can only be secured by the cooperation of, at least, England, France, and Germany. In both the latter countries, the working-class movement is well ahead of England. In Germany, it is even within measurable distance of success. The progress it has there made during the last 25 years is unparalleled. It advances with ever-increasing velocity. If the German middle-class have shown themselves lamentably deficient in political capacity, discipline, courage, energy, and perseverance, the German working-class have given ample proof of all these qualities. Four hundred years ago, Germany was the starting-point of the first upheaval of the European middle-class; as things are now, is it outside the limits of possibility that Germany will be the scene, too, of the first great victory of the European proletariat?

Frederick Engels
London
April 20, 1892

I The Development of Utopian Socialism

Modern Socialism is, in its essence, the direct product of the recognition, on the one hand, of the class antagonisms existing in the society of today between proprietors and non-proprietors, between capitalists and wage-workers; on the other hand, of the anarchy existing in production. But, in its theoretical form, modern Socialism originally appears ostensibly as a more logical extension of the principles laid down by the great French philosophers of the 18th century. Like every new theory, modern Socialism had, at first, to connect itself with the intellectual stock-in-trade ready to its hand, however deeply its roots lay in material economic facts.

The great men, who in France prepared men's minds for the coming revolution, were themselves extreme revolutionists. They recognized no external authority of any kind whatever. Religion, natural science, society, political institutions – everything was subjected to the most unsparing criticism: everything must justify its existence before the judgment-seat of reason or give up existence. Reason became the sole measure of everything. It was the time when, as Hegel says, the world stood upon its head; first in the sense that the human head, and the principles arrived at by its thought, claimed to be the basis of all human action and association; but by and by, also, in the wider sense that the reality which was in contradiction to these principles had, in fact, to be turned upside down. Every form of society and government then existing, every old traditional notion, was flung into the lumber-room as irrational; the world had hitherto allowed itself to be led solely by prejudices; everything in the past deserved only pity and contempt. Now, for the first time, appeared the light of day, the kingdom of reason; henceforth superstition, injustice, privilege, oppression, were to be superseded by eternal truth, eternal Right, equality based on Nature and the inalienable rights of man.

We know today that this kingdom of reason was nothing more than the idealized kingdom of the bourgeoisie; that this eternal Right found its realization in bourgeois justice; that this equality reduced itself to bourgeois equality before the law; that bourgeois property was proclaimed as one of the essential rights of man; and that the government of reason, the *Contrat Social* of Rousseau, came into being, and only could come into being, as a democratic bourgeois republic. The great thinkers of the 18th century could, no more than their predecessors, go beyond the limits imposed upon them by their epoch.

But, side by side with the antagonisms of the feudal nobility and the burghers, who claimed to represent all the rest of society, was the general antagonism of exploiters and exploited, of rich idlers and poor workers. It was this very circumstance that made it possible for the representatives of the bourgeoisie to put themselves forward as representing not one special class, but the whole of suffering humanity. Still further. From its origin the bourgeoisie was saddled with its antithesis: capitalists cannot exist without wage-workers, and, in the same proportion as the mediaeval burgher of the guild developed into the modern bourgeois, the guild journeyman and the day-laborer, outside the guilds, developed into the proletarian. And although, upon the whole, the bourgeoisie, in their struggle with the nobility, could claim to represent at the same time the interests of the different working-classes of that period, yet in every great bourgeois movement there were independent outbursts of that class which was the forerunner, more or less developed, of the modern proletariat. For example, at the time of the German Reformation and the Peasants' War, the Anabaptists and Thomas Münzer; in the great English Revolution, the Levellers; in the great French Revolution, Babeuf.

These were theoretical enunciations, corresponding with these revolutionary uprisings of a class not yet developed; in the 16th and 17th centuries, Utopian pictures of ideal social conditions; in the 18th century, actual communistic theories (Morelly and Mably). The demand for equality was no longer limited to political rights; it was extended also to the social conditions of individuals. It was not simply class privileges that were to be abolished, but class distinctions themselves. A Communism, ascetic, denouncing all the pleasures of life, Spartan, was the first form of the new teaching. Then came the three great Utopians: Saint-Simon, to whom the middle-class movement, side by side with the proletarian, still had a certain significance; Fourier; and Owen, who in the country where capitalist production was most developed, and under the influence of the antagonisms begotten of this, worked out his proposals for the removal of class distinction systematically and in direct relation to French materialism.

One thing is common to all three. Not one of them appears as a representative of the interests of that proletariat which historical development had, in the meantime, produced. Like the French philosophers, they do not claim to emancipate a particular class to begin with, but all humanity at once. Like them, they wish to bring in the kingdom of reason and eternal justice, but this kingdom, as they see it, is as far as Heaven from Earth, from that of the French philosophers.

For, to our three social reformers, the bourgeois world, based upon the principles of these philosophers, is quite as irrational and unjust, and, therefore, finds its way to the dust-hole quite as readily as feudalism and all the earlier stages of society. If pure reason and justice have not, hitherto, ruled the world, this has been the case only because men have not rightly understood them. What was wanted was the individual man of genius, who has now arisen and who understands the truth. That he has now arisen, that the truth has now been clearly understood, is not an inevitable event, following of necessity in the chains of historical development, but a mere happy accident. He might just as well have been born 500 years earlier, and might then have spared humanity 500 years of error, strife, and suffering.

We saw how the French philosophers of the 18th century, the forerunners of the Revolution, appealed to reason as the sole judge of all that is. A rational government, rational society, were to be founded; everything that ran counter to eternal reason was to be remorselessly done away with. We saw also that this eternal reason was in reality nothing but the idealized understanding of the 18th century citizen, just then evolving into the bourgeois. The French Revolution had realized this rational society and government.

But the new order of things, rational enough as compared with earlier conditions, turned out to be by no means absolutely rational. The state based upon reason completely collapsed. Rousseau's *Contrat Social* had found its realization in the Reign of Terror, from which the bourgeoisie, who had lost confidence in their own political capacity, had taken refuge first in the corruption of the Directorate, and, finally, under the wing of the Napoleonic despotism. The promised eternal peace was turned into an endless war of conquest. The society based upon reason had fared no better. The antagonism between rich and poor, instead of dissolving into general prosperity, had become intensified by the removal of the guild and other privileges, which had to some extent bridged it over, and by the removal of the charitable institutions of the Church. The "freedom of property" from feudal fetters, now veritably accomplished, turned out to be, for the small capitalists and small proprietors, the freedom to sell their small property, crushed under the overmastering competition of the large capitalists and landlords, to these great lords, and thus, as far as the small capitalists and peasant proprietors were concerned, became "freedom from property". The development of industry upon a capitalistic basis made poverty and misery of the working masses conditions of existence of society. Cash payment became more and more, in Carlyle's phrase (See Thomas Carlyle, *Past and Present*, London 1843), the sole nexus between man and man. The number of crimes increased from year to year. Formerly, the feudal vices had openly stalked about in broad daylight; though not eradicated, they were now at any rate thrust into the background. In their stead, the bourgeois vices, hitherto practiced in secret, began to blossom all the more luxuriantly. Trade became to a greater and greater extent cheating. The "fraternity" of the revolutionary motto was realized in the chicanery and rivalries of the battle of competition. Oppression by force was replaced by corruption; the sword, as the first social lever, by gold. The right of the first night was transferred from the feudal lords to the bourgeois manufacturers. Prostitution increased to an extent never heard of. Marriage itself remained, as before, the legally recognized form, the official cloak of prostitution, and, moreover, was supplemented by rich crops of adultery.

In a word, compared with the splendid promises of the philosophers, the social and political institutions born of the "triumph of reason" were bitterly disappointing caricatures. All that was wanting was the men to formulate this disappointment, and they came with the turn of the century. In 1802, Saint-Simon's Geneva letters appeared; in 1808 appeared Fourier's first work, although the groundwork of his theory dated from 1799; on January 1, 1800, Robert Owen undertook the direction of New Lanark.

At this time, however, the capitalist mode of production, and with it the antagonism between the bourgeoisie and the proletariat, was still very incompletely developed. Modern Industry, which had just arisen in England, was still unknown in France. But Modern Industry develops, on the one hand, the conflicts which make absolutely necessary a revolution in the mode of production, and the doing away with its capitalistic character – conflicts not only between the classes begotten of it, but also between the very productive forces and the forms of exchange created by it. And, on the other hand, it develops, in these very gigantic productive forces, the means of ending these conflicts. If, therefore, about the year 1800, the conflicts arising from the new social order were only just beginning to take shape, this holds still more fully as to the means of ending them. The "have-nothing" masses of Paris, during the Reign of Terror, were able for a moment to gain the mastery, and thus to lead the bourgeois revolution to victory in spite of the bourgeoisie themselves. But, in doing so, they only proved how impossible it was for their domination to last under the conditions then obtaining. The proletariat, which then for the first time evolved itself from these "have-nothing" masses as the nucleus of a new class, as yet quite incapable of independent political action, appeared as an oppressed, suffering order, to whom, in its incapacity to help itself, help could, at best, be brought in from without or down from above.

This historical situation also dominated the founders of Socialism. To the crude conditions of capitalistic production and the crude class conditions correspond crude theories. The solution of the social problems, which as yet lay hidden in undeveloped economic conditions, the Utopians attempted to evolve out of the human brain. Society presented nothing but wrongs; to remove these was the task of reason. It was necessary, then, to discover a new and more perfect system of social order and to impose this upon society from without by propaganda, and, wherever it was possible, by the example of model experiments. These new social systems were foredoomed as Utopian; the more completely they were worked out in detail, the more they could not avoid drifting off into pure phantasies.

These facts once established, we need not dwell a moment longer upon this side of the question, now wholly belonging to the past. We can leave it to the literary small fry to solemnly quibble over these phantasies, which today only make us smile, and to crow over the superiority of their own bald reasoning, as compared with such "insanity". For ourselves, we delight in the stupendously grand thoughts and germs of thought that everywhere break out through their phantastic covering, and to which these Philistines are blind.

Saint-Simon was a son of the great French Revolution, at the outbreak of which he was not yet 30. The Revolution was the victory of the 3rd estate – i.e., of the great masses of the nation, working in production and in trade, over the privileged idle classes, the nobles and the priests. But the victory of the 3rd estate soon revealed itself as exclusively the victory of a smaller part of this "estate", as the conquest of political power by the socially privileged section of it – i.e., the propertied bourgeoisie. And the bourgeoisie had certainly developed rapidly during the Revolution, partly by speculation in the lands of the nobility and of the Church, confiscated and afterwards put up for sale, and partly by frauds upon the nation by means of army contracts. It was the domination of these swindlers that, under the Directorate, brought France to the verge of ruin, and thus gave Napoleon the pretext for his coup d'état.

Hence, to Saint-Simon the antagonism between the 3rd Estate and the privileged classes took the form of an antagonism between "workers" and "idlers". The idlers were not merely the old privileged classes, but also all who, without taking any part in production or distribution, lived on their incomes. And the workers were not only the wage-workers, but also the manufacturers, the merchants, the bankers. That the idlers had lost the capacity for intellectual leadership and political supremacy had been proved, and was by the

Revolution finally settled. That the non-possessing classes had not this capacity seemed to Saint-Simon proved by the experiences of the Reign of Terror. Then, who was to lead and command? According to Saint-Simon, science and industry, both united by a new religious bond, destined to restore that unity of religious ideas which had been lost since the time of the Reformation – a necessarily mystic and rigidly hierarchic "new Christianity". But science, that was the scholars; and industry, that was, in the first place, the working bourgeois, manufacturers, merchants, bankers. These bourgeois were, certainly, intended by Saint-Simon to transform themselves into a kind of public officials, of social trustees; but they were still to hold, vis-à-vis of the workers, a commanding and economically privileged position. The bankers especially were to be called upon to direct the whole of social production by the regulation of credit. This conception was in exact keeping with a time in which Modern Industry in France and, with it, the chasm between bourgeoisie and proletariat, was only just coming into existence. But what Saint-Simon especially lays stress upon is this: what interests him first, and above all other things, is the lot of the class that is the most numerous and the most poor ("*la classe la plus nombreuse et la plus pauvre*").

Already in his Geneva letters, Saint-Simon lays down the proposition that "all men ought to work". In the same work he recognizes also that the Reign of Terror was the reign of the non-possessing masses.

"See," says he to them, "what happened in France at the time when your comrades held sway there; they brought about a famine." (*Lettres d'un habitant de Genève à ses contemporains,* Saint-Simon, 1803)

But to recognize the French Revolution as a class war, and not simply one between nobility and bourgeoisie, but between nobility, bourgeoisie, and the non-possessors, was, in the year 1802, a most pregnant discovery. In 1816, he declares that politics is the science of production, and foretells the complete absorption of politics by economics. The knowledge that economic conditions are the basis of political institutions appears here only in embryo. Yet what is here already very plainly expressed is the idea of the future conversion of political rule over men into an administration of things and a direction of processes of production – that is to say, the "abolition of the state", about which recently there has been so much noise.

Saint-Simon shows the same superiority over his contemporaries, when in 1814, immediately after the entry of the allies into Paris, and again in 1815, during the Hundred Days' War, he proclaims the alliance of France and England, and then of both of these countries, with Germany, as the only guarantee for the prosperous development and peace of Europe. To preach to the French in 1815 an alliance with the victors of Waterloo required as much courage as historical foresight.

If in Saint-Simon we find a comprehensive breadth of view, by virtue of which almost all the ideas of later Socialists that are not strictly economic are found in him in embryo, we find in Fourier a criticism of the existing conditions of society, genuinely French and witty, but not upon that account any the less thorough. Fourier takes the bourgeoisie, their inspired prophets before the Revolution, and their interested eulogists after it, at their own word. He lays bare remorselessly the material and moral misery of the bourgeois world. He confronts it with the earlier philosophers' dazzling promises of a society in which reason alone should reign, of a civilization in which happiness should be universal, of an illimitable human perfectibility, and with the rose-colored phraseology of the bourgeois ideologists of his time. He points out how everywhere the most pitiful reality corresponds with the most high-sounding phrases, and he overwhelms this hopeless fiasco of phrases with his mordant sarcasm.

Fourier is not only a critic, his imperturbably serene nature makes him a satirist, and assuredly one of the greatest satirists of all time. He depicts, with equal power and charm, the swindling speculations that blossomed out upon the downfall of the Revolution, and the shopkeeping spirit prevalent in, and characteristic of, French commerce at that time. Still more masterly is his criticism of the bourgeois form of the relations between sexes, and the position of woman in bourgeois society. He was the first to declare that in any given society the degree of woman's emancipation is the natural measure of the general emancipation.

But Fourier is at his greatest in his conception of the history of society. He divides its whole course, thus far, into four stages of evolution – savagery, barbarism, the patriarchate, civilization. This last is identical with the so-called civil, or bourgeois, society of today – i.e., with the social order that came in with the 16th century. He proves "that the civilized stage raises every vice practiced by barbarism in a simple fashion into a form of existence, complex, ambiguous, equivocal, hypocritical" – that civilization moves "in a vicious circle", in contradictions which it constantly reproduces without being able to solve them; hence it constantly arrives at the very opposite to that which it wants to attain, or pretends to want to attain, so that, e.g., "under civilization poverty is born of superabundance itself". (*Théorie de l'unite universelle*, Fourier, 1843 and *Le nouveau monde industriel et sociétaire, ou invention du procédé d'industrie attrayante et enaturelle distribuée en séries passionnées*, Fourier, 1845)

Fourier, as we see, uses the dialectic method in the same masterly way as his contemporary, Hegel. Using these same dialectics, he argues against talk about illimitable human perfectibility, that every historical phase has its period of ascent and also its period of descent, and he applies this observation to the future of the whole human race. As Kant introduced into natural science the idea of the ultimate destruction of the Earth, Fourier introduced into historical science that of the ultimate destruction of the human race.

Whilst in France the hurricane of the Revolution swept over the land, in England a quieter, but not on that account less tremendous, revolution was going on. Steam and the new tool-making machinery were transforming manufacture into modern industry, and thus revolutionizing the whole foundation of bourgeois society. The sluggish march of development of the manufacturing period changed into a veritable storm and stress period of production. With constantly increasing swiftness the splitting-up into large capitalists and non-possessing proletarians went on. Between these, instead of the former stable middle-class, an unstable mass of artisans and small shopkeepers, the most fluctuating portion of the population, now led a precarious existence.

The new mode of production was, as yet, only at the beginning of its period of ascent; as yet it was the normal, regular method of production – the only one possible under existing conditions. Nevertheless, even then it was producing crying social abuses – the herding together of a homeless population in the worst quarters of the large towns; the loosening of all traditional moral bonds, of patriarchal subordination, of family relations; overwork, especially of women and children, to a frightful extent; complete demoralization of the working-class, suddenly flung into altogether new conditions, from the country into the town, from agriculture into modern industry, from stable conditions of existence into insecure ones that change from day to day.

At this juncture, there came forward as a reformer a manufacturer 29-years-old – a man of almost sublime, childlike simplicity of character, and at the same time one of the few born leaders of men. Robert Owen had adopted the teaching of the materialistic philosophers: that man's character is the product, on the one hand, of heredity; on the other, of the environment of the individual during his lifetime, and especially during his period of development. In the industrial revolution most of his class saw only chaos and confusion, and the opportunity of fishing in these troubled waters and making large fortunes quickly. He saw in it the opportunity of putting into practice his favorite theory, and so of bringing order out of chaos. He had already tried it with success, as superintendent of more than 500 men in a Manchester factory. From 1800 to 1829, he directed the great cotton mill at New Lanark, in Scotland, as managing partner, along the same lines, but with greater freedom of action and with a success that made him a European reputation. A population, originally consisting of the most diverse and, for the most part, very demoralized elements, a population that gradually grew to 2,500, he turned into a model colony, in which drunkenness, police, magistrates, lawsuits, poor laws, charity, were unknown. And all this simply by placing the people in conditions worthy of human beings, and especially by carefully bringing up the rising generation. He was the founder of infant schools, and introduced them first at New Lanark. At the age of two, the children came to school, where they enjoyed themselves so much that they could scarely be got home again. Whilst his competitors worked their people 13 or 14 hours a day, in New Lanark the working-day was only 10 and a half hours. When a crisis in cotton stopped work for four months, his workers received their full wages all the time. And with all this the business more than doubled in value, and to the last yielded large profits to its proprietors.

In spite of all this, Owen was not content. The existence which he secured for his workers was, in his eyes, still far from being worthy of human beings. "The people were slaves at my mercy." The relatively favorable conditions in which he had placed them were still far from allowing a rational development of the character and of the intellect in all directions, much less of the free exercise of all their faculties.

"And yet, the working part of this population of 2,500 persons was daily producing as much real wealth for society as, less than half a century before, it would have required the working part of a population of 600,000 to create. I asked myself, what became of the difference between the wealth consumed by 2,500 persons and that which would have been consumed by 600,000?"

The answer was clear. It had been used to pay the proprietors of the establishment 5 per cent on the capital they had laid out, in addition to over £300,000 clear profit. And that which held for New Lanark held to a still greater extent for all the factories in England.

"If this new wealth had not been created by machinery, imperfectly as it has been applied, the wars of Europe, in opposition to Napoleon, and to support the aristocratic principles of society, could not have been maintained. And yet this new power was the creation of the working-classes."

To them, therefore, the fruits of this new power belonged. The newly-created gigantic productive forces, hitherto used only to enrich individuals and to enslave the masses, offered to Owen the foundations for a reconstruction of society; they were destined, as the common property of all, to be worked for the common good of all.

Owen's communism was based upon this purely business foundation, the outcome, so to say, of commercial calculation. Throughout, it maintained this practical character. Thus, in 1823, Owen proposed the relief of the distress in Ireland by Communist colonies, and drew up complete estimates of costs of founding them, yearly expenditure, and probable revenue. And in his definite plan for the future, the technical working out of details is managed with such practical knowledge – ground plan, front and side and bird's-eye views all included – that the Owen method of social reform once accepted, there is from the practical point of view little to be said against the actual arrangement of details.

His advance in the direction of Communism was the turning-point in Owen's life. As long as he was simply a philanthropist, he was rewarded with nothing but wealth, applause, honor, and glory. He was the most popular man in Europe. Not only men of his own class, but statesmen and princes listened to him approvingly. But when he came out with his Communist theories, that was quite another thing. Three great obstacles seemed to him especially to block the path to social reform: private property, religion, the present form of marriage.

He knew what confronted him if he attacked these – outlawry, excommunication from official society, the loss of his whole social position. But nothing of this prevented him from attacking them without fear of consequences, and what he had foreseen happened. Banished from official society, with a conspiracy of silence against him in the press, ruined by his unsuccessful Communist experiments in America, in which he sacrificed all his fortune, he turned directly to the working-class and continued working in their midst for 30 years. Every social movement, every real advance in England on behalf of the workers, links itself on to the name of Robert Owen. He forced through in 1819, after five years' fighting, the first law limiting the hours of labor of women and children in factories. He was president of the first Congress at which all the Trade Unions of England united in a single great trade association. He introduced as transition measures to the complete communistic organization of society, on the one hand, cooperative societies for retail trade and production. These have since that time, at least, given practical proof that the merchant and the manufacturer are socially quite unnecessary. On the other hand, he introduced labor bazaars for the exchange of the products of labor through the medium of labor-notes, whose unit was a single hour of work; institutions necessarily doomed to failure, but completely anticipating Proudhon's bank of exchange of a much later period, and differing entirely from this in that it did not claim to be the panacea for all social ills, but only a first step towards a much more radical revolution of society.

The Utopians' mode of thought has for a long time governed the Socialist ideas of the 19th century, and still governs some of them. Until very recently, all French and English Socialists did homage to it. The earlier German Communism, including that of Weitling, was of the same school. To all these, Socialism is the expression of absolute truth, reason and justice, and has only to be discovered to conquer all the world by virtue of its own power. And as an absolute truth is independent of time, space, and of the historical development of man, it is a mere accident when and where it is discovered. With all this, absolute truth, reason, and justice are different with the founder of each different school. And as each one's special kind of absolute truth, reason, and justice is again conditioned by his subjective understanding, his conditions of existence, the measure of his knowledge and his intellectual training, there is no other ending possible in this conflict of absolute truths than that they shall be mutually exclusive of one another. Hence, from this nothing could come but a kind of eclectic, average Socialism, which, as a matter of fact, has up to the present time dominated the minds of most of the socialist workers in France and England. Hence, a mish-mash allowing of the most manifold shades of opinion: a mish-mash of such critical statements, economic theories, pictures of future society by the founders of different sects, as excite a minimum of opposition; a mish-mash which is the more easily brewed the more definite sharp edges of the individual constituents are rubbed down in the stream of debate, like rounded pebbles in a brook.

To make a science of Socialism, it had first to be placed upon a real basis.

II Dialectics
In the meantime, along with and after the French philosophy of the 18th century, had arisen the new German philosophy, culminating in Hegel.

Its greatest merit was the taking up again of dialectics as the highest form of reasoning. The old Greek philosophers were all born natural dialecticians, and Aristotle, the most encyclopaedic of them, had already analyzed the most essential forms of dialectic thought. The newer philosophy, on the other hand, although in it also dialectics had brilliant exponents (e.g. Descartes and Spinoza), had, especially through English influence, become more and more rigidly fixed in the so-called metaphysical mode of reasoning, by which also the French of the 18th century were almost wholly dominated, at all events in their special philosophical work. Outside philosophy in the restricted sense, the French nevertheless produced masterpieces of dialectic. We need only call to mind Diderot's *Le Neveu de Rameau*, and Rousseau's *Discours sur l'origine et les fondements de l'inegalite parmi less hommes*. We give here, in brief, the essential character of these two modes of thought.

When we consider and reflect upon Nature at large, or the history of mankind, or our own intellectual activity, at first we see the picture of an endless entanglement of relations and reactions, permutations and combinations, in which nothing remains what, where and as it was, but everything moves, changes, comes into being and passes away. We see, therefore, at first the picture as a whole, with its individual parts still more or less kept in the background; we observe the movements, transitions, connections, rather than the things that move, combine, and are connected. This primitive, naive but intrinsically correct conception of the world is that of ancient Greek philosophy, and was first clearly formulated by Heraclitus:

everything is and is not, for everything is fluid, is constantly changing, constantly coming into being and passing away.

But this conception, correctly as it expresses the general character of the picture of appearances as a whole, does not suffice to explain the details of which this picture is made up, and so long as we do not understand these, we have not a clear idea of the whole picture. In order to understand these details, we must detach them from their natural, special causes, effects, etc. This is, primarily, the task of natural science and historical research: branches of science which the Greek of classical times, on very good grounds, relegated to a subordinate position, because they had first of all to collect materials for these sciences to work upon. A certain amount of natural and historical material must be collected before there can be any critical analysis, comparison, and arrangement in classes, orders, and species. The foundations of the exact natural sciences were, therefore, first worked out by the Greeks of the Alexandrian period, and later on, in the Middle Ages, by the Arabs. Real natural science dates from the second half of the 15th century, and thence onward it had advanced with constantly increasing rapidity. The analysis of Nature into its individual parts, the grouping of the different natural processes and objects in definite classes, the study of the internal anatomy of organized bodies in their manifold forms — these were the fundamental conditions of the gigantic strides in our knowledge of Nature that have been made during the last 400 years. But this method of work has also left us as legacy the habit of observing natural objects and processes in isolation, apart from their connection with the vast whole; of observing them in repose, not in motion; as constraints, not as essentially variables; in their death, not in their life. And when this way of looking at things was transferred by Bacon and Locke from natural science to philosophy, it begot the narrow, metaphysical mode of thought peculiar to the last century.

To the metaphysician, things and their mental reflexes, ideas, are isolated, are to be considered one after the other and apart from each other, are objects of investigation fixed, rigid, given once for all. He thinks in absolutely irreconcilable antitheses. His communication is 'yea, yea; nay, nay'; for whatsoever is more than these cometh of evil." For him, a thing either exists or does not exist; a thing cannot at the same time be itself and something else. Positive and negative absolutely exclude one another; cause and effect stand in a rigid antithesis, one to the other.

At first sight, this mode of thinking seems to us very luminous, because it is that of so-called sound commonsense. Only sound commonsense, respectable fellow that he is, in the homely realm of his own four walls, has very wonderful adventures directly he ventures out into the wide world of research. And the metaphysical mode of thought, justifiable and necessary as it is in a number of domains whose extent varies according to the nature of the particular object of investigation, sooner or later reaches a limit, beyond which it becomes one-sided, restricted, abstract, lost in insoluble contradictions. In the contemplation of individual things, it forgets the connection between them; in the contemplation of their existence, it forgets the beginning and end of that existence; of their repose, it forgets their motion. It cannot see the woods for the trees.

For everyday purposes, we know and can say, e.g., whether an animal is alive or not. But, upon closer inquiry, we find that this is, in many cases, a very complex question, as the jurists know very well. They have cudgelled their brains in vain to discover a rational limit beyond which the killing of the child in its mother's womb is murder. It is just as impossible to determine absolutely the moment of death, for physiology proves that death is not an instantaneous, momentary phenomenon, but a very protracted process.

In like manner, every organized being is every moment the same and not the same; every moment, it assimilates matter supplied from without, and gets rid of other matter; every moment, some cells of its body die and others build themselves anew; in a longer or shorter time, the matter of its body is completely renewed, and is replaced by other molecules of matter, so that every organized being is always itself, and yet something other than itself.

Further, we find upon closer investigation that the two poles of an antithesis, positive and negative, e.g., are as inseparable as they are opposed, and that despite all their opposition, they mutually interpenetrate. And we find, in like manner, that cause and effect are conceptions which only hold good in their application to individual cases; but as soon as we consider the individual cases in their general connection with the universe as a whole, they run into each other, and they become confounded when we contemplate that universal action and reaction in which causes and effects are eternally changing places, so that what is effect here and now will be cause there and then, and vice versa.

None of these processes and modes of thought enters into the framework of metaphysical reasoning. Dialectics, on the other hand, comprehends things and their representations, ideas, in their essential connection, concatenation, motion, origin and ending. Such processes as those mentioned above are, therefore, so many corroborations of its own method of procedure.

Nature is the proof of dialectics, and it must be said for modern science that it has furnished this proof with very rich materials increasingly daily, and thus has shown that, in the last resort, Nature works dialectically and not metaphysically; that she does not move in the eternal oneness of a perpetually recurring circle, but goes through a real historical evolution. In this connection, Darwin must be named before all others. He dealt the metaphysical conception of Nature the heaviest blow by his proof that all organic beings, plants, animals, and man himself, are the products of a process of evolution going on through millions of years. But, the naturalists, who have learned to think dialectically, are few and far between, and this conflict of the results of discovery with preconceived modes of thinking, explains the endless confusion now reigning in theoretical natural science, the despair of teachers as well as learners, of authors and readers alike.

An exact representation of the universe, of its evolution, of the development of mankind, and of the reflection of this evolution in the minds of men, can therefore only be obtained by the methods of dialectics with its constant regard to the innumerable actions and reactions of life and death, of progressive or retrogressive changes. And in this spirit, the new German philosophy has worked. Kant began his career by resolving the stable Solar system of Newton and its eternal duration, after the famous initial impulse had once been given, into the result of a historical process, the formation of the Sun and all the planets out of a rotating, nebulous mass. From this, he at the same time drew the conclusion that, given this origin of the Solar system, its future death followed of necessity. His theory, half a century later, was established mathematically by Laplace, and half a century after that, the spectroscope proved the existence in space of such incandescent masses of gas in various stages of condensation.

This new German philosophy culminated in the Hegelian system. In this system — and herein is its great merit — for the first time the whole world, natural, historical, intellectual, is represented as a process — i.e., as in constant motion, change, transformation, development; and the attempt is made to trace out the internal connection that makes a continuous whole of all this movement and development. From this point of view, the history of mankind no longer appeared as a wild whirl of senseless deeds of violence, all equally condemnable at the judgment seat of mature philosophic reason and which are best forgotten as quickly as possible, but as the process of evolution of man himself. It was now the task of the intellect to follow the gradual march of this process through all its devious ways, and to trace out the inner law running through all its apparently accidental phenomena.

That the Hegelian system did not solve the problem it propounded is here immaterial. Its epoch-making merit was that it propounded the problem. This problem is one that no single individual will ever be able to solve. Although Hegel was — with Saint-Simon — the most encyclopaedic mind of his time, yet he was limited, first, by the necessary limited extent of his own knowledge and, second, by the limited extent and depth of the knowledge and conceptions of his age. To these limits, a third must be added; Hegel was an idealist. To him, the thoughts within his brain were not the more or less abstract pictures of actual things and processes, but, conversely, things and their evolution were only the realized pictures of the "Idea", existing somewhere from eternity before the world was. This way of thinking turned everything upside down, and completely reversed the actual connection of things in the world. Correctly and ingeniously as many groups of facts were grasped by Hegel, yet, for the reasons just given, there is much that is botched, artificial, labored, in a word, wrong in point of detail. The Hegelian system, in itself, was a colossal miscarriage — but it was also the last of its kind.

It was suffering, in fact, from an internal and incurable contradiction. Upon the one hand, its essential proposition was the conception that human history is a process of evolution, which, by its very nature, cannot find its intellectual final term in the discovery of any so-called absolute truth. But, on the other hand, it laid claim to being the very essence of this absolute truth. A system of natural and historical knowledge, embracing everything, and final for all time, is a contradiction to the fundamental law of dialectic reasoning.

This law, indeed, by no means excludes, but, on the contrary, includes the idea that the systematic knowledge of the external universe can make giant strides from age to age.

The perception of the fundamental contradiction in German idealism led necessarily back to materialism, but — *nota bene* — not to the simply metaphysical, exclusively mechanical materialism of the 18th century. Old materialism looked upon all previous history as a crude heap of irrationality and violence; modern materialism sees in it the process of evolution of humanity, and aims at discovering the laws thereof. With the French of the 18th century, and even with Hegel, the conception obtained of Nature as a whole — moving in narrow circles, and forever immutable, with its eternal celestial bodies, as Newton, and unalterable organic species, as Linnaeus, taught. Modern materialism embraces the more recent discoveries of natural science, according to which Nature also has its history in time, the celestial bodies, like the organic species that, under favorable conditions, people them, being born and perishing. And even if Nature, as a whole, must still be said to move in recurrent cycles, these cycles assume infinitely larger dimensions. In both aspects, modern materialism is essentially dialectic, and no longer requires the assistance of that sort of philosophy which, queen-like, pretended to rule the remaining mob of sciences. As soon as each special science is bound to make clear its position in the great totality of things and of our knowledge of things, a special science dealing with this totality is superfluous or unnecessary. That which still survives of all earlier philosophy is the science of thought and its law — formal logic and dialectics. Everything else is subsumed in the positive science of Nature and history.

Whilst, however, the revolution in the conception of Nature could only be made in proportion to the corresponding positive materials furnished by research, already much earlier certain historical facts had occurred which led to a decisive change in the conception of history. In 1831, the first working-class rising took place in Lyons; between 1838 and 1842, the first national working-class movement, that of the English Chartists, reached its height. The class struggle between proletariat and bourgeoisie came to the front in the history of the most advanced countries in Europe, in proportion to the development, upon the one hand, of modern industry, upon the other, of the newly-acquired political supremacy of the bourgeoisie. Facts more and more strenuously gave the lie to the teachings of bourgeois economy as to the identity of the interests of capital and labor, as to the universal harmony and universal prosperity that would be the consequence of unbridled competition. All these things could no longer be ignored, any more than the French and English

Socialism, which was their theoretical, though very imperfect, expression.

But the old idealist conception of history, which was not yet dislodged, knew nothing of class struggles based upon economic interests, knew nothing of economic interests; production and all economic relations appeared in it only as incidental, subordinate elements in the "history of civilization".

The new facts made imperative a new examination of all past history. Then it was seen that all past history, with the exception of its primitive stages, was the history of class struggles; that these warring classes of society are always the products of the modes of production and of exchange — in a word, of the economic conditions of their time; that the economic structure of society always furnishes the real basis, starting from which we can alone work out the ultimate explanation of the whole superstructure of juridical and political institutions as well as of the religious, philosophical, and other ideas of a given historical period. Hegel has freed history from metaphysics — he made it dialectic; but his conception of history was essentially idealistic. But now idealism was driven from its last refuge, the philosophy of history; now a materialistic treatment of history was propounded, and a method found of explaining man's "knowing" by his "being", instead of, as heretofore, his "being" by his "knowing".

From that time forward, Socialism was no longer an accidental discovery of this or that ingenious brain, but the necessary outcome of the struggle between two historically developed classes — the proletariat and the bourgeoisie. Its task was no longer to manufacture a system of society as perfect as possible, but to examine the historico-economic succession of events from which these classes and their antagonism had of necessity sprung, and to discover in the economic conditions thus created the means of ending the conflict. But the Socialism of earlier days was as incompatible with this materialist conception as the conception of Nature of the French materialists was with dialectics and modern natural science. The Socialism of earlier days certainly criticized the existing capitalistic mode of production and its consequences. But it could not explain them, and, therefore, could not get the mastery of them. It could only simply reject them as bad. The more strongly this earlier Socialism denounced the exploitations of the working-class, inevitable under Capitalism, the less able was it clearly to show in what this exploitation consisted and how it arose. but for this it was necessary-to present the capitalistic mode of production in its historical connection and its inevitableness during a particular historical period, and therefore, also, to present its inevitable downfall; and —

to lay bare its essential character, which was still a secret. This was done by the discovery of surplus-value.

It was shown that the appropriation of unpaid labor is the basis of the capitalist mode of production and of the exploitation of the worker that occurs under it; that even if the capitalist buys the labor power of his laborer at its full value as a commodity on the market, he yet extracts more value from it than he paid for; and that in the ultimate analysis, this surplus-value forms those sums of value from which are heaped up constantly increasing masses of capital in the hands of the possessing classes. The genesis of capitalist production and the production of capital were both explained.

These two great discoveries, the materialistic conception of history and the revelation of the secret of capitalistic production through surplus-value, we owe to Marx. With these discoveries, Socialism became a science. The next thing was to work out all its details and relations.

III Historical Materialism

The materialist conception of history starts from the proposition that the production of the means to support human life and, next to production, the exchange of things produced, is the basis of all social structure; that in every society that has appeared in history, the manner in which wealth is distributed and society divided into classes or orders is dependent upon what is produced, how it is produced, and how the products are exchanged. From this point of view, the final causes of all social changes and political revolutions are to be sought, not in men's brains, not in men's better insights into eternal truth and justice, but in changes in the modes of production and exchange. They are to be sought, not in the philosophy, but in the economics of each particular epoch. The growing perception that existing social institutions are unreasonable and unjust, that reason has become unreason, and right wrong, is only proof that in the modes of production and exchange changes have silently taken place with which the social order, adapted to earlier economic conditions, is no longer in keeping. From this it also follows that the means of getting rid of the incongruities that have been brought to light must also be present, in a more or less developed condition, within the changed modes of production themselves. These means are not to be invented by deduction from fundamental principles, but are to be discovered in the stubborn facts of the existing system of production.

What is, then, the position of modern Socialism in this connection?

The present situation of society — this is now pretty generally conceded — is the creation of the ruling class of today, of the bourgeoisie. The mode of production peculiar to the bourgeoisie, known, since Marx, as the capitalist mode of production, was incompatible with the feudal system, with the privileges it conferred upon individuals, entire social ranks and local corporations, as well as with the hereditary ties of subordination which constituted the framework of its social organization. The bourgeoisie broke up the feudal system and built upon its ruins the capitalist order of society, the kingdom of free competition, of personal liberty, of the equality, before the law, of all commodity owners, of all the rest of the capitalist blessings. Thenceforward, the capitalist mode of production could develop in freedom. Since steam, machinery, and the making of machines by machinery transformed the older manufacture into modern industry, the productive forces, evolved under the guidance of the bourgeoisie, developed with a rapidity and in a degree unheard of before. But just as the older manufacture, in its time, and handicraft, becoming more developed under its influence, had come into collision with the feudal trammels of the guilds, so now modern industry, in its complete development, comes into collision with the bounds within which the capitalist mode of production holds it confined. The new productive forces have already outgrown the capitalistic mode of using them. And this conflict between productive forces and modes of production is not a conflict engendered in the mind of man, like that between original sin and divine justice. It exists, in fact, objectively, outside us, independently of the will and actions even of the men that have brought it on. Modern Socialism is nothing but the reflex, in thought, of this conflict in fact; its ideal reflection in the minds, first, of the class directly suffering under it, the working class.

Now, in what does this conflict consist?

Before capitalist production — i.e., in the Middle Ages — the system of petty industry obtained generally, based upon the private property of the laborers in their means of production; in the country, the agriculture of the small peasant, freeman, or serf; in the towns, the handicrafts organized in guilds. The instruments of labor — land, agricultural implements, the workshop, the tool — were the instruments of labor of single individuals, adapted for the use of one worker, and, therefore, of necessity, small, dwarfish, circumscribed. But, for this very reason, they belonged as a rule to the producer himself. To concentrate these scattered, limited means of production, to enlarge them, to turn them into the powerful levers of production of the present day — this was precisely the historic role of capitalist production and of its upholder, the bourgeoisie. In the fourth section of *Capital*, Marx has explained in detail how since the 15th century this has been historically worked out through the three phases of simple co-operation, manufacture, and modern industry. But the bourgeoisie, as is shown there, could not transform these puny means of production into mighty productive forces without transforming them, at the same time, from means of production of the individual into social means of production only workable by a collectivity of men. The spinning wheel, the handloom, the blacksmith's hammer, were replaced by the spinning-machine, the power-loom, the steam-hammer; the individual workshop, by the factory implying the co-operation of hundreds and thousands of workmen. In like manner, production itself changed from a series of individual into a series of social acts, and the production from individual to social products. The yarn, the cloth, the metal articles that now come out of the factory were the joint product of many workers, through whose hands they had successively to pass before they were ready. No one person could say of them: "I made that; this is my product."

But where, in a given society, the fundamental form of production is that spontaneous division of labor which creeps in gradually and not upon any preconceived plan, there the products take on the form of commodities, whose mutual exchange, buying and selling, enable the individual producers to satisfy their manifold wants. And this was the case in the Middle Ages. The peasant, e.g., sold to the artisan agricultural products and bought from him the products of handicraft. Into this society of individual producers, of commodity producers, the new mode of production thrust itself. In the midst of the old division of labor, grown up spontaneously and upon no definite plan, which had governed the whole of society, now arose division of labor upon a definite plan, as organized in the factory; side by side with individual production appeared social production. The products of both were sold in the same market, and, therefore, at prices at least approximately equal. But organization upon a definite plan was stronger than spontaneous division of labor. The factories working with the combined social forces of a collectivity of individuals produced their commodities far more cheaply than the individual small producers. Individual producers succumbed in one department after another. Socialized production revolutionized all the old methods of production. But its revolutionary character was, at the same time, so little recognized that it was, on the contrary, introduced as a means of increasing and developing the production of commodities. When it arose, it found ready-made, and made liberal use of, certain machinery for the production and exchange of commodities: merchants' capital, handicraft, wage-labor. Socialized production thus introducing itself as a new form of the production of commodities, it was a matter of course that under it the old forms of appropriation remained in full swing, and were applied to its products as well.

In the medieval stage of evolution of the production of commodities, the question as to the owner of the product of labor could not arise. The individual producer, as a rule, had, from raw material belonging to himself, and generally his own handiwork, produced it with his own tools, by the labor of his own hands or of his family. There was no need for him to appropriate the new product. It belonged wholly to him, as a matter of course. His property in the product was, therefore, based upon his own labor. Even where external help was used, this was, as a rule, of little importance, and very generally was compensated by something other than wages. The apprentices and journeymen of the guilds worked less for board and wages than for education, in order that they might become master craftsmen themselves.

Then came the concentration of the means of production and of the producers in large workshops and manufactories, their transformation into actual socialized means of production and socialized producers. But the socialized producers and means of production and their products were still treated, after this change, just as they had been before — i.e., as the means of production and the products of individuals. Hitherto, the owner of the instruments of labor had himself appropriated the product, because, as a rule, it was his own product and the assistance of others was the exception. Now, the owner of the instruments of labor always appropriated to himself the product, although it was no longer his product but exclusively the product of the labor of others. Thus, the products now produced socially were not appropriated by those who had actually set in motion the means of production and actually produced the commodities, but by the capitalists. The means of production, and production itself, had become in essence socialized. But they were subjected to a form of appropriation which presupposes the private production of individuals, under which, therefore, every one owns his own product and brings it to market. The mode of production is subjected to this form of appropriation, although it abolishes the conditions upon which the latter rests.

This contradiction, which gives to the new mode of production its capitalistic character, contains the germ of the whole of the social antagonisms of today. The greater the mastery obtained by the new mode of production over all important fields of production and in all manufacturing countries, the more it reduced individual production to an insignificant residuum, the more clearly was brought out the incompatibility of socialized production with capitalistic appropriation.

The first capitalists found, as we have said, alongside of other forms of labor, wage-labor ready-made for them on the market. But it was exceptional, complementary, accessory, transitory wage-labor. The agricultural laborer, though, upon occasion, he hired himself out by the day, had a few acres of his own land on which he could at all events live at a pinch. The guilds were so organized that the journeyman of today became the master of tomorrow.

But all this changed, as soon as the means of production became socialized and concentrated in the hands of capitalists. The means of production, as well as the product, of the individual producer became more and more worthless; there was nothing left for him but to turn wage-worker under the capitalist. Wage-labor, aforetime the exception and accessory, now became the rule and basis of all production; aforetime complementary, it now became the sole remaining function of the worker. The wage-worker for a time became a wage-worker for life. The number of these permanent was further enormously increased by the breaking-up of the feudal system that occurred at the same time, by the disbanding of the retainers of the feudal lords, the eviction of the peasants from their homesteads, etc. The separation was made complete between the means of production concentrated in the hands of the capitalists, on the one side, and the producers, possessing nothing but their labor-power, on the other. The contradiction between socialized production and capitalistic appropriation manifested itself as the antagonism of proletariat and bourgeoisie.

We have seen that the capitalistic mode of production thrust its way into a society of commodity-producers, of individual producers, whose social bond was the exchange of their products. But every society based upon the production of commodities has this peculiarity: that the producers have lost control over their own social inter-relations. Each man produces for himself with such means of production as he may happen to have, and for such exchange as he may require to satisfy his remaining wants. No one knows how much of his particular article is coming on the market, nor how much of it will be wanted. No one knows whether his individual product will meet an actual demand, whether he will be able to make good his costs of production or even to sell his commodity at all. Anarchy reigns in socialized production.

But the production of commodities, like every other form of production, has it peculiar, inherent laws inseparable from it; and these laws work, despite anarchy, in and through anarchy. They reveal themselves in the only persistent form of social inter-relations — i.e., in exchange — and here they affect the individual producers as compulsory laws of competition. They are, at first, unknown to these producers themselves, and have to be discovered by them gradually and as the result of experience. They work themselves out, therefore, independently of the producers, and in antagonism to them, as inexorable natural laws of their particular form of production. The product governs the producers.

In mediaeval society, especially in the earlier centuries, production was essentially directed toward satisfying the wants of the individual. It satisfied, in the main, only the wants of the producer and his family. Where relations of personal dependence existed, as in the country, it also helped to satisfy the wants of the feudal lord. In all this there was, therefore, no exchange; the products, consequently, did not assume the character of commodities. The family of the peasant produced almost everything they wanted: clothes and furniture, as well as the means of subsistence. Only when it began to produce more than was sufficient to supply its own wants and the payments in kind to the feudal lords, only then did it also produce commodities. This surplus, thrown into socialized exchange and offered for sale, became commodities.

The artisan in the towns, it is true, had from the first to produce for exchange. But they, also, themselves supplied the greatest part of their individual wants. They had gardens and plots of land. They turned their cattle out into the communal forest, which, also, yielded them timber and firing. The women spun flax, wool, and so forth. Production for the purpose of exchange, production of commodities, was only in its infancy. Hence, exchange was restricted, the market narrow, the methods of production stable; there was local exclusiveness without, local unity within; the mark in the country; in the town, the guild.

But with the extension of the production of commodities, and especially with the introduction of the capitalist mode of production, the laws of commodity-production, hitherto latent, came into action more openly and with greater force. The old bonds were loosened, the old exclusive limits broken through, the producers were more and more turned into independent, isolated producers of commodities. It became apparent that the production of society at large was ruled by absence of plan, by accident, by anarchy; and this anarchy grew to greater and greater height. But the chief means by aid of which the capitalist mode of production intensified this anarchy of socialized production was the exact opposite of anarchy. It was the increasing organization of production, upon a social basis, in every individual productive establishment. By this, the old, peaceful, stable condition of things was ended. Wherever this organization of production was introduced into a branch of industry, it brooked no other method of production by its side. The field of labor became a battle-ground. The great geographical discoveries, and the colonization following them, multiplied markets and quickened the transformation of handicraft into manufacture. The war did not simply break out between the individual producers of particular localities. The local struggles begat, in their turn, national conflicts, the commercial wars of the 17th and 18th centuries.

Finally, modern industry and the opening of the world-market made the struggle universal, and at the same time gave it an unheard-of virulence. Advantages in natural or artificial conditions of production now decide the existence or non-existence of individual capitalists, as well as of whole industries and countries. He that falls is remorselessly cast aside. It is the Darwinian struggle of the individual for existence transferred from Nature to society with intensified violence. The conditions of existence natural to the animal appear as the final term of human development. The contradiction between socialized production and capitalistic appropriation now presents itself as an antagonism between the organization of production in the individual workshop and the anarchy of production in society generally.

The capitalistic mode of production moves in these two forms of the antagonism immanent to it from its very origin. It is never able to get out of that "vicious circle" which Fourier had already discovered. What Fourier could not, indeed, see in his time is that this circle is gradually narrowing; that the movement becomes more and more a spiral, and must come to an end, like the movement of planets, by collision with the centre. It is the compelling force of anarchy in the production of society at large that more and more completely turns the great majority of men into proletarians; and it is the masses of the proletariat again who will finally put an end to anarchy in production. It is the compelling force of anarchy in social production that turns the limitless perfectibility of machinery under modern industry into a compulsory law by which every individual industrial capitalist must perfect his machinery more and more, under penalty of ruin.

But the perfecting of machinery is making human labor superfluous. If the introduction and increase of machinery means the displacement of millions of manual by a few machine-workers, improvement in machinery means the displacement of more and more of the machine-workers themselves. It means, in the last instance, the production of a number of available wage workers in excess of the average needs of capital, the formation of a complete industrial reserve army, as I called it in 1845, available at the times when industry is working at high pressure, to be cast out upon the street when the inevitable crash comes, a constant dead weight upon the limbs of the working-class in its struggle for existence with capital, a regulator for keeping of wages down to the low level that suits the interests of capital.

Thus it comes about, to quote Marx, that machinery becomes the most powerful weapon in the war of capital against the working-class; that the instruments of labor constantly tear the means of subsistence out of the hands of the laborer; that they very product of the worker is turned into an instrument for his subjugation.

Thus it comes about that the economizing of the instruments of labor becomes at the same time, from the outset, the most reckless waste of labor-power, and robbery based upon the normal conditions under which labor functions; that machinery, "the most powerful instrument for shortening labor time, becomes the most unfailing means for placing every moment of the laborer's time and that of his family at the disposal of the capitalist for the purpose of expanding the value of his capital." (*Capital*, English edition, p. 406)

Thus it comes about that the overwork of some becomes the preliminary condition for the idleness of others, and that modern industry, which hunts after new consumers over the whole world, forces the consumption of the masses at home down to a starvation minimum, and in doing thus destroys its own home market.

"The law that always equilibrates the relative surplus- population, or industrial reserve army, to the extent and energy of accumulation, this law rivets the laborer to capital more firmly than the wedges of Vulcan did Prometheus to the rock. It establishes an accumulation of misery, corresponding with the accumulation of capital. Accumulation of wealth at one pole is, therefore, at the same time accumulation of misery, agony of toil, slavery, ignorance, brutality, mental degradation, at the opposite pole, i.e., on the side of the class that produces its own product in the form of capital (Marx's *Capital*, p. 661)

And to expect any other division of the products from the capitalist mode of production is the same as expecting the electrodes of a battery not to decompose acidulated water, not to liberate oxygen at the positive, hydrogen at the negative pole, so long as they are connected with the battery.

We have seen that the ever-increasing perfectibility of modern machinery is, by the anarchy of social production, turned into a compulsory law that forces the individual industrial capitalist always to improve his machinery, always to increase its productive force. The bare possibility of extending the field of production is transformed for him into a similarly compulsory law. The enormous expansive force of modern industry, compared with which that of gases is mere child's play, appears to us now as a necessity for expansion, both qualitative and quantative, that laughs at all resistance. Such resistance is offered by consumption, by sales, by the markets for the products of modern industry. But the capacity for extension, extensive and intensive, of the markets is primarily governed by quite different laws that work much less energetically. The extension of the markets cannot keep pace with the extension of production. The collision becomes inevitable, and as this cannot produce any real solution so long as it does not break in pieces the capitalist mode of production, the collisions become periodic. Capitalist production has begotten another "vicious circle".

As a matter of fact, since 1825, when the first general crisis broke out, the whole industrial and commercial world, production and exchange among all civilized peoples and their more or less barbaric hangers-on, are thrown out of joint about once every 10 years. Commerce is at a stand-still, the markets are glutted, products accumulate, as multitudinous as they are unsaleable, hard cash disappears, credit vanishes, factories are closed, the mass of the workers are in want of the means of subsistence, because they have produced too much of the means of subsistence; bankruptcy follows upon bankruptcy, execution upon execution. The stagnation lasts for years; productive forces and products are wasted and destroyed wholesale, until the accumulated mass of commodities finally filter off, more or less depreciated in value, until production and exchange gradually begin to move again. Little by little, the pace quickens. It becomes a trot. The industrial trot breaks into a canter, the canter in turn grows into the headlong gallop of a perfect steeplechase of industry, commercial credit, and speculation, which finally, after breakneck leaps, ends where it began — in the ditch of a crisis. And so over and over again. We have now, since the year 1825, gone through this five times, and at the present moment (1877), we are going through it for the sixth time. And the character of these crises is so clearly defined that Fourier hit all of them off when he described the first *"crise plethorique"*, a crisis from plethora.

In these crises, the contradiction between socialized production and capitalist appropriation ends in a violent explosion. The circulation of commodities is, for the time being, stopped. Money, the means of circulation, becomes a hindrance to circulation. All the laws of production and circulation of commodities are turned upside down. The economic collision has reached its apogee. The mode of production is in rebellion against the mode of exchange.

The fact that the socialized organization of production within the factory has developed so far that it has become incompatible with the anarchy of production in society, which exists side by side with and dominates it, is brought home to the capitalist themselves by the violent concentration of capital that occurs during crises, through the ruin of many large, and a still greater number of small, capitalists. The whole mechanism of the capitalist mode of production breaks down under the pressure of the productive forces, its own creations. It is no longer able to turn all this mass of means of production into capital. They lie fallow, and for that very reason the industrial reserve army must also lie fallow. Means of production, means of subsistence, available laborers, all the elements of production and of general wealth, are present in abundance. But "abundance becomes the source of distress and want" (Fourier), because it is the very thing that prevents the transformation of the means of production and subsistence into capital. For in capitalistic society, the means of production can only function when they have undergone a preliminary transformation into capital, into the means of exploiting human labor-power. The necessity of this transformation into capital of the means of production and subsistence stands like a ghost between these and the workers. It alone prevents the coming together of the material and personal levers of production; it alone forbids the means of production to function, the workers to work and live. On the one hand, therefore, the capitalistic mode of production stands convicted of its own incapacity to further direct these productive forces. On the other, these productive forces themselves, with increasing energy, press forward to the removal of the existing contradiction, to the abolition of their quality as capital, to the practical recognition of their character as social production forces.

This rebellion of the productive forces, as they grow more and more powerful, against their quality as capital, this stronger and stronger command that their social character shall be recognized, forces the capital class itself to treat them more and more as social productive forces, so far as this is possible under capitalist conditions. The period of industrial high pressure, with its unbounded inflation of credit, not less than the crash itself, by the collapse of great capitalist establishments, tends to bring about that form of the socialization of great masses of the means of production which we meet with in the different kinds of joint-stock companies. Many of these means of production and of distribution are, from the outset, so colossal that, like the railways, they exclude all other forms of capitalistic expansion. At a further stage of evolution, this form also becomes insufficient. The producers on a large scale in a particular branch of an industry in a particular country unite in a "Trust", a union for the purpose of regulating production. They determine the total amount to be produced, parcel it out among themselves, and thus enforce the selling price fixed beforehand. But trusts of this kind, as soon as business becomes bad, are generally liable to break up, and on this very account compel a yet greater concentration of association. The whole of a particular industry is turned into one gigantic joint-stock company; internal competition gives place to the internal monopoly of this one company. This has happened in 1890 with the English alkali production, which is now, after the fusion of 48 large works, in the hands of one company, conducted upon a single plan, and with a capital of 6,000,000 pounds.

In the trusts, freedom of competition changes into its very opposite — into monopoly; and the production without any definite plan of capitalistic society capitulates to the production upon a definite plan of the invading socialistic society. Certainly, this is so far still to the benefit and advantage of the capitalists. But, in this case, the exploitation is so palpable, that it must break down. No nation will put up with production conducted by trusts, with so barefaced an exploitation of the community by a small band of dividend-mongers.

In any case, with trusts or without, the official representative of capitalist society — the state — will ultimately have to undertake the direction of production. This necessity for conversion into State property is felt first in the great institutions for intercourse and communication — the post office, the telegraphs, the railways.

If the crises demonstrate the incapacity of the bourgeoisie for managing any longer modern productive forces, the transformation of the great establishments for production and distribution into joint-stock companies, trusts, and State property, show how unnecessary the bourgeoisie are for that purpose. All the social functions of the capitalist has no further social function than that of pocketing dividends, tearing off coupons, and gambling on the Stock Exchange, where the different capitalists despoil one another of their capital. At first, the capitalistic mode of production forces out the workers. Now, it forces out the capitalists, and reduces them, just as it reduced the workers, to the ranks of the surplus-population, although not immediately into those of the industrial reserve army.

But, the transformation — either into joint-stock companies and trusts, or into State-ownership — does not do away with the capitalistic nature of the productive forces. In the joint-stock companies and trusts, this is obvious. And the modern State, again, is only the organization that bourgeois society takes on in order to support the external conditions of the capitalist mode of production against the encroachments as well of the workers as of individual capitalists. The modern state, no matter what its form, is essentially a capitalist machine — the state of the capitalists, the ideal personification of the total national capital. The more it proceeds to the taking over of productive forces, the more does it actually become the national capitalist, the more citizens does it exploit. The workers remain wage-workers — proletarians. The capitalist relation is not done away with. It is, rather, brought to a head. But, brought to a head, it topples over. State-ownership of the productive forces is not the solution of the conflict, but concealed within it are the technical conditions that form the elements of that solution.

This solution can only consist in the practical recognition of the social nature of the modern forces of production, and therefore in the harmonizing with the socialized character of the means of production. And this can only come about by society openly and directly taking possession of the productive forces which have outgrown all control, except that of society as a whole. The social character of the means of production and of the products today reacts against the producers, periodically disrupts all production and exchange, acts only like a law of Nature working blindly, forcibly, destructively. But, with the taking over by society of the productive forces, the social character of the means of production and of the products will be utilized by the producers with a perfect understanding of its nature, and instead of being a source of disturbance and periodical collapse, will become the most powerful lever of production itself.

Active social forces work exactly like natural forces: blindly, forcibly, destructively, so long as we do not understand, and reckon with, them. But, when once we understand them, when once we grasp their action, their direction, their effects, it depends only upon ourselves to subject them more and more to our own will, and, by means of them, to reach our own ends. And this holds quite especially of the mighty productive forces of today. As long as we obstinately refuse to understand the nature and the character of these social means of action — and this understanding goes against the grain of the capitalist mode of production, and its defenders — so long these forces are at work in spite of us, in opposition to us, so long they master us, as we have shown above in detail.

But when once their nature is understood, they can, in the hand working together, be transformed from master demons into willing servants. The difference is as that between the destructive force of electricity in the lightning in the storm, and electricity under command in the telegraph and the voltaic arc; the difference between a conflagration, and fire working in the service of man. With this recognition, at last, of the real nature of the productive forces of today, the social anarchy of production gives place to a social regulation of production upon a definite plan, according to the needs of the community and of each individual. Then the capitalist mode of appropriation, in which the product enslaves first the producer, and then the appropriator, is replaced by the mode of appropriation of the products that is based upon the nature of the modern means of production; upon the one hand, direct social appropriation, as means to the maintenance and extension of production — on the other, direct individual appropriation, as means of subsistence and of enjoyment.

Whilst the capitalist mode of production more and more completely transforms the great majority of the population into proletarians, it creates the power which, under penalty of its own destruction, is forced to accomplish this revolution. Whilst it forces on more and more of the transformation of the vast means of production, already socialized, into State property, it shows itself the way to accomplishing this revolution. The proletariat seizes political power and turns the means of production into State property.

But, in doing this, it abolishes itself as proletariat, abolishes all class distinction and class antagonisms, abolishes also the State as State. Society, thus far, based upon class antagonisms, had need of the State. That is, of an organization of the particular class which was, *pro tempore*, the exploiting class, an organization for the purpose of preventing any interference from without with the existing conditions of production, and, therefore, especially, for the purpose of forcibly keeping the exploited classes in the condition of oppression corresponding with the given mode of production (slavery, serfdom, wage-labor). The State was the official representative of society as a whole; the gathering of it together into a visible embodiment. But, it was this only in so far as it was the State of that class which itself represented, for the time being, society as a whole:

in ancient times, the State of slaveowning citizens;

in the Middle Ages, the feudal lords;

in our own times, the bourgeoisie.

When, at last, it becomes the real representative of the whole of society, it renders itself unnecessary. As soon as there is no longer any social class to be held in subjection; as soon as class rule, and the individual struggle for existence based upon our present anarchy in production, with the collisions and excesses arising from these, are removed, nothing more remains to be repressed, and a special repressive force, a State, is no longer necessary. The first act by virtue of which the State really constitutes itself the representative of the whole of society — the taking possession of the means of production in the name of society — this is, at the same time, its last independent act as a State. State interference in social relations becomes, in one domain after another, superfluous, and then dies out of itself; the government of persons is replaced by the administration of things, and by the conduct of processes of production. The State is not "abolished". It dies out. This gives the measure of the value of the phrase: "a free State", both as to its justifiable use at times by agitators, and as to its ultimate scientific inefficiency; and also of the demands of the so-called anarchists for the abolition of the State out of hand.

Since the historical appearance of the capitalist mode of production, the appropriation by society of all the means of production has often been dreamed of, more or less vaguely, by individuals, as well as by sects, as the ideal of the future. But it could become possible, could become a historical necessity, only when the actual conditions for its realization were there. Like every other social advance, it becomes practicable, not by men understanding that the existence of classes is in contradiction to justice, equality, etc., not by the mere willingness to abolish these classes, but by virtue of certain new economic conditions. The separation of society into an exploiting and an exploited class, a ruling and an oppressed class, was the necessary consequences of the deficient and restricted development of production in former times. So long as the total social labor only yields a produce which but slightly exceeds that barely necessary for the existence of all; so long, therefore, as labor engages all or almost all the time of the great majority of the members of society — so long, of necessity, this society is divided into classes. Side by side with the great majority, exclusively bond slaves to labor, arises a class freed from directly productive labor, which looks after the general affairs of society: the direction of labor, State business, law, science, art, etc. It is, therefore, the law of division of labor that lies at the basis of the division into classes. But this does not prevent this division into classes from being carried out by means of violence and robbery, trickery and fraud. It does not prevent the ruling class, once having the upper hand, from consolidating its power at the expense of the working-class, from turning its social leadership into an intensified exploitation of the masses.

But if, upon this showing, division into classes has a certain historical justification, it has this only for a given period, only under given social conditions. It was based upon the insufficiency of production. It will be swept away by the complete development of modern productive forces. And, in fact, the abolition of classes in society presupposes a degree of historical evolution at which the existence, not simply of this or that particular ruling class, but of any ruling class at all, and, therefore, the existence of class distinction itself, has become a obsolete anachronism. It presupposes, therefore, the development of production carried out to a degree at which appropriation of the means of production and of the products, and, with this, of political domination, of the monopoly of culture, and of intellectual leadership by a particular class of society, has become not only superfluous but economically, politically, intellectually, a hindrance to development.

This point is now reached. Their political and intellectual bankruptcy is scarcely any longer a secret to the bourgeoisie themselves. Their economic bankruptcy recurs regularly every 10 years. In every crisis, society is suffocated beneath the weight of its own productive forces and products, which it cannot use, and stands helpless, face-to-face with the absurd contradiction that the producers have nothing to consume, because consumers are wanting. The expansive force of the means of production burst the bonds that the capitalist mode of production had imposed upon them. Their deliverance from these bonds is the one precondition for an unbroken, constantly-accelerated development of the productive forces, and therewith for a practically unlimited increase of production itself. Nor is this all. The socialized appropriation of the means of production does away, not only with the present artificial restrictions upon production, but also with the positive waste and devastation of productive forces and products that are at the present time the inevitable concomitants of production, and that reach their height in the crises. Further, it sets free for the community at large a mass of means of production and of products, by doing away with the senseless extravagance of the ruling classes of today, and their political representatives. The possibility of securing for every member of society, by means of socialized production, an existence not only fully sufficient materially, and becoming day-by-day more full, but an existence guaranteeing to all the free development and exercise of their physical and mental faculties — this possibility is now, for the first time, here, but it is here.

With the seizing of the means of production by society, production of commodities is done away with, and, simultaneously, the mastery of the product over the producer. Anarchy in social production is replaced by systematic, definite organization. The struggle for individual existence disappears. Then, for the first time, man, in a certain sense, is finally marked off from the rest of the animal kingdom, and emerges from mere animal conditions of existence into really human ones. The whole sphere of the conditions of life which environ man, and which have hitherto ruled man, now comes under the dominion and control of man, who for the first time becomes the real, conscious lord of nature, because he has now become master of his own social organization. The laws of his own social action, hitherto standing face-to-face with man as laws of Nature foreign to, and dominating him, will then be used with full understanding, and so mastered by him. Man's own social organization, hitherto confronting him as a necessity imposed by Nature and history, now becomes the result of his own free action. The extraneous objective forces that have, hitherto, governed history, pass under the control of man himself. Only from that time will man himself, more and more consciously, make his own history — only from that time will the social causes set in movement by him have, in the main and in a constantly growing measure, the results intended by him. It is the ascent of man from the kingdom of necessity to the kingdom of freedom.

Let us briefly sum up our sketch of historical evolution.

I. Mediaeval Society — Individual production on a small scale. Means of production adapted for individual use; hence primitive, ungainly, petty, dwarfed in action. Production for immediate consumption, either of the producer himself or his feudal lord. Only where an excess of production over this consumption occurs is such excess offered for sale, enters into exchange. Production of commodities, therefore, only in its infancy. But already it contains within itself, in embryo, anarchy in the production of society at large.

II. Capitalist Revolution — transformation of industry, at first be means of simple cooperation and manufacture. Concentration of the means of production, hitherto scattered, into great workshops. As a consequence, their transformation from individual to social means of production — a transformation which does not, on the whole, affect the form of exchange. The old forms of appropriation remain in force. The capitalist appears. In his capacity as owner of the means of production, he also appropriates the products and turns them into commodities. Production has become a social act. Exchange and appropriation continue to be individual acts, the acts of individuals. The social product is appropriated by the individual capitalist. Fundamental contradiction, whence arise all the contradictions in which our present-day society moves, and which modern industry brings to light.

A. Severance of the producer from the means of production. Condemnation of the worker to wage-labor for life. Antagonism between the proletariat and the bourgeoisie.

B. Growing predominance and increasing effectiveness of the laws governing the production of commodities. Unbridled competition. Contradiction between socialized organization in the individual factory and social anarchy in the production as a whole.

C. On the one hand, perfecting of machinery, made by competition compulsory for each individual manufacturer, and complemented by a constantly growing displacement of laborers. Industrial reserve-army. On the other hand, unlimited extension of production, also compulsory under competition, for every manufacturer. On both sides, unheard-of development of productive forces, excess of supply over demand, over-production and products — excess there, of laborers, without employment and without means of existence. But these two levers of production and of social well-being are unable to work together, because the capitalist form of production prevents the productive forces from working and the products from circulating, unless they are first turned into capital — which their very superabundance prevents. The contradiction has grown into an absurdity. The mode of production rises in rebellion against the form of exchange.

D. Partial recognition of the social character of the productive forces forced upon the capitalists themselves. Taking over of the great institutions for production and communication, first by joint-stock companies, later in by trusts, then by the State. The bourgeoisie demonstrated to be a superfluous class. All its social functions are now performed by salaried employees.

III. Proletarian Revolution — Solution of the contradictions. The proletariat seizes the public power, and by means of this transforms the socialized means of production, slipping from the hands of the bourgeoisie, into public property. By this act, the proletariat frees the means of production from the character of capital they have thus far borne, and gives their socialized character complete freedom to work itself out. Socialized production upon a predetermined plan becomes henceforth possible. The development of production makes the existence of different classes of society thenceforth an anachronism. In proportion as anarchy in social production vanishes, the political authority of the State dies out. Man, at last the master of his own form of social organization, becomes at the same time the lord over Nature, his own master — free.

To accomplish this act of universal emancipation is the historical mission of the modern proletariat. To thoroughly comprehend the historical conditions and this the very nature of this act, to impart to the now oppressed proletarian class a full knowledge of the conditions and of the meaning of the momentous act it is called upon to accomplish, this is the task of the theoretical expression of the proletarian movement, scientific Socialism.

The Principles of Communism

1 — What is Communism?
Communism is the doctrine of the conditions of the liberation of the proletariat.

2 — What is the proletariat?
The proletariat is that class in society which lives entirely from the sale of its labor and does not draw profit from any kind of capital; whose weal and woe, whose life and death, whose sole existence depends on the demand for labor – hence, on the changing state of business, on the vagaries of unbridled competition. The proletariat, or the class of proletarians, is, in a word, the working class of the 19th century.

3 — Proletarians, then, have not always existed?
No. There have always been poor and working classes; and the working class have mostly been poor. But there have not always been workers and poor people living under conditions as they are today; in other words, there have not always been proletarians, any more than there has always been free unbridled competitions.

4 — How did the proletariat originate?

The Proletariat originated in the industrial revolution, which took place in England in the last half of the last (18th) century, and which has since then been repeated in all the civilized countries of the world.

This industrial revolution was precipitated by the discovery of the steam engine, various spinning machines, the mechanical loom, and a whole series of other mechanical devices. These machines, which were very expensive and hence could be bought only by big capitalists, altered the whole mode of production and displaced the former workers, because the machines turned out cheaper and better commodities than the workers could produce with their inefficient spinning wheels and handlooms. The machines delivered industry wholly into the hands of the big capitalists and rendered entirely worthless the meagre property of the workers (tools, looms, etc.). The result was that the capitalists soon had everything in their hands and nothing remained to the workers. This marked the introduction of the factory system into the textile industry.

Once the impulse to the introduction of machinery and the factory system had been given, this system spread quickly to all other branches of industry, especially cloth- and book-printing, pottery, and the metal industries.

Labor was more and more divided among the individual workers so that the worker who previously had done a complete piece of work now did only a part of that piece. This division of labor made it possible to produce things faster and cheaper. It reduced the activity of the individual worker to simple, endlessly repeated mechanical motions which could be performed not only as well but much better by a machine. In this way, all these industries fell, one after another, under the dominance of steam, machinery, and the factory system, just as spinning and weaving had already done.

But at the same time, they also fell into the hands of big capitalists, and their workers were deprived of whatever independence remained to them. Gradually, not only genuine manufacture but also handicrafts came within the province of the factory system as big capitalists increasingly displaced the small master craftsmen by setting up huge workshops, which saved many expenses and permitted an elaborate division of labor.

This is how it has come about that in civilized countries at the present time nearly all kinds of labor are performed in factories – and, in nearly all branches of work, handicrafts and manufacture have been superseded. This process has, to an ever greater degree, ruined the old middle class, especially the small handicraftsmen; it has entirely transformed the condition of the workers; and two new classes have been created which are gradually swallowing up all the others. These are:

(i) The class of big capitalists, who, in all civilized countries, are already in almost exclusive possession of all the means of subsistence and of the instruments (machines, factories) and materials necessary for the production of the means of subsistence. This is the bourgeois class, or the bourgeoisie.

(ii) The class of the wholly propertyless, who are obliged to sell their labor to the bourgeoisie in order to get, in exchange, the means of subsistence for their support. This is called the class of proletarians, or the proletariat.

5 — Under what conditions does this sale of the labor of the proletarians to the bourgeoisie take place?

Labor is a commodity, like any other, and its price is therefore determined by exactly the same laws that apply to other commodities. In a regime of big industry or of free competition – as we shall see, the two come to the same thing – the price of a commodity is, on the average, always equal to its cost of production. Hence, the price of labor is also equal to the cost of production of labor.

But, the costs of production of labor consist of precisely the quantity of means of subsistence necessary to enable the worker to continue working, and to prevent the working class from dying out. The worker will therefore get no more for his labor than is necessary for this purpose; the price of labor, or the wage, will, in other words, be the lowest, the minimum, required for the maintenance of life.

However, since business is sometimes better and sometimes worse, it follows that the worker sometimes gets more and sometimes gets less for his commodities. But, again, just as the industrialist, on the average of good times and bad, gets no more and no less for his commodities than what they cost, similarly on the average the worker gets no more and no less than his minimum.

This economic law of wages operates the more strictly the greater the degree to which big industry has taken possession of all branches of production.

6 — What working classes were there before the industrial revolution?

The working classes have always, according to the different stages of development of society, lived in different circumstances and had different relations to the owning and ruling classes.

In antiquity, the workers were the slaves of the owners, just as they still are in many backward countries and even in the southern part of the United States.

In the Middle Ages, they were the serfs of the land-owning nobility, as they still are in Hungary, Poland, and Russia. In the Middle Ages, and indeed right up to the industrial revolution, there were also journeymen in the cities who worked in the service of petty bourgeois masters. Gradually, as manufacture developed, these journeymen became manufacturing workers who were even then employed by larger capitalists.

7 — In what way do proletarians differ from slaves?

The slave is sold once and for all; the proletarian must sell himself daily and hourly.

The individual slave, property of one master, is assured an existence, however miserable it may be, because of the master's interest. The individual proletarian, property as it were of the entire bourgeois class which buys his labor only when someone has need of it, has no secure existence. This existence is assured only to the class as a whole.

The slave is outside competition; the proletarian is in it and experiences all its vagaries.

The slave counts as a thing, not as a member of society. Thus, the slave can have a better existence than the proletarian, while the proletarian belongs to a higher stage of social development and, himself, stands on a higher social level than the slave.

The slave frees himself when, of all the relations of private property, he abolishes only the relation of slavery and thereby becomes a proletarian; the proletarian can free himself only by abolishing private property in general.

8 — In what way do proletarians differ from serfs?

The serf possesses and uses an instrument of production, a piece of land, in exchange for which he gives up a part of his product or part of the services of his labor.

The proletarian works with the instruments of production of another, for the account of this other, in exchange for a part of the product.

The serf gives up, the proletarian receives. The serf has an assured existence, the proletarian has not. The serf is outside competition, the proletarian is in it.

The serf liberates himself in one of three ways: either he runs away to the city and there becomes a handicraftsman; or, instead of products and services, he gives money to his lord and thereby becomes a free tenant; or he overthrows his feudal lord and himself becomes a property owner. In short, by one route or another, he gets into the owning class and enters into competition. The proletarian liberates himself by abolishing competition, private property, and all class differences.

9 — In what way do proletarians differ from handicraftsmen?

In contrast to the proletarian, the so-called handicraftsman, as he still existed almost everywhere in the past (eighteenth) century and still exists here and there at present, is a proletarian at most temporarily. His goal is to acquire capital himself wherewith to exploit other workers. He can often achieve this goal where guilds still exist or where freedom from guild restrictions has not yet led to the introduction of factory-style methods into the crafts nor yet to fierce competition But as soon as the factory system has been introduced into the crafts and competition flourishes fully, this perspective dwindles away and the handicraftsman becomes more and more a proletarian. The handicraftsman therefore frees himself by becoming either bourgeois or entering the middle class in general, or becoming a proletarian because of competition (as is now more often the case). In which case he can free himself by joining the proletarian movement, i.e., the more or less communist movement.

10 — In what way do proletarians differ from manufacturing workers?

The manufacturing worker of the 16th to the 18th centuries still had, with but few exception, an instrument of production in his own possession – his loom, the family spinning wheel, a little plot of land which he cultivated in his spare time. The proletarian has none of these things.

The manufacturing worker almost always lives in the countryside and in a more or less patriarchal relation to his landlord or employer; the proletarian lives, for the most part, in the city and his relation to his employer is purely a cash relation.

The manufacturing worker is torn out of his patriarchal relation by big industry, loses whatever property he still has, and in this way becomes a proletarian.

11 — What were the immediate consequences of the industrial revolution and of the division of society into bourgeoisie and proletariat?

First, the lower and lower prices of industrial products brought about by machine labor totally destroyed, in all countries of the world, the old system of manufacture or industry based upon hand labor.

In this way, all semi-barbarian countries, which had hitherto been more or less strangers to historical development, and whose industry had been based on manufacture, were violently forced out of their isolation. They bought the cheaper commodities of the English and allowed their own manufacturing workers to be ruined. Countries which had known no progress for thousands of years – for example, India – were thoroughly revolutionized, and even China is now on the way to a revolution.

We have come to the point where a new machine invented in England deprives millions of Chinese workers of their livelihood within a year's time.

In this way, big industry has brought all the people of the Earth into contact with each other, has merged all local markets into one world market, has spread civilization and progress everywhere and has thus ensured that whatever happens in civilized countries will have repercussions in all other countries.

It follows that if the workers in England or France now liberate themselves, this must set off revolution in all other countries – revolutions which, sooner or later, must accomplish the liberation of their respective working class.

Second, wherever big industries displaced manufacture, the bourgeoisie developed in wealth and power to the utmost and made itself the first class of the country. The result was that wherever this happened, the bourgeoisie took political power into its own hands and displaced the hitherto ruling classes, the aristocracy, the guildmasters, and their representative, the absolute monarchy.

The bourgeoisie annihilated the power of the aristocracy, the nobility, by abolishing the entailment of estates – in other words, by making landed property subject to purchase and sale, and by doing away with the special privileges of the nobility. It destroyed the power of the guildmasters by abolishing guilds and handicraft privileges. In their place, it put competition – that is, a state of society in which everyone has the right to enter into any branch of industry, the only obstacle being a lack of the necessary capital.

The introduction of free competition is thus public declaration that from now on the members of society are unequal only to the extent that their capitals are unequal, that capital is the decisive power, and that therefore the capitalists, the bourgeoisie, have become the first class in society.

Free competition is necessary for the establishment of big industry, because it is the only condition of society in which big industry can make its way.

Having destroyed the social power of the nobility and the guildmasters, the bourgeois also destroyed their political power. Having raised itself to the actual position of first class in society, it proclaims itself to be also the dominant political class. This it does through the introduction of the representative system which rests on bourgeois equality before the law and the recognition of free competition, and in European countries takes the form of constitutional monarchy. In these constitutional monarchies, only those who possess a certain capital are voters – that is to say, only members of the bourgeoisie. These bourgeois voters choose the deputies, and these bourgeois deputies, by using their right to refuse to vote taxes, choose a bourgeois government.

Third, everywhere the proletariat develops in step with the bourgeoisie. In proportion, as the bourgeoisie grows in wealth, the proletariat grows in numbers. For, since the proletarians can be employed only by capital, and since capital extends only through employing labor, it follows that the growth of the proletariat proceeds at precisely the same pace as the growth of capital.

Simultaneously, this process draws members of the bourgeoisie and proletarians together into the great cities where industry can be carried on most profitably, and by thus throwing great masses in one spot it gives to the proletarians a consciousness of their own strength.

Moreover, the further this process advances, the more new labor-saving machines are invented, the greater is the pressure exercised by big industry on wages, which, as we have seen, sink to their minimum and therewith render the condition of the proletariat increasingly unbearable. The growing dissatisfaction of the proletariat thus joins with its rising power to prepare a proletarian social revolution.

12—What were the further consequences of the industrial revolution?

Big industry created in the steam engine, and other machines, the means of endlessly expanding industrial production, speeding it up, and cutting its costs. With production thus facilitated, the free competition, which is necessarily bound up with big industry, assumed the most extreme forms; a multitude of capitalists invaded industry, and, in a short while, more was produced than was needed.

As a consequence, finished commodities could not be sold, and a so-called commercial crisis broke out. Factories had to be closed, their owners went bankrupt, and the workers were without bread. Deepest misery reigned everywhere.

After a time, the superfluous products were sold, the factories began to operate again, wages rose, and gradually business got better than ever.

But it was not long before too many commodities were again produced and a new crisis broke out, only to follow the same course as its predecessor.

Ever since the beginning of this (19th) century, the condition of industry has constantly fluctuated between periods of prosperity and periods of crisis; nearly every five to seven years, a fresh crisis has intervened, always with the greatest hardship for workers, and always accompanied by general revolutionary stirrings and the direct peril to the whole existing order of things.

13 — What follows from these periodic commercial crises?

First: That, though big industry in its earliest stage created free competition, it has now outgrown free competition;

that, for big industry, competition and generally the individualistic organization of production have become a fetter which it must and will shatter;

that, so long as big industry remains on its present footing, it can be maintained only at the cost of general chaos every seven years, each time threatening the whole of civilization and not only plunging the proletarians into misery but also ruining large sections of the bourgeoisie;

hence, either that big industry must itself be given up, which is an absolute impossibility, or that it makes unavoidably necessary an entirely new organization of society in which production is no longer directed by mutually competing individual industrialists but rather by the whole society operating according to a definite plan and taking account of the needs of all.

Second: That big industry, and the limitless expansion of production which it makes possible, bring within the range of feasibility a social order in which so much is produced that every member of society will be in a position to exercise and develop all his powers and faculties in complete freedom.

It thus appears that the very qualities of big industry which, in our present-day society, produce misery and crises are those which, in a different form of society, will abolish this misery and these catastrophic depressions.

We see with the greatest clarity:

(i) That all these evils are from now on to be ascribed solely to a social order which no longer corresponds to the requirements of the real situation; and

(ii) That it is possible, through a new social order, to do away with these evils altogether.

14 — What will this new social order have to be like?

Above all, it will have to take the control of industry and of all branches of production out of the hands of mutually competing individuals, and instead institute a system in which all these branches of production are operated by society as a whole – that is, for the common account, according to a common plan, and with the participation of all members of society.

It will, in other words, abolish competition and replace it with association.

Moreover, since the management of industry by individuals necessarily implies private property, and since competition is in reality merely the manner and form in which the control of industry by private property owners expresses itself, it follows that private property cannot be separated from competition and the individual management of industry. Private property must, therefore, be abolished and in its place must come the common utilization of all instruments of production and the distribution of all products according to common agreement – in a word, what is called the communal ownership of goods.

In fact, the abolition of private property is, doubtless, the shortest and most significant way to characterize the revolution in the whole social order which has been made necessary by the development of industry – and for this reason it is rightly advanced by communists as their main demand.

15 — Was not the abolition of private property possible at an earlier time?

No. Every change in the social order, every revolution in property relations, is the necessary consequence of the creation of new forces of production which no longer fit into the old property relations.

Private property has not always existed.

When, towards the end of the Middle Ages, there arose a new mode of production which could not be carried on under the then existing feudal and guild forms of property, this manufacture, which had outgrown the old property relations, created a new property form, private property. And for manufacture and the earliest stage of development of big industry, private property was the only possible property form; the social order based on it was the only possible social order.

So long as it is not possible to produce so much that there is enough for all, with more left over for expanding the social capital and extending the forces of production – so long as this is not possible, there must always be a ruling class directing the use of society's productive forces, and a poor, oppressed class. How these classes are constituted depends on the stage of development.

The agrarian Middle Ages give us the baron and the serf; the cities of the later Middle Ages show us the guildmaster and the journeyman and the day laborer; the 17th century has its manufacturing workers; the 19th has big factory owners and proletarians.

It is clear that, up to now, the forces of production have never been developed to the point where enough could be developed for all, and that private property has become a fetter and a barrier in relation to the further development of the forces of production.

Now, however, the development of big industry has ushered in a new period. Capital and the forces of production have been expanded to an unprecedented extent, and the means are at hand to multiply them without limit in the near future. Moreover, the forces of production have been concentrated in the hands of a few bourgeois, while the great mass of the people are more and more falling into the proletariat, their situation becoming more wretched and intolerable in proportion to the increase of wealth of the bourgeoisie. And finally, these mighty and easily extended forces of production have so far outgrown private property and the bourgeoisie, that they threaten at any moment to unleash the most violent disturbances of the social order. Now, under these conditions, the abolition of private property has become not only possible but absolutely necessary.

16 — Will the peaceful abolition of private property be possible?

It would be desirable if this could happen, and the communists would certainly be the last to oppose it. Communists know only too well that all conspiracies are not only useless, but even harmful. They know all too well that revolutions are not made intentionally and arbitrarily, but that, everywhere and always, they have been the necessary consequence of conditions which were wholly independent of the will and direction of individual parties and entire classes.

But they also see that the development of the proletariat in nearly all civilized countries has been violently suppressed, and that in this way the opponents of communism have been working toward a revolution with all their strength. If the oppressed proletariat is finally driven to revolution, then we communists will defend the interests of the proletarians with deeds as we now defend them with words.

17 — Will it be possible for private property to be abolished at one stroke?

No, no more than existing forces of production can at one stroke be multiplied to the extent necessary for the creation of a communal society.

In all probability, the proletarian revolution will transform existing society gradually and will be able to abolish private property only when the means of production are available in sufficient quantity.

18 — What will be the course of this revolution?

Above all, it will establish a democratic constitution, and through this, the direct or indirect dominance of the proletariat. Direct in England, where the proletarians are already a majority of the people. Indirect in France and Germany, where the majority of the people consists not only of proletarians, but also of small peasants and petty bourgeois who are in the process of falling into the proletariat, who are more and more dependent in all their political interests on the proletariat, and who must, therefore, soon adapt to the demands of the proletariat. Perhaps this will cost a second struggle, but the outcome can only be the victory of the proletariat.

Democracy would be wholly valueless to the proletariat if it were not immediately used as a means for putting through measures directed against private property and ensuring the livelihood of the proletariat. The main measures, emerging as the necessary result of existing relations, are the following:

(i) Limitation of private property through progressive taxation, heavy inheritance taxes, abolition of inheritance through collateral lines (brothers, nephews, etc.) forced loans, etc.

(ii) Gradual expropriation of landowners, industrialists, railroad magnates and shipowners, partly through competition by state industry, partly directly through compensation in the form of bonds.

(iii) Confiscation of the possessions of all emigrants and rebels against the majority of the people.

(iv) Organization of labor or employment of proletarians on publicly owned land, in factories and workshops, with competition among the workers being abolished and with the factory owners, in so far as they still exist, being obliged to pay the same high wages as those paid by the state.

(v) An equal obligation on all members of society to work until such time as private property has been completely abolished. Formation of industrial armies, especially for agriculture.

(vi) Centralization of money and credit in the hands of the state through a national bank with state capital, and the suppression of all private banks and bankers.

(vii) Increase in the number of national factories, workshops, railroads, ships; bringing new lands into cultivation and improvement of land already under cultivation – all in proportion to the growth of the capital and labor force at the disposal of the nation.

(viii) Education of all children, from the moment they can leave their mother's care, in national establishments at national cost. Education and production together.

(ix) Construction, on public lands, of great palaces as communal dwellings for associated groups of citizens engaged in both industry and agriculture and combining in their way of life the advantages of urban and rural conditions while avoiding the one-sidedness and drawbacks of each.

(x) Destruction of all unhealthy and jerry-built dwellings in urban districts.

(xi) Equal inheritance rights for children born in and out of wedlock.

(xii) Concentration of all means of transportation in the hands of the nation.

It is impossible, of course, to carry out all these measures at once. But one will always bring others in its wake. Once the first radical attack on private property has been launched, the proletariat will find itself forced to go ever further, to concentrate increasingly in the hands of the state all capital, all agriculture, all transport, all trade. All the foregoing measures are directed to this end; and they will become practicable and feasible, capable of producing their centralizing effects to precisely the degree that the proletariat, through its labor, multiplies the country's productive forces.

Finally, when all capital, all production, all exchange have been brought together in the hands of the nation, private property will disappear of its own accord, money will become superfluous, and production will so expand and man so change that society will be able to slough off whatever of its old economic habits may remain.

19—Will it be possible for this revolution to take place in one country alone?

No. By creating the world market, big industry has already brought all the peoples of the Earth, and especially the civilized peoples, into such close relation with one another that none is independent of what happens to the others.

Further, it has co-ordinated the social development of the civilized countries to such an extent that, in all of them, bourgeoisie and proletariat have become the decisive classes, and the struggle between them the great struggle of the day. It follows that the communist revolution will not merely be a national phenomenon but must take place simultaneously in all civilized countries – that is to say, at least in England, America, France, and Germany.

It will develop in each of the these countries more or less rapidly, according as one country or the other has a more developed industry, greater wealth, a more significant mass of productive forces. Hence, it will go slowest and will meet most obstacles in Germany, most rapidly and with the fewest difficulties in England. It will have a powerful impact on the other countries of the world, and will radically alter the course of development which they have followed up to now, while greatly stepping up its pace.

It is a universal revolution and will, accordingly, have a universal range.

20 — What will be the consequences of the ultimate disappearance of private property?

Society will take all forces of production and means of commerce, as well as the exchange and distribution of products, out of the hands of private capitalists and will manage them in accordance with a plan based on the availability of resources and the needs of the whole society. In this way, most important of all, the evil consequences which are now associated with the conduct of big industry will be abolished.

There will be no more crises; the expanded production, which for the present order of society is overproduction and hence a prevailing cause of misery, will then be insufficient and in need of being expanded much further. Instead of generating misery, overproduction will reach beyond the elementary requirements of society to assure the satisfaction of the needs of all; it will create new needs and, at the same time, the means of satisfying them. It will become the condition of, and the stimulus to, new progress, which will no longer throw the whole social order into confusion, as progress has always done in the past. Big industry, freed from the pressure of private property, will undergo such an expansion that what we now see will seem as petty in comparison as manufacture seems when put beside the big industry of our own day. This development of industry will make available to society a sufficient mass of products to satisfy the needs of everyone.

The same will be true of agriculture, which also suffers from the pressure of private property and is held back by the division of privately owned land into small parcels. Here, existing improvements and scientific procedures will be put into practice, with a resulting leap forward which will assure to society all the products it needs.

In this way, such an abundance of goods will be able to satisfy the needs of all its members.

The division of society into different, mutually hostile classes will then become unnecessary. Indeed, it will be not only unnecessary but intolerable in the new social order. The existence of classes originated in the division of labor, and the division of labor, as it has been known up to the present, will completely disappear. For mechanical and chemical processes are not enough to bring industrial and agricultural production up to the level we have described; the capacities of the men who make use of these processes must undergo a corresponding development.

Just as the peasants and manufacturing workers of the last century changed their whole way of life and became quite different people when they were drawn into big industry, in the same way, communal control over production by society as a whole, and the resulting new development, will both require an entirely different kind of human material.

People will no longer be, as they are today, subordinated to a single branch of production, bound to it, exploited by it; they will no longer develop one of their faculties at the expense of all others; they will no longer know only one branch, or one branch of a single branch, of production as a whole. Even industry as it is today is finding such people less and less useful.

Industry controlled by society as a whole, and operated according to a plan, presupposes well-rounded human beings, their faculties developed in balanced fashion, able to see the system of production in its entirety.

The form of the division of labor which makes one a peasant, another a cobbler, a third a factory worker, a fourth a stock-market operator, has already been undermined by machinery and will completely disappear. Education will enable young people quickly to familiarize themselves with the whole system of production and to pass from one branch of production to another in response to the needs of society or their own inclinations. It will, therefore, free them from the one-sided character which the present-day division of labor impresses upon every individual. Communist society will, in this way, make it possible for its members to put their comprehensively developed faculties to full use. But, when this happens, classes will necessarily disappear. It follows that society organized on a communist basis is incompatible with the existence of classes on the one hand, and that the very building of such a society provides the means of abolishing class differences on the other.

A corollary of this is that the difference between city and country is destined to disappear. The management of agriculture and industry by the same people rather than by two different classes of people is, if only for purely material reasons, a necessary condition of communist association. The dispersal of the agricultural population on the land, alongside the crowding of the industrial population into the great cities, is a condition which corresponds to an undeveloped state of both agriculture and industry and can already be felt as an obstacle to further development.

The general co-operation of all members of society for the purpose of planned exploitation of the forces of production, the expansion of production to the point where it will satisfy the needs of all, the abolition of a situation in which the needs of some are satisfied at the expense of the needs of others, the complete liquidation of classes and their conflicts, the rounded development of the capacities of all members of society through the elimination of the present division of labor, through industrial education, through engaging in varying activities, through the participation by all in the enjoyments produced by all, through the combination of city and country – these are the main consequences of the abolition of private property.

21 – What will be the influence of communist society on the family?

It will transform the relations between the sexes into a purely private matter which concerns only the persons involved and into which society has no occasion to intervene. It can do this since it does away with private property and educates children on a communal basis, and in this way removes the two bases of traditional marriage – the dependence, rooted in private property, of the women on the man, and of the children on the parents.

And here is the answer to the outcry of the highly moral philistines against the "community of women". Community of women is a condition which belongs entirely to bourgeois society and which today finds its complete expression in prostitution. But prostitution is based on private property and falls with it. Thus, communist society, instead of introducing community of women, in fact abolishes it.

22 — What will be the attitude of communism to existing nationalities?

The nationalities of the peoples associating themselves in accordance with the principle of community will be compelled to mingle with each other as a result of this association and thereby to dissolve themselves, just as the various estate and class distinctions must disappear through the abolition of their basis, private property.

23 — What will be its attitude to existing religions?

All religions so far have been the expression of historical stages of development of individual peoples or groups of peoples. But communism is the stage of historical development which makes all existing religions superfluous and brings about their disappearance.

24 — How do communists differ from socialists?

The so-called socialists are divided into three categories.

Reactionary Socialists

The first category consists of adherents of a feudal and patriarchal society which has already been destroyed, and is still daily being destroyed, by big industry and world trade and their creation, bourgeois society. This category concludes, from the evils of existing society, that feudal and patriarchal society must be restored because it was free of such evils. In one way or another, all their proposals are directed to this end.

This category of reactionary socialists, for all their seeming partisanship and their scalding tears for the misery of the proletariat, is nevertheless energetically opposed by the communists for the following reasons:

(i) It strives for something which is entirely impossible.

(ii) It seeks to establish the rule of the aristocracy, the guildmasters, the small producers, and their retinue of absolute or feudal monarchs, officials, soldiers, and priests – a society which was, to be sure, free of the evils of present-day society but which brought it at least as many evils without even offering to the oppressed workers the prospect of liberation through a communist revolution.

(iii) As soon as the proletariat becomes revolutionary and communist, these reactionary socialists show their true colors by immediately making common cause with the bourgeoisie against the proletarians.

Bourgeois Socialists

The second category consists of adherents of present-day society who have been frightened for its future by the evils to which it necessarily gives rise. What they want, therefore, is to maintain this society while getting rid of the evils which are an inherent part of it.

To this end, some propose mere welfare measures – while others come forward with grandiose systems of reform which, under the pretense of re-organizing society, are in fact intended to preserve the foundations, and hence the life, of existing society.

Communists must unremittingly struggle against these bourgeois socialists because they work for the enemies of communists and protect the society which communists aim to overthrow.

Democractic Socialists

Finally, the third category consists of democratic socialists who favor some of the same measures the communists advocate, as described in Question 18, not as part of the transition to communism, however, but as measures which they believe will be sufficient to abolish the misery and evils of present-day society.

These democratic socialists are either proletarians who are not yet sufficiently clear about the conditions of the liberation of their class, or they are representatives of the petty bourgeoisie, a class which, prior to the achievement of democracy and the socialist measures to which it gives rise, has many interests in common with the proletariat.

It follows that, in moments of action, the communists will have to come to an understanding with these democratic socialists, and in general to follow as far as possible a common policy with them – provided that these socialists do not enter into the service of the ruling bourgeoisie and attack the communists.

It is clear that this form of co-operation in action does not exclude the discussion of differences.

25 — What is the attitude of the communists to the other political parties of our time?

This attitude is different in the different countries.

In England, France, and Belgium, where the bourgeoisie rules, the communists still have a common interest with the various democratic parties, an interest which is all the greater the more closely the socialistic measures they champion approach the aims of the communists – that is, the more clearly and definitely they represent the interests of the proletariat and the more they depend on the proletariat for support. In England, for example, the working-class Chartists are infinitely closer to the communists than the democratic petty bourgeoisie or the so-called Radicals.

In America, where a democratic constitution has already been established, the communists must make the common cause with the party which will turn this constitution against the bourgeoisie and use it in the interests of the proletariat – that is, with the agrarian National Reformers.

In Switzerland, the Radicals, though a very mixed party, are the only group with which the communists can co-operate, and, among these Radicals, the Vaudois and Genevese are the most advanced.

In Germany, finally, the decisive struggle now on the order of the day is that between the bourgeoisie and the absolute monarchy. Since the communists cannot enter upon the decisive struggle between themselves and the bourgeoisie until the bourgeoisie is in power, it follows that it is in the interest of the communists to help the bourgeoisie to power as soon as possible in order the sooner to be able to overthrow it. Against the governments, therefore, the communists must continually support the radical liberal party, taking care to avoid the self-deceptions of the bourgeoisie and not fall for the enticing promises of benefits which a victory for the bourgeoisie would allegedly bring to the proletariat. The sole advantages which the proletariat would derive from a bourgeois victory would consist

(i) in various concessions which would facilitate the unification of the proletariat into a closely knit, battle-worthy, and organized class; and

(ii) in the certainly that, on the very day the absolute monarchies fall, the struggle between bourgeoisie and proletariat will start. From that day on, the policy of the communists will be the same as it now is in the countries where the bourgeoisie is already in power.

The Part Played By Labour In The Transition From Ape To Man

I

Labour is the source of all wealth, the political economists assert. And it really is the source – next to nature, which supplies it with the material that it converts into wealth. But it is even infinitely more than this. It is the prime basic condition for all human existence, and this to such an extent that, in a sense, we have to say that labour created man himself.

Many hundreds of thousands of years ago, during an epoch, not yet definitely determinable, of that period of the earth's history known to geologists as the Tertiary period, most likely towards the end of it, a particularly highly-developed race of anthropoid apes lived somewhere in the tropical zone – probably on a great continent that has now sunk to the bottom of the Indian Ocean. Darwin has given us an approximate description of these ancestors of ours. They were completely covered with hair, they had beards and pointed ears, and they lived in bands in the trees.

First, owing to their way of living which meant that the hands had different functions than the feet when climbing, these apes began to lose the habit of using their hands to walk and adopted a more and more erect posture. This was the decisive step in the transition from ape to man.

All extant anthropoid apes can stand erect and move about on their feet alone, but only in case of urgent need and in a very clumsy way. Their natural gait is in a half-erect posture and includes the use of the hands. The majority rest the knuckles of the fist on the ground and, with legs drawn up, swing the body through their long arms, much as a cripple moves on crutches. In general, all the transition stages from walking on all fours to walking on two legs are still to be observed among the apes today. The latter gait, however, has never become more than a makeshift for any of them.

It stands to reason that if erect gait among our hairy ancestors became first the rule and then, in time, a necessity, other diverse functions must, in the meantime, have devolved upon the hands. Already among the apes there is some difference in the way the hands and the feet are employed. In climbing, as mentioned above, the hands and feet have different uses. The hands are used mainly for gathering and holding food in the same way as the fore paws of the lower mammals are used. Many apes use their hands to build themselves nests in the trees or even to construct roofs between the branches to protect themselves against the weather, as the chimpanzee, for example, does. With their hands they grasp sticks to defend themselves against enemies, or bombard their enemies with fruits and stones. In captivity they use their hands for a number of simple operations copied from human beings. It is in this that one sees the great gulf between the undeveloped hand of even the most man-like apes and the human hand that has been highly perfected by hundreds of thousands of years of labour. The number and general arrangement of the bones and muscles are the same in both hands, but the hand of the lowest savage can perform hundreds of operations that no simian hand can imitate – no simian hand has ever fashioned even the crudest stone knife.

The first operations for which our ancestors gradually learned to adapt their hands during the many thousands of years of transition from ape to man could have been only very simple ones. The lowest savages, even those in whom regression to a more animal-like condition with a simultaneous physical degeneration can be assumed, are nevertheless far superior to these transitional beings. Before the first flint could be fashioned into a knife by human hands, a period of time probably elapsed in comparison with which the historical period known to us appears insignificant. But the decisive step had been taken, the hand had become free and could henceforth attain ever greater dexterity; the greater flexibility thus acquired was inherited and increased from generation to generation.

Thus the hand is not only the organ of labour, it is also the product of labour. Only by labour, by adaptation to ever new operations, through the inheritance of muscles, ligaments, and, over longer periods of time, bones that had undergone special development and the ever-renewed employment of this inherited finesse in new, more and more complicated operations, have given the human hand the high degree of perfection required to conjure into being the pictures of a Raphael, the statues of a Thorwaldsen, the music of a Paganini.

But the hand did not exist alone, it was only one member of an integral, highly complex organism. And what benefited the hand, benefited also the whole body it served; and this in two ways.

In the first place, the body benefited from the law of correlation of growth, as Darwin called it. This law states that the specialised forms of separate parts of an organic being are always bound up with certain forms of other parts that apparently have no connection with them. Thus all animals that have red blood cells without cell nuclei, and in which the head is attached to the first vertebra by means of a double articulation (condyles), also without exception possess lacteal glands for suckling their young. Similarly, cloven hoofs in mammals are regularly associated with the possession of a multiple stomach for rumination. Changes in certain forms involve changes in the form of other parts of the body, although we cannot explain the connection. Perfectly white cats with blue eyes are always, or almost always, deaf. The gradually increasing perfection of the human hand, and the commensurate adaptation of the feet for erect gait, have undoubtedly, by virtue of such correlation, reacted on other parts of the organism. However, this action has not as yet been sufficiently investigated for us to be able to do more here than to state the fact in general terms.

Much more important is the direct, demonstrable influence of the development of the hand on the rest of the organism. It has already been noted that our simian ancestors were gregarious; it is obviously impossible to seek the derivation of man, the most social of all animals, from non-gregarious immediate ancestors. Mastery over nature began with the development of the hand, with labour, and widened man's horizon at every new advance. He was continually discovering new, hitherto unknown properties in natural objects. On the other hand, the development of labour necessarily helped to bring the members of society closer together by increasing cases of mutual support and joint activity, and by making clear the advantage of this joint activity to each individual. In short, men in the making arrived at the point where they had something to say to each other. Necessity created the organ; the undeveloped larynx of the ape was slowly but surely transformed by modulation to produce constantly more developed modulation, and the organs of the mouth gradually learned to pronounce one articulate sound after another.

Comparison with animals proves that this explanation of the origin of language from and in the process of labour is the only correct one. The little that even the most highly-developed animals need to communicate to each other does not require articulate speech. In its natural state, no animal feels handicapped by its inability to speak or to understand human speech. It is quite different when it has been tamed by man. The dog and the horse, by association with man, have developed such a good ear for articulate speech that they easily learn to understand any language within their range of concept. Moreover they have acquired the capacity for feelings such as affection for man, gratitude, etc., which were previously foreign to them. Anyone who has had much to do with such animals will hardly be able to escape the conviction that in many cases they now feel their inability to speak as a defect, although, unfortunately, it is one that can no longer be remedied because their vocal organs are too specialised in a definite direction. However, where vocal organs exist, within certain limits even this inability disappears. The buccal organs of birds are as different from those of man as they can be, yet birds are the only animals that can learn to speak; and it is the bird with the most hideous voice, the parrot, that speaks best of all. Let no one object that the parrot does not understand what it says. It is true that for the sheer pleasure of talking and associating with human beings, the parrot will chatter for hours at a stretch, continually repeating its whole vocabulary. But within the limits of its range of concepts it can also learn to understand what it is saying. Teach a parrot swear words in such a way that it gets an idea of their meaning (one of the great amusements of sailors returning from the tropics); tease it and you will soon discover that it knows how to use its swear words just as correctly as a Berlin costermonger. The same is true of begging for titbits.

First labour, after it and then with it speech – these were the two most essential stimuli under the influence of which the brain of the ape gradually changed into that of man, which, for all its similarity, is far larger and more perfect. Hand in hand with the development of the brain went the development of its most immediate instruments – the senses. Just as the gradual development of speech is inevitably accompanied by a corresponding refinement of the organ of hearing, so the development of the brain as a whole is accompanied by a refinement of all the senses. The eagle sees much farther than man, but the human eye discerns considerably more in things than does the eye of the eagle. The dog has a far keener sense of smell than man, but it does not distinguish a hundredth part of the odours that for man are definite signs denoting different things. And the sense of touch, which the ape hardly possesses in its crudest initial form, has been developed only side by side with the development of the human hand itself, through the medium of labour.

The reaction on labour and speech of the development of the brain and its attendant senses, of the increasing clarity of consciousness, power of abstraction and of conclusion, gave both labour and speech an ever-renewed impulse to further development. This development did not reach its conclusion when man finally became distinct from the ape, but on the whole made further powerful progress, its degree and direction varying among different peoples and at different times, and here and there even being interrupted by local or temporary regression. This further development has been strongly urged forward, on the one hand, and guided along more definite directions, on the other, by a new element which came into play with the appearance of fully-fledged man, namely, society.

Hundreds of thousands of years – of no greater significance in the history of the earth than one second in the life of man (a leading authority in this respect, Sir William Thomson, has calculated that little more than a hundred million years could have elapsed since the time when the earth had cooled sufficiently for plants and animals to be able to live on it) certainly elapsed before human society arose out of a troupe of tree-climbing monkeys. Yet it did finally appear. And what do we find once more as the characteristic difference between the troupe of monkeys and human society? Labour. The ape herd was satisfied to browse over the feeding area determined for it by geographical conditions or the resistance of neighbouring herds; it undertook migrations and struggles to win new feeding grounds, but it was incapable of extracting from them more than they offered in their natural state, except that it unconsciously fertilised the soil with its own excrement. As soon as all possible feeding grounds were occupied, there could be no further increase in the ape population; the number of animals could at best remain stationary. But all animals waste a great deal of food, and, in addition, destroy in the germ the next generation of the food supply. Unlike the hunter, the wolf does not spare the doe which would provide it with the young the next year; the goats in Greece, that eat away the young bushes before they grow to maturity, have eaten bare all the mountains of the country. This "predatory economy" of animals plays an important part in the gradual transformation of species by forcing them to adapt themselves to other than the usual food, thanks to which their blood acquires a different chemical composition and the whole physical constitution gradually alters, while species that have remained unadapted die out. There is no doubt that this predatory economy contributed powerfully to the transition of our ancestors from ape to man. In a race of apes that far surpassed all others in intelligence and adaptability, this predatory economy must have led to a continual increase in the number of plants used for food and the consumption of more and more edible parts of food plants. In short, food became more and more varied, as did also the substances entering the body with it, substances that were the chemical premises for the transition to man.

But all that was not yet labour in the proper sense of the word. Labour begins with the making of tools. And what are the most ancient tools that we find – the most ancient judging by the heirlooms of prehistoric man that have been discovered, and by the mode of life of the earliest historical peoples and of the rawest of contemporary savages? They are hunting and fishing implements, the former at the same time serving as weapons. But hunting and fishing presuppose the transition from an exclusively vegetable diet to the concomitant use of meat, and this is another important step in the process of transition from ape to man. A meat diet contained in an almost ready state the most essential ingredients required by the organism for its metabolism. By shortening the time required for digestion, it also shortened the other vegetative bodily processes that correspond to those of plant life, and thus gained further time, material and desire for the active manifestation of animal life proper. And the farther man in the making moved from the vegetable kingdom the higher he rose above the animal. Just as becoming accustomed to a vegetable diet side by side with meat converted wild cats and dogs into the servants of man, so also adaptation to a meat diet, side by side with a vegetable diet, greatly contributed towards giving bodily strength and independence to man in the making. The meat diet, however, had its greatest effect on the brain, which now received a far richer flow of the materials necessary for its nourishment and development, and which, therefore, could develop more rapidly and perfectly from generation to generation. With all due respect to the vegetarians, man did not come into existence without a meat diet, and if the latter, among all peoples known to us, has led to cannibalism at some time or other (the forefathers of the Berliners, the Weletabians or Wilzians, used to eat their parents as late as the tenth century), that is of no consequence to us today.

The meat diet led to two new advances of decisive importance – the harnessing of fire and the domestication of animals. The first still further shortened the digestive process, as it provided the mouth with food already, as it were, half-digested; the second made meat more copious by opening up a new, more regular source of supply in addition to hunting, and moreover provided, in milk and its products, a new article of food at least as valuable as meat in its composition. Thus both these advances were, in themselves, new means for the emancipation of man. It would lead us too far afield to dwell here in detail on their indirect effects notwithstanding the great importance they have had for the development of man and society.

Just as man learned to consume everything edible, he also learned to live in any climate. He spread over the whole of the habitable world, being the only animal fully able to do so of its own accord. The other animals that have become accustomed to all climates – domestic animals and vermin – did not become so independently, but only in the wake of man. And the transition from the uniformly hot climate of the original home of man to colder regions, where the year was divided into summer and winter, created new requirements – shelter and clothing as protection against cold and damp, and hence new spheres of labour, new forms of activity, which further and further separated man from the animal.

By the combined functioning of hand, speech organs and brain, not only in each individual but also in society, men became capable of executing more and more complicated operations, and were able to set themselves, and achieve, higher and higher aims. The work of each generation itself became different, more perfect and more diversified. Agriculture was added to hunting and cattle raising; then came spinning, weaving, metalworking, pottery and navigation. Along with trade and industry, art and science finally appeared. Tribes developed into nations and states. Law and politics arose, and with them that fantastic reflection of human things in the human mind – religion. In the face of all these images, which appeared in the first place to be products of the mind and seemed to dominate human societies, the more modest productions of the working hand retreated into the background, the more so since the mind that planned the labour was able, at a very early stage in the development of society (for example, already in the primitive family), to have the labour that had been planned carried out by other hands than its own. All merit for the swift advance of civilisation was ascribed to the mind, to the development and activity of the brain. Men became accustomed to explain their actions as arising out of thought instead of their needs (which in any case are reflected and perceived in the mind); and so in the course of time there emerged that idealistic world outlook which, especially since the fall of the world of antiquity, has dominated men's minds. It still rules them to such a degree that even the most materialistic natural scientists of the Darwinian school are still unable to form any clear idea of the origin of man, because under this ideological influence they do not recognise the part that has been played therein by labour.

Animals, as has already been pointed out, change the environment by their activities in the same way, even if not to the same extent, as man does, and these changes, as we have seen, in turn react upon and change those who made them. In nature nothing takes place in isolation. Everything affects and is affected by every other thing, and it is mostly because this manifold motion and interaction is forgotten that our natural scientists are prevented from gaining a clear insight into the simplest things. We have seen how goats have prevented the regeneration of forests in Greece; on the island of St. Helena, goats and pigs brought by the first arrivals have succeeded in exterminating its old vegetation almost completely, and so have prepared the ground for the spreading of plants brought by later sailors and colonists. But animals exert a lasting effect on their environment unintentionally and, as far as the animals themselves are concerned, accidentally. The further removed men are from animals, however, the more their effect on nature assumes the character of premeditated, planned action directed towards definite preconceived ends. The animal destroys the vegetation of a locality without realising what it is doing. Man destroys it in order to sow field crops on the soil thus released, or to plant trees or vines which he knows will yield many times the amount planted. He transfers useful plants and domestic animals from one country to another and thus changes the flora and fauna of whole continents. More than this. Through artificial breeding both plants and animals are so changed by the hand of man that they become unrecognisable. The wild plants from which our grain varieties originated are still being sought in vain. There is still some dispute about the wild animals from which our very different breeds of dogs or our equally numerous breeds of horses are descended.

It goes without saying that it would not occur to us to dispute the ability of animals to act in a planned, premeditated fashion. On the contrary, a planned mode of action exists in embryo wherever protoplasm, living albumen, exists and reacts, that is, carries out definite, even if extremely simple, movements as a result of definite external stimuli. Such reaction takes place even where there is yet no cell at all, far less a nerve cell. There is something of the planned action in the way insect-eating plants capture their prey, although they do it quite unconsciously. In animals the capacity for conscious, planned action is proportional to the development of the nervous system, and among mammals it attains a fairly high level. While fox-hunting in England one can daily observe how unerringly the fox makes use of its excellent knowledge of the locality in order to elude its pursuers, and how well it knows and turns to account all favourable features of the ground that cause the scent to be lost. Among our domestic animals, more highly developed thanks to association with man, one can constantly observe acts of cunning on exactly the same level as those of children. For, just as the development history of the human embryo in the mother's womb is only an abbreviated repetition of the history, extending over millions of years, of the bodily development of our animal ancestors, starting from the worm, so the mental development of the human child is only a still more abbreviated repetition of the intellectual development of these same ancestors, at least of the later ones. But all the planned action of all animals has never succeeded in impressing the stamp of their will upon the earth. That was left for man.

In short, the animal merely uses its environment, and brings about changes in it simply by its presence; man by his changes makes it serve his ends, masters it. This is the final, essential distinction between man and other animals, and once again it is labour that brings about this distinction.

Let us not, however, flatter ourselves overmuch on account of our human victories over nature. For each such victory nature takes its revenge on us. Each victory, it is true, in the first place brings about the results we expected, but in the second and third places it has quite different, unforeseen effects which only too often cancel the first. The people who, in Mesopotamia, Greece, Asia Minor and elsewhere, destroyed the forests to obtain cultivable land, never dreamed that by removing along with the forests the collecting centres and reservoirs of moisture they were laying the basis for the present forlorn state of those countries. When the Italians of the Alps used up the pine forests on the southern slopes, so carefully cherished on the northern slopes, they had no inkling that by doing so they were cutting at the roots of the dairy industry in their region; they had still less inkling that they were thereby depriving their mountain springs of water for the greater part of the year, and making it possible for them to pour still more furious torrents on the plains during the rainy seasons. Those who spread the potato in Europe were not aware that with these farinaceous tubers they were at the same time spreading scrofula. Thus at every step we are reminded that we by no means rule over nature like a conqueror over a foreign people, like someone standing outside nature – but that we, with flesh, blood and brain, belong to nature, and exist in its midst, and that all our mastery of it consists in the fact that we have the advantage over all other creatures of being able to learn its laws and apply them correctly.

And, in fact, with every day that passes we are acquiring a better understanding of these laws and getting to perceive both the more immediate and the more remote consequences of our interference with the traditional course of nature. In particular, after the mighty advances made by the natural sciences in the present century, we are more than ever in a position to realise, and hence to control, also the more remote natural consequences of at least our day-to-day production activities. But the more this progresses the more will men not only feel but also know their oneness with nature, and the more impossible will become the senseless and unnatural idea of a contrast between mind and matter, man and nature, soul and body, such as arose after the decline of classical antiquity in Europe and obtained its highest elaboration in Christianity.

It required the labour of thousands of years for us to learn a little of how to calculate the more remote natural effects of our actions in the field of production, but it has been still more difficult in regard to the more remote social effects of these actions. We mentioned the potato and the resulting spread of scrofula. But what is scrofula compared to the effects which the reduction of the workers to a potato diet had on the living conditions of the popular masses in whole countries, or compared to the famine the potato blight brought to Ireland in 1847, which consigned to the grave a million Irishmen, nourished solely or almost exclusively on potatoes, and forced the emigration overseas of two million more? When the Arabs learned to distil spirits, it never entered their heads that by so doing they were creating one of the chief weapons for the annihilation of the aborigines of the then still undiscovered American continent. And when afterwards Columbus discovered this America, he did not know that by doing so he was giving a new lease of life to slavery, which in Europe had long ago been done away with, and laying the basis for the Negro slave trade. The men who in the seventeenth and eighteenth centuries laboured to create the steam-engine had no idea that they were preparing the instrument which more than any other was to revolutionise social relations throughout the world. Especially in Europe, by concentrating wealth in the hands of a minority and dispossessing the huge majority, this instrument was destined at first to give social and political domination to the bourgeoisie, but later, to give rise to a class struggle between bourgeoisie and proletariat which can end only in the overthrow of the bourgeoisie and the abolition of all class antagonisms. But in this sphere too, by long and often cruel experience and by collecting and analysing historical material, we are gradually learning to get a clear view of the indirect, more remote social effects of our production activity, and so are afforded an opportunity to control and regulate these effects as well.

This regulation, however, requires something more than mere knowledge. It requires a complete revolution in our hitherto existing mode of production, and simultaneously a revolution in our whole contemporary social order.

All hitherto existing modes of production have aimed merely at achieving the most immediately and directly useful effect of labour. The further consequences, which appear only later and become effective through gradual repetition and accumulation, were totally neglected. The original common ownership of land corresponded, on the one hand, to a level of development of human beings in which their horizon was restricted in general to what lay immediately available, and presupposed, on the other hand, a certain superfluity of land that would allow some latitude for correcting the possible bad results of this primeval type of economy. When this surplus land was exhausted, common ownership also declined. All higher forms of production, however, led to the division of the population into different classes and thereby to the antagonism of ruling and oppressed classes. Thus the interests of the ruling class became the driving factor of production, since production was no longer restricted to providing the barest means of subsistence for the oppressed people. This has been put into effect most completely in the capitalist mode of production prevailing today in Western Europe. The individual capitalists, who dominate production and exchange, are able to concern themselves only with the most immediate useful effect of their actions. Indeed, even this useful effect – inasmuch as it is a question of the usefulness of the article that is produced or exchanged – retreats far into the background, and the sole incentive becomes the profit to be made on selling.

Classical political economy, the social science of the bourgeoisie, in the main examines only social effects of human actions in the fields of production and exchange that are actually intended. This fully corresponds to the social organisation of which it is the theoretical expression. As individual capitalists are engaged in production and exchange for the sake of the immediate profit, only the nearest, most immediate results must first be taken into account. As long as the individual manufacturer or merchant sells a manufactured or purchased commodity with the usual coveted profit, he is satisfied and does not concern himself with what afterwards becomes of the commodity and its purchasers. The same thing applies to the natural effects of the same actions. What cared the Spanish planters in Cuba, who burned down forests on the slopes of the mountains and obtained from the ashes sufficient fertiliser for one generation of very highly profitable coffee trees – what cared they that the heavy tropical rainfall afterwards washed away the unprotected upper stratum of the soil, leaving behind only bare rock! In relation to nature, as to society, the present mode of production is predominantly concerned only about the immediate, the most tangible result; and then surprise is expressed that the more remote effects of actions directed to this end turn out to be quite different, are mostly quite the opposite in character; that the harmony of supply and demand is transformed into the very reverse opposite, as shown by the course of each ten years' industrial cycle – even Germany has had a little preliminary experience of it in the "crash"; that private ownership based on one's own labour must of necessity develop into the expropriation of the workers, while all wealth becomes more and more concentrated in the hands of non-workers; that

[the manuscript ends here]

Ludwig Feuerbach and the End of Classical German Philosophy

Foreword

In the preface to *A Contribution to the Critique of Political Economy*, published in Berlin, 1859, Karl Marx relates how the two of us in Brussels in the year 1845 set about: "to work out in common the opposition of our view" — the materialist conception of history which was elaborated mainly by Marx — "to the ideological view of German philosophy, in fact, to settle accounts with our erstwhile philosophical conscience. The resolve was carried out in the form of a criticism of post-Hegelian philosophy. The manuscript, two large octavo volumes, had long reached its place of publication in Westphalia when we received the news that altered circumstances did not allow of its being printed. We abandoned the manuscript to the gnawing criticism of the mice, all the more willingly as we had achieved our main purpose — self-clarification!"

Since then more than 40 years have elapsed and Marx died without either of us having had an opportunity of returning to the subject. We have expressed ourselves in various places regarding our relation to Hegel, but nowhere in a comprehensive, connected account. To Feuerbach, who after all in many respects forms an intermediate link between Hegelian philosophy and our conception, we never returned.

In the meantime, the Marxist world outlook has found representatives far beyond the boundaries of Germany and Europe and in all the literary languages of the world. On the other hand, classical German philosophy is experiencing a kind of rebirth abroad, especially in England and Scandinavia, and even in Germany itself people appear to be getting tired of the pauper's broth of eclecticism which is ladled out in the universities there under the name of philosophy.

In these circumstances, a short, coherent account of our relation to the Hegelian philosophy, of how we proceeded, as well as of how we separated, from it, appeared to me to be required more and more. Equally, a full acknowledgement of the influence which Feuerbach, more than any other post-Hegelian philosopher, had upon us during our period of storm and stress, appeared to me to be an undischarged debt of honor. I therefore willingly seized the opportunity when the editors of *Neue Zeit* asked me for a critical review of Starcke's book on Feuerbach. My contribution was published in that journal in the fourth and fifth numbers of 1886 and appears here in revised form as a separate publication.

Before sending these lines to press, I have once again ferreted out and looked over the old manuscript of 1845–46 (*The German Ideology*).

The section dealing with Feuerbach is not completed. The finished portion consists of an exposition of the materialist conception of history which proves only how incomplete our knowledge of economic history still was at that time. It contains no criticism of Feuerbach's doctrine itself; for the present purposes, therefore, it was unusable. On the other hand, in an old notebook of Marx's I have found the 11 Theses on Feuerbach, printed here as an appendix.

These are notes hurriedly scribbled down for later elaboration, absolutely not intended for publication, but invaluable as the first document in which is deposited the brilliant germ of the new world outlook.

Frederick Engels
London
February 21, 1888

Part 1: Hegel

The volume before us carries us back to a period which, although in time no more than a generation behind us, has become as foreign to the present generation in Germany as if it were already a hundred years old. Yet it was the period of Germany's preparation for the Revolution of 1848; and all that has happened since then in our country has been merely a continuation of 1848, merely the execution of the last will and testament of the revolution.

Just as in France in the 18th century, so in Germany in the 19th, a philosophical revolution ushered in the political collapse. But how different the two looked! The French were in open combat against all official science, against the church and often also against the state; their writings were printed across the frontier, in Holland or England, while they themselves were often in jeopardy of imprisonment in the Bastille. On the other hand, the Germans were professors, state-appointed instructors of youth; their writings were recognized textbooks, and the termination system of the whole development — the Hegelian system — was even raised, as it were, to the rank of a royal Prussian philosophy of state! Was it possible that a revolution could hide behind these professors, behind their obscure, pedantic phrases, their ponderous, wearisome sentences? Were not precisely these people who were then regarded as the representatives of the revolution, the liberals, the bitterest opponents of this brain-confusing philosophy? But what neither the government nor the liberals saw was seen at least by one man as early as 1833, and this man was indeed none other than Heinrich Heine.

Let us take an example. No philosophical proposition has earned more gratitude from narrow-minded governments and wrath from equally narrow-minded liberals than Hegel's famous statement: "All that is real is rational; and all that is rational is real." That was tangibly a sanctification of things that be, a philosophical benediction bestowed upon despotism, police government, Star Chamber proceedings and censorship. That is how Frederick William III and how his subjects understood it. But according to Hegel certainly not everything that exists is also real, without further qualification. For Hegel the attribute of reality belongs only to that which at the same time is necessary: "In the course of its development reality proves to be necessity." A particular governmental measure — Hegel himself cites the example of "a certain tax regulation" — is therefore for him by no means real without qualification. That which is necessary, however, proves itself in the last resort to be also rational; and, applied to the Prussian state of that time, the Hegelian proposition, therefore, merely means: this state is rational, corresponds to reason, insofar as it is necessary; and if it nevertheless appears to us to be evil, but still, in spite of its evil character, continues to exist, then the evil character of the government is justified and explained by the corresponding evil character of its subjects. The Prussians of that day had the government that they deserved.

Now, according to Hegel, reality is, however, in no way an attribute predictable of any given state of affairs, social or political, in all circumstances and at all times. On the contrary. The Roman Republic was real, but so was the Roman Empire, which superseded it. In 1789, the French monarchy had become so unreal, that is to say, so robbed of all necessity, so irrational, that it had to be destroyed by the Great Revolution, of which Hegel always speaks with the greatest enthusiasm. In this case, therefore, the monarchy was the unreal and the revolution the real. And so, in the course of development, all that was previously real becomes unreal, loses it necessity, its right of existence, its rationality. And in the place of moribund reality comes a new, viable reality — peacefully if the old has enough intelligence to go to its death without a struggle; forcibly if it resists this necessity. Thus the Hegelian proposition turns into its opposite through Hegelian dialectics itself: All that is real in the sphere of human history, becomes irrational in the process of time, is therefore irrational by its very destination, is tainted beforehand with irrationality, and everything which is rational in the minds of men is destined to become real, however much it may contradict existing apparent reality. In accordance with all the rules of the Hegelian method of thought, the proposition of the rationality of everything which is real resolves itself into the other proposition: All that exists deserves to perish.

But precisely therein lay the true significance and the revolutionary character of the Hegelian philosophy (to which, as the close of the whole movement since Kant, we must here confine ourselves), that it once and for all dealt the death blow to the finality of all product of human thought and action. Truth, the cognition of which is the business of philosophy, was in the hands of Hegel no longer an aggregate of finished dogmatic statements, which, once discovered, had merely to be learned by heart. Truth lay now in the process of cognition itself, in the long historical development of science, which mounts from lower to ever higher levels of knowledge without ever reaching, by discovering so-called absolute truth, a point at which it can proceed no further, where it would have nothing more to do than to fold its hands and gaze with wonder at the absolute truth to which it had attained. And what holds good for the realm of philosophical knowledge holds good also for that of every other kind of knowledge and also for practical action. Just as knowledge is unable to reach a complete conclusion in a perfect, ideal condition of humanity, so is history unable to do so; a perfect society, a perfect "state", are things which can only exist in imagination. On the contrary, all successive historical systems are only transitory stages in the endless course of development of human society from the lower to the higher. Each stage is necessary, and therefore justified for the time and conditions to which it owes its origin. But in the face of new, higher conditions which gradually develop in its own womb, it loses vitality and justification. It must give way to a higher stage which will also in its turn decay and perish. Just as the bourgeoisie by large-scale industry, competition, and the world market dissolves in practice all stable time-honored institutions, so this dialectical philosophy dissolves all conceptions of final, absolute truth and of absolute states of humanity corresponding to it. For it (dialectical philosophy), nothing is final, absolute, sacred. It reveals the transitory character of everything and in everything; nothing can endure before it except the uninterrupted process of becoming and of passing away, of endless ascendancy from the lower to the higher. And dialectical philosophy itself is nothing more than the mere reflection of this process in the thinking brain. It has, of course, also a conservative side; it recognizes that definite stages of knowledge and society are justified for their time and circumstances; but only so far. The conservatism of this mode of outlook is relative; its revolutionary character is absolute — the only absolute dialectical philosophy admits.

It is not necessary, here, to go into the question of whether this mode of outlook is thoroughly in accord with the present state of natural science, which predicts a possible end even for the Earth, and for its habitability a fairly certain one; which therefore recognizes that for the history of mankind, too, there is not only an ascending but also a descending branch. At any rate, we still find ourselves a considerable distance from the turning-point at which the historical course of society becomes one of descent, and we cannot expect

Hegelian philosophy to be concerned with a subject which natural science, in its time, had not at all placed upon the agenda as yet.

But what must, in fact, be said here is this: that in Hegel the views developed above are not so sharply delineated. They are a necessary conclusion from his method, but one which he himself never drew with such explicitness. And this, indeed, for the simple reason that he was compelled to make a system and, in accordance with traditional requirements, a system of philosophy must conclude with some sort of absolute truth. Therefore, however much Hegel, especially in his Logic, emphasized that this eternal truth is nothing but the logical, or, the historical, process itself, he nevertheless finds himself compelled to supply this process with an end, just because he has to bring his system to a termination at some point or other. In his Logic, he can make this end a beginning again, since here the point of the conclusion, the absolute idea — which is only absolute insofar as he has absolutely nothing to say about it — "alienates", that is, transforms, itself into nature and comes to itself again later in the mind, that is, in thought and in history. But at the end of the whole philosophy, a similar return to the beginning is possible only in one way. Namely, by conceiving of the end of history as follows: mankind arrives at the cognition of the self-same absolute idea, and declares that this cognition of the absolute idea is reached in Hegelian philosophy. In this way, however, the whole dogmatic content of the Hegelian system is declared to be absolute truth, in contradiction to his dialectical method, which dissolves all dogmatism. Thus the revolutionary side is smothered beneath the overgrowth of the conservative side. And what applies to philosophical cognition applies also to historical practice. Mankind, which, in the person of Hegel, has reached the point of working out the absolute idea, must also in practice have gotten so far that it can carry out this absolute idea in reality. Hence the practical political demands of the absolute idea on contemporaries may not be stretched too far. And so we find at the conclusion of the Philosophy of Right that the absolute idea is to be realized in that monarchy based on social estates which Frederick William III so persistently but vainly promised to his subjects, that is, in a limited, moderate, indirect rule of the possessing classes suited to the petty-bourgeois German conditions of that time; and, moreover, the necessity of the nobility is demonstrated to us in a speculative fashion.

The inner necessities of the system are, therefore, of themselves sufficient to explain why a thoroughly revolutionary method of thinking produced an extremely tame political conclusion. As a matter of fact, the specific form of this conclusion springs from this, that Hegel was a German, and like his contemporary Goethe had a bit of the philistine's queue dangling behind. Each of them was an Olympian Zeus in his own sphere, yet neither of them ever quite freed himself from German philistinism.

But all this did not prevent the Hegelian system from covering an incomparably greater domain than any earlier system, nor from developing in this domain a wealth of thought, which is astounding even today. The phenomenology of mind (which one may call a parallel of the embryology and palaeontology of the mind, a development of individual consciousness through its different stages, set in the form of an abbreviated reproduction of the stages through which the consciousness of man has passed in the course of history), logic, natural philosophy, philosophy of mind, and the latter worked out in its separate, historical subdivisions: philosophy of history, of right, of religion, history of philosophy, aesthetics, etc. — in all these different historical fields Hegel labored to discover and demonstrate the pervading thread of development. And as he was not only a creative genius but also a man of encyclopaedic erudition, he played an epoch-making role in every sphere. It is self-evident that owing to the needs of the "system" he very often had to resort to those forced constructions about which his pigmy opponents make such a terrible fuss even today. But these constructions are only the frame and scaffolding of his work. If one does not loiter here needlessly, but presses on farther into the immense building, one finds innumerable treasures which today still possess undiminshed value. With all philosophers it is precisely the "system" which is perishable; and for the simple reason that it springs from an imperishable desire of the human mind — the desire to overcome all contradictions. But if all contradictions are once and for all disposed of, we shall have arrived at so-called absolute truth — world history will be at an end. And yet it has to continue, although there is nothing left for it to do — hence, a new, insoluble contradiction. As soon as we have once realized — and in the long run no one has helped us to realize it more than Hegel himself — that the task of philosophy thus stated means nothing but the task that a single philosopher should accomplish that which can only be accomplished by the entire human race in its progressive development — as soon as we realize that, there is an end to all philosophy in the hitherto accepted sense of the word. One leaves alone "absolute truth", which is unattainable along this path or by any single individual; instead, one pursues attainable relative truths along the path of the positive sciences, and the summation of their results by means of dialectical thinking. At any rate, with Hegel philosophy comes to an end; on the one hand, because in his system he summed up its whole development in the most splendid fashion; and on the other hand, because, even though unconsciously, he showed us the way out of the labyrinth of systems to real positive knowledge of the world.

One can imagine what a tremendous effect this Hegelian system must have produced in the philosophy-tinged atmosphere of Germany. It was a triumphant procession which lasted for decades and which by no means came to a standstill on the death of Hegel. On the contrary, it was precisely from 1830 to 1840 that "Hegelianism" reigned most exclusively, and to a greater or lesser extent infected even its opponents. It was precisely in this period that Hegelian views, consciously or unconsciously, most extensively penetrated the most diversified sciences and leavened even popular literature and the daily press, from which the average "educated consciousness" derives its mental pabulum. But this victory along the whole front was only the prelude to an internal struggle.

As we have seen, the doctrine of Hegel, taken as a whole, left plenty of room for giving shelter to the most diverse practical party views. And in the theoretical Germany of that time, two things above all were practical: religion and politics. Whoever placed the chief emphasis on the Hegelian system could be fairly conservative in both spheres; whoever regarded the dialectical method as the main thing could belong to the most extreme opposition, both in politics and religion. Hegel himself, despite the fairly frequent outbursts of revolutionary wrath in his works, seemed on the whole to be more inclined to the conservative side. Indeed, his system had cost him much more "hard mental plugging" than his method. Towards the end of the thirties, the cleavage in the school became more and more apparent. The Left wing, the so-called Young Hegelians, in their fight with the pietist orthodox and the feudal reactionaries, abandoned bit by bit that philosophical-genteel reserve in regard to the burning questions of the day which up to that time had secured state toleration and even protection for their teachings. And when in 1840, orthodox pietism and absolutist feudal reaction ascended the throne with Frederick William IV, open partisanship became unavoidable. The fight was still carried on with philosophical weapons, but no longer for abstract philosophical aims. It turned directly on the destruction of traditional religion and of the existing state. And while in the *Deutsche Jahrbucher* the practical ends were still predominantly put forward in philosophical disguise, in the *Rheinische Zeitung* of 1842 the Young Hegelian school revealed itself directly as the philosophy of the aspiring radical bourgeoisie and used the meagre cloak of philosophy only to deceive the censorship.

At that time, however, politics was a very thorny field, and hence the main fight came to be directed against religion; this fight, particularly since 1840, was indirectly also political. Strauss' Life of Jesus, published in 1835, had provided the first impulse. The theory therein developed of the formation of the gospel myths was combated later by Bruno Bauer with proof that a whole series of evangelic stories had been fabricated by the authors themselves. The controversy between these two was carried out in the philosophical disguise of a battle between "self-consciousness" and "substance". The question whether the miracle stories of the gospels came into being through unconscious-traditional myth-creation within the bosom of the community or whether they were fabricated by the evangelists themselves was magnified into the question whether, in world history, "substance" or "self-consciousness" was the decisive operative force. Finally came Stirner, the prophet of contemporary anarchism — Bakunin has taken a great deal from him — and capped the sovereign "self-consciousness" by his sovereign "ego".

We will not go further into this side of the decomposition process of the Hegelian school. More important for us is the following: the main body of the most determined Young Hegelians was, by the practical necessities of its fight against positive religion, driven back to Anglo-French materialism. This brought them into conflict with the system of their school. While materialism conceives nature as the sole reality, nature in the Hegelian system represents merely the "alienation" of the absolute idea, so to say, a degradation of the idea. At all events, thinking and its thought-product, the idea, is here the primary, nature the derivative, which only exists at all by the condescension of the idea. And in this contradiction they floundered as well or as ill as they could.

Then came Feuerbach's *Essence of Christianity*. With one blow, it pulverized the contradiction, in that without circumlocutions it placed materialism on the throne again. Nature exists independently of all philosophy. It is the foundation upon which we human beings, ourselves products of nature, have grown up. Nothing exists outside nature and man, and the higher beings our religious fantasies have created are only the fantastic reflection of our own essence. The spell was broken; the "system" was exploded and cast aside, and the contradiction, shown to exist only in our imagination, was dissolved. One must himself have experienced the liberating effect of this book to get an idea of it. Enthusiasm was general; we all became at once Feuerbachians. How enthusiastically Marx greeted the new conception and how much — in spite of all critical reservations — he was influenced by it, one may read in the *The Holy Family*.

Even the shortcomings of the book contributed to its immediate effect. Its literary, sometimes even high-flown, style secured for it a large public and was at any rate refreshing after long years of abstract and abstruse Hegelianizing. The same is true of its extravagant deification of love, which, coming after the now intolerable sovereign rule of "pure reason", had its excuse, if not justification. But what we must not forget is that it was precisely these two weaknesses of Feuerbach that "true Socialism", which had been spreading like a plague in educated Germany since 1844, took as its starting-point, putting literary phrases in the place of scientific knowledge, the liberation of mankind by means of "love" in place of the emancipation of the proletariat through the economic transformation of production — in short, losing itself in the nauseous fine writing and ecstacies of love typified by Herr Karl Grun.

Another thing we must not forget is this: the Hegelian school disintegrated, but Hegelian philosophy was not overcome through criticism; Strauss and Bauer each took one of its sides and set it polemically against the other. Feuerbach smashed the system and simply discarded it. But a philosophy is not disposed of by the mere assertion that it is false. And so powerful a work as Hegelian philosophy, which had exercised so enormous an influence on the intellectual development of the nation, could not be disposed of by simply being ignored. It had to be "sublated" in its own sense, that is, in the sense that while its form had to be annihilated through criticism, the new content which had been won through it had to be saved. How this was brought about we shall see below.

But in the meantime, the Revolution of 1848 thrust the whole of philosophy aside as unceremoniously as Feuerbach had thrust aside Hegel. And in the process, Feuerbach himself was also pushed into the background.

Part 2: Materialism

The great basic question of all philosophy, especially of more recent philosophy, is that concerning the relation of thinking and being. From the very early times when men, still completely ignorant of the structure of their own bodies, under the stimulus of dream apparitions, came to believe that their thinking and sensation were not activities of their bodies, but of a distinct soul which inhabits the body and leaves it at death — from this time men have been driven to reflect about the relation between this soul and the outside world. If, upon death, it took leave of the body and lived on, there was no occasion to invent yet another distinct death for it. Thus arose the idea of immortality, which at that stage of development appeared not at all as a consolation but as a fate against which it was no use fighting, and often enough, as among the Greeks, as a positive misfortune. The quandary arising from the common universal ignorance of what to do with this soul, once its existence had been accepted, after the death of the body, and not religious desire for consolation, led in a general way to the tedious notion of personal immortality. In an exactly similar manner, the first gods arose through the personification of natural forces. And these gods in the further development of religions assumed more and more extramundane form, until finally by a process of abstraction, I might almost say of distillation, occurring naturally in the course of man's intellectual development, out of the many more or less limited and mutually limiting gods there arose in the minds of men the idea of the one exclusive God of the monotheistic religions.

Thus the question of the relation of thinking to being, the relation of the spirit to nature — the paramount question of the whole of philosophy — has, no less than all religion, its roots in the narrow-minded and ignorant notions of savagery. But this question could for the first time be put forward in its whole acuteness, could achieve its full significance, only after humanity in Europe had awakened from the long hibernation of the Christian Middle Ages. The question of the position of thinking in relation to being, a question which, by the way, had played a great part also in the scholasticism of the Middle Ages, the question: which is primary, spirit or nature — that question, in relation to the church, was sharpened into this: Did God create the world or has the world been in existence eternally?

The answers which the philosophers gave to this question split them into two great camps. Those who asserted the primacy of spirit to nature and, therefore, in the last instance, assumed world creation in some form or other — and among the philosophers, Hegel, for example, this creation often becomes still more intricate and impossible than in Christianity — comprised the camp of idealism. The others, who regarded nature as primary, belong to the various schools of materialism.

These two expressions, idealism and materialism, originally signify nothing else but this; and here too they are not used in any other sense. What confusion arises when some other meaning is put to them will be seen below.

But the question of the relation of thinking and being had yet another side: in what relation do our thoughts about the world surrounding us stand to this world itself? Is our thinking capable of the cognition of the real world? Are we able in our ideas and notions of the real world to produce a correct reflection of reality? In philosophical language this question is called the question of identity of thinking and being, and the overwhelming majority of philosophers give an affirmative answer to this question. With Hegel, for example, its affirmation is self-evident; for what we cognize in the real world is precisely its thought-content — that which makes the world a gradual realization of the absolute idea, which absolute idea has existed somewhere from eternity, independent of the world and before the world. But it is manifest without further proof that thought can know a content which is from the outset a thought-content. It is equally manifest that what is to be proved here is already tacitly contained in the premises. But that in no way prevents Hegel from drawing the further conclusion from his proof of the identity of thinking and being that his philosophy, because it is correct for his thinking, is therefore the only correct one, and that the identity of thinking and being must prove its validity by mankind immediately translating his philosophy from theory into practice and transforming the whole world according to Hegelian principles. This is an illusion which he shares with well-nigh all philosophers.

In addition, there is yet a set of different philosophers — those who question the possibility of any cognition, or at least of an exhaustive cognition, of the world. To them, among the more modern ones, belong Hume and Kant, and they played a very important role in philosophical development. What is decisive in the refutation of this view has already been said by Hegel, in so far as this was possible from an idealist standpoint. The materialistic additions made by Feuerbach are more ingenious than profound. The most telling refutation of this as of all other philosophical crotchets is practice — namely, experiment and industry. If we are able to prove the correctness of our conception of a natural process by making it ourselves, bringing it into being out of its conditions and making it serve our own purposes into the bargain, then there is an end to the Kantian ungraspable "thing-in-itself". The chemical substances produced in the bodies of plants and animals remained just such "things-in-themselves" until organic chemistry began to produce them one after another, whereupon the "thing-in-itself" became a thing for us — as, for instance, alizarin, the coloring matter of the madder, which we no longer trouble to grow in the madder roots in the field, but produce much more cheaply and simply from coal tar. For 300 years, the Copernican solar system was a hypothesis with 100, 1,000, 10,000 to 1 chances in its favor, but still always a hypothesis. But then Leverrier, by means of the data provided by this system, not only deduced the necessity of the existence of an unknown planet, but also calculated the position in the heavens which this planet must necessarily occupy, and when (Johann) Galle really found this planet (Neptune, discovered 1846, at Berlin Observatory), the Copernican system was proved. If, nevertheless, the neo-Kantians are attempting to resurrect the Kantian conception in Germany, and the agnostics that of Hume in England (where in fact it never became extinct), this is, in view of their theoretical and practical refutation accomplished long ago, scientifically a regression and practically merely a shamefaced way of surreptitiously accepting materialism, while denying it before the world.

But during this long period from Descartes to Hegel and from Hobbes to Feuerbach, these philosophers were by no means impelled, as they thought they were, solely by the force of pure reason. On the contrary, what really pushed them forward most was the powerful and ever more rapidly onrushing progress of natural science and industry. Among the materialists this was plain on the surface, but the idealist systems also filled themselves more and more with a materialist content and attempted pantheistically to reconcile the antithesis between mind and matter. Thus, ultimately, the Hegelian system represents merely a materialism idealistically turned upside down in method and content.

It is, therefore, comprehensible that Starcke in his characterization of Feuerbach first of all investigates the latter's position in regard to this fundamental question of the relation of thinking and being. After a short introduction, in which the views of the preceding philosophers, particularly since Kant, are described in unnecessarily ponderous philosophical language, and in which Hegel, by an all too formalistic adherence to certain passages of his works, gets far less his due, there follows a detailed description of the course of development of Feuerbach's "metaphysics" itself, as this course was successively reflected in those writings of this philosopher which have a bearing here. This description is industriously and lucidly elaborated; only, like the whole book, it is loaded with a ballast of philosophical phraseology by no means everywhere unavoidable, which is the more disturbing in its effect the less the author keeps to the manner of expression of one and the same school, or even of Feuerbach himself, and the more he interjects expressions of very different tendencies, especially of the tendencies now rampant and calling themselves philosophical.

The course of evolution of Feuerbach is that of a Hegelian — a never quite orthodox Hegelian, it is true — into a materialist; an evolution which at a definite stage necessitates a complete rupture with the idealist system of his predecessor. With irresistible force, Feuerbach is finally driven to the realization that the Hegelian premundane existence of the "absolute idea", the "pre-existence of the logical categories" before the world existed, is nothing more than the fantastic survival of the belief in the existence of an extra-mundane creator; that the material, sensuously perceptible world to which we ourselves belong is the only reality; and that our consciousness and thinking, however supra-sensuous they may seem, are the product of a material, bodily organ, the brain. Matter is not a product of mind, but mind itself is merely the highest product of matter. This is, of course, pure materialism. But, having got so far, Feuerbach stops short. He cannot overcome the customary philosophical prejudice, prejudice not against the thing but against the name materialism. He says:

"To me materialism is the foundation of the edifice of human essence and knowledge; but to me it is not what it is to the physiologist, to the natural scientists in the narrower sense, for example, to Moleschott, and necessarily is from their standpoint and profession, namely, the edifice itself. Backwards I fully agree with the materialists; but not forwards."

Here, Feuerbach lumps together the materialism that is a general world outlook resting upon a definite conception of the relation between matter and mind, and the special form in which this world outlook was expressed at a definite historical stage — namely, in the 18th century. More than that, he lumps it with the shallow, vulgarized form in which the materialism of the 18th century continues to exist today in the heads of naturalists and physicians, the form which was preached on their tours in the fifties by Buchner, Vogt, and Moleschott. But just as idealism underwent a series of stages of development, so also did materialism. With each epoch-making discovery even in the sphere of natural science, it has to change its form; and after history was also subjected to materialistic treatment, a new avenue of development has opened here, too.

The materialism of the last century was predominantly mechanical, because at that time, of all natural sciences, only mechanics, and indeed only the mechanics of solid bodies — celestial and terrestrial — in short, the mechanics of gravity, had come to any definite close. Chemistry at that time existed only in its infantile, phlogistic form. Biology still lay in swaddling clothes; vegetable and animal organisms had been only roughly examined and were explained by purely mechanical causes. What the animal was to Descartes, man was to the materialists of the 18th century — a machine. This exclusive application of the standards of mechanics to processes of a chemical and organic nature — in which processes the laws of mechanics are, indeed, also valid, but are pushed into the backgrounds by other, higher laws — constitutes the first specific but at that time inevitable limitations of classical French materialism.

The second specific limitation of this materialism lay in its inability to comprehend the universe as a process, as matter undergoing uninterrupted historical development. This was in accordance with the level of the natural science of that time, and with the metaphysical, that is, anti-dialectical manner of philosophizing connected with it. Nature, so much was known, was in eternal motion. But according to the ideas of that time, this motion turned, also eternally, in a circle and therefore never moved from the spot; it produced the same results over and over again. This conception was at that time inevitable. The Kantian theory of the origin of the Solar System (that the Sun and planets originated from incandescent rotating nebulous masses) had been put forward but recently and was still regarded merely as a curiosity. The history of the development of the Earth, geology, was still totally unknown, and the conception that the animate natural beings of today are the result of a long sequence of development from the simple to the complex could not at that time scientifically be put forward at all. The unhistorical view of nature was therefore inevitable. We have the less reason to reproach the philosophers of the 18th century on this account since the same thing is found in Hegel. According to him, nature, as a mere "alienation" of the idea, is incapable of development in time — capable only of extending its manifoldness in space, so that it displays simultaneously and alongside of one another all the stages of development comprised in it, and is condemned to an eternal repetition of the same processes. This absurdity of a development in space, but outside of time — the fundamental condition of all development — Hegel imposes upon nature just at the very time when geology, embryology, the physiology of plants and animals, and organic chemistry were being built up, and when everywhere on the basis of these new sciences brilliant foreshadowings of the later theory of evolution were appearing (for instance, Goethe and Lamarck). But the system demanded it; hence the method, for the sake of the system, had to become untrue to itself.

This same unhistorical conception prevailed also in the domain of history. Here the struggle against the remnants of the Middle Ages blurred the view. The Middle Ages were regarded as a mere interruption of history by a thousand years of universal barbarism. The great progress made in the Middle Ages — the extension of the area of European culture, the viable great nations taking form there next to each other, and finally the enormous technical progress of the 14th and 15th centuries — all this was not seen. Thus a rational insight into the great historical interconnectedness was made impossible, and history served at best as a collection of examples and illustrations for the use of philosophers.

The vulgarizing pedlars, who in Germany in the fifties dabbled in materialism, by no means overcame this limitation of their teachers. All the advances of natural science which had been made in the meantime served them only as new proofs against the existence of a creator of the world; and, indeed, they did not in the least make it their business to develop the theory any further. Though idealism was at the end of its tether and was dealt a death-blow by the Revolution of 1848, it had the satisfaction of seeing that materialism had for the moment fallen lower still. Feuerbach was unquestionably right when he refused to take responsibility for this materialism; only he should not have confounded the doctrines of these itinerant preachers with materialism in general.

Here, however, there are two things to be pointed out. First, even during Feuerbach's lifetime, natural science was still in that process of violent fermentation which only during the last 15 years had reached a clarifying, relative conclusion. New scientific data were acquired to a hitherto unheard-of extent, but the establishing of interrelations, and thereby the bringing of order into this chaos of discoveries following closely upon each other's heels, has only quite recently become possible. It is true that Feuerbach had lived to see all three of the decisive discoveries — that of the cell, the transformation of energy, and the theory of evolution named after Darwin. But how could the lonely philosopher, living in rural solitude, be able sufficiently to follow scientific developments in order to appreciate at their full value discoveries which natural scientists themselves at that time either still contested or did not know how to make adequate use of? The blame for this falls solely upon the wretched conditions in Germany, in consequence of which cobweb-spinning eclectic flea-crackers had taken possession of the chairs of philosophy, while Feuerbach, who towered above them all, had to rusticate and grow sour in a little village. It is therefore not Feuerbach's fault that this historical conception of nature, which had now become possible and which removed all the one-sidedness of French materialism, remained inaccessible to him.

Secondly, Feuerbach is quite correct in asserting that exclusively natural-scientific materialism is indeed "the foundation of the edifice of human knowledge, but not the edifice itself". For we live not only in nature but also in human society, and this also no less than nature has its history of development and its science. It was therefore a question of bringing the science of society, that is, the sum total of the so-called historical and philosophical sciences, into harmony with the materialist foundation, and of reconstructing it thereupon. But it did not fall to Feuerbach's lot to do this. In spite of the "foundation", he remained here bound by the traditional idealist fetters, a fact which he recognizes in these words: "Backwards I agree with the materialists, but not forwards!"

But it was Feuerbach himself who did not go "forwards" here; in the social domain, who did not get beyond his standpoint of 1840 or 1844. And this was again chiefly due to this reclusion which compelled him, who, of all philosophers, was the most inclined to social intercourse, to produce thoughts out of his solitary head instead of in amicable and hostile encounters with other men of his calibre. Later, we shall see in detail how much he remained an idealist in this sphere.

It need only be added here that Starcke looks for Feuerbach's idealism in the wrong place.

"Feuerbach is an idealist; he believes in the progress of mankind." (p.19)

"The foundation, the substructure of the whole, remains nevertheless idealism. Realism for us is nothing more than a protection again aberrations, while we follow our ideal trends. Are not compassion, love, and enthusiasm for truth and justice ideal forces?" (p.VIII)

In the first place, idealism here means nothing, but the pursuit of ideal aims. But these necessarily have to do at the most with Kantian idealism and its "categorical imperative"; however, Kant himself called his philosophy "transcendental idealism" by no means because he dealt therein also with ethical ideals, but for quite other reasons, as Starcke will remember. The superstition that philosophical idealism is pivoted round a belief in ethical, that is, social, ideals, arose outside philosophy, among the German philistines, who learned by heart from Schiller's poems the few morsels of philosophical culture they needed. No one has criticized more severely the impotent "categorical imperative" of Kant — impotent because it demands the impossible, and therefore never attains to any reality — no one has more cruelly derided the philistine sentimental enthusiasm for unrealizable ideals purveyed by Schiller than precisely the complete idealist Hegel (see, for example, his *Phenomenology*).

In the second place, we simply cannot get away from the fact that everything that sets men acting must find its way through their brains — even eating and drinking, which begins as a consequence of the sensation of hunger or thirst transmitted through the brain, and ends as a result of the sensation of satisfaction likewise transmitted through the brain. The influences of the external world upon man express themselves in his brain, are reflected therein as feelings, impulses, volitions — in short, as "ideal tendencies", and in this form become "ideal powers". If, then, a man is to be deemed an idealist because he follows "ideal tendencies" and admits that "ideal powers" have an influence over him, then every person who is at all normally developed is a born idealist, and how, in that case, can there still be any materialists?

In the third place, the conviction that humanity, at least at the present moment, moves on the whole in a progressive direction has absolutely nothing to do with the antagonism between materialism and idealism. The French materialists no less than the deists Voltaire and Rousseau held this conviction to an almost fanatical degree, and often enough made the greatest personal sacrifices for it. If ever anybody dedicated his whole life to the "enthusiasm for truth and justice" — using this phrase in the good sense — it was Diderot, for instance. If, therefore, Starcke declares all this to be idealism, this merely proves that the word *materialism*, and the whole antagonism between the two trends, has lost all meaning for him here.

The fact is that Starcke, although perhaps unconsciously, in this makes an unpardonable concession to the traditional philistine prejudice against the word materialism resulting from its long-continued defamation by the priests. By the word materialism, the philistine understands gluttony, drunkenness, lust of the eye, lust of the flesh, arrogance, cupidity, avarice, covetousness, profit-hunting, and stock-exchange swindling — in short, all the filthy vices in which he himself indulges in private. By the word idealism he understands the belief in virtue, universal philanthropy, and in a general way a "better world", of which he boasts before others but in which he himself at the utmost believes only so long as he is having the blues or is going through the bankruptcy consequent upon his customary "materialist" excesses. It is then that he sings his favorite song, What is man? — Half beast, half angel.

For the rest, Starcke takes great pains to defend Feuerbach against the attacks and doctrines of the vociferous assistant professors who today go by the name of philosophers in Germany. For people who are interested in this afterbirth of classical German philosophy this is, of course, a matter of importance; for Starcke himself it may have appeared necessary. We, however, will spare the reader this.

The real idealism of Feuerbach becomes evident as soon as we come to his philosophy of religion and ethics. He by no means wishes to abolish religion; he wants to perfect it. Philosophy itself must be absorbed in religion.

"The periods of humanity are distinguished only by religious changes. A historical movement is fundamental only when it is rooted in the hearts of men. The heart is not a form of religion, so that the latter should exist also in the heart; the heart is the essence of religion." (Quoted by Starcke, p.168.)

According to Feuerbach, religion is the relation between human beings based on the affections, the relation based on the heart, which relation until now has sought its truth in a fantastic mirror image of reality — in the mediation of one or many gods, the fantastic mirror images of human qualities — but now finds it directly and without any mediation in the love between "I" and "Thou". Thus, finally, with Feuerbach sex love becomes one of the highest forms, if not the highest form, of the practice of his new religion.

Now relations between human beings, based on affection, and especially between the two sexes, have existed as long as mankind has. Sex love in particular has undergone a development and won a place during the last 800 years which has made it a compulsory pivotal point of all poetry during this period. The existing positive religions have limited themselves to the bestowal of a higher consecration upon state-regulated sex love — that is, upon the marriage laws — and they could all disappear tomorrow without changing in the slightest the practice of love and friendship. Thus the Christian religion in France, as a matter of fact, so completely disappeared in the year 1793–95 that even Napoleon could not re-introduce it without opposition and difficulty; and this without any need for a substitute in Feuerbach's sense, making itself in the interval.

Feuerbach's idealism consists here in this: he does not simply accept mutual relations based on reciprocal inclination between human beings, such as sex love, friendship, compassion, self-sacrifice, etc., as what they are in themselves — without associating them with any particular religion which to him, too, belongs to the past; but instead he asserts that they will attain their full value only when consecrated by the name of religion. The chief thing for him is not that these purely human relations exist, but that they shall be conceived of as the new, true, religion. They are to have full value only after they have been marked with a religious stamp. Religion is derived from *religare* ("to bind") and meant, originally, a bond. Therefore, every bond between two people is a religion. Such etymological tricks are the last resort of idealist philosophy. Not what the word means according to the historical development of its actual use, but what it ought to mean according to its derivation is what counts. And so sex love, and the intercourse between the sexes, is apotheosized to a religion, merely in order that the word *religion*, which is so dear to idealistic memories, may not disappear from the language. The Parisian reformers of the Louis Blanc trend used to speak in precisely the same way in the forties. They, likewise, could conceive of a man without religion only as a monster, and used to say to us: "*Donc, l'atheisme c'est votre religion!*" ("Well, then atheism is your religion!") If Feuerbach wishes to establish a true religion upon the basis of an essentially materialist conception of nature, that is the same as regarding modern chemistry as true alchemy. If religion can exist without its god, alchemy can exist without its philosopher's stone. By the way, there exists a very close connection between alchemy and religion. The philosopher's stone has many godlike properties and the Egyptian-Greek alchemists of the first two centuries of our era had a hand in the development of Christian doctrines, as the data given by Kopp and Bertholet have proved.

Feuerbach's assertion that "the periods of humanity are distinguished only by religious changes" is decidedly false. Great historical turning-points have been accompanied by religious changes only so far as the three world religions which have existed up to the present — Buddhism, Christianity, and Islam — are concerned. The old tribal and national religions, which arose spontaneously, did not proselytize and lost all their power of resistance as soon as the independence of the tribe or people was lost. For the Germans, it was sufficient to have simple contact with the decaying Roman world empire and with its newly adopted Christian world religion which fitted its economic, political, and ideological conditions. Only with these world religions, arisen more or less artificially, particularly Christianity and Islam, do we find that the more general historical movements acquire a religious imprint. Even in regard to Christianity, the religious stamp in revolutions of really universal significance is restricted to the first stages of the bourgeoisie's struggle for emancipation — from the 13th to the 17th century — and is to be accounted for, not as Feuerbach thinks by the hearts of men and their religious needs, but by the entire previous history of the Middle Ages, which knew no other form of ideology than religion and theology. But when the bourgeoisie of the 18th century was strengthened enough likewise to posses an ideology of its own, suited to its own class standpoint, it made its great and conclusive revolution — the French — appealing exclusively to juristic and political ideas, and troubling itself with religion only in so far as it stood in its way. But it never occurred to it to put a new religion in place of the old. Everyone knows how Robespierre failed in his attempt (to set up a religion of the "highest being").

The possibility of purely human sentiments in our intercourse with other human beings has nowadays been sufficiently curtailed by the society in which we must live, which is based upon class antagonism and class rule. We have no reason to curtail it still more by exalting these sentiments to a religion. And similarly the understanding of the great historical class struggles has already been sufficiently obscured by current historiography, particularly in Germany, so that there is also no need for us to make such an understanding totally impossible by transforming the history of these struggles into a mere appendix of ecclesiastical history. Already here it becomes evident how far today we have moved beyond Feuerbach. His "finest" passages in glorification of his new religion of love are totally unreadable today.

The only religion which Feuerbach examines seriously is Christianity, the world religion of the Occident, based upon monotheism. He proves that the Christian god is only a fantastic reflection, a mirror image, of man. Now, this god is, however, himself the product of a tedious process of abstraction, the concentrated quintessence of the numerous earlier tribal and national gods. And man, whose image this god is, is therefore also not a real man, but likewise the quintessence of the numerous real men, man in the abstract, therefore himself again a mental image. Feuerbach, who on every page preaches sensuousness, absorption in the concrete, in actuality, becomes thoroughly abstract as soon as he begins to talk of any other than mere sex relations between human beings.

Of these relations, only one aspect appeals to him: morality. And here we are again struck by Feuerbach's astonishing poverty when compared to Hegel. The latter's ethics, or doctrine of moral conduct, is the philosophy of right, and embraces: (1) abstract right; (2) morality; (3) social ethics (*Sittlichkeit*), under which are comprised: the family, civil society, and the state.

Here the content is as realistic as the form is idealistic. Besides morality, the whole sphere of law, economy, politics is here included. With Feuerbach, it is just the reverse. In the form he is realistic since he takes his start from man; but there is absolutely no mention of the world in which this man lives; hence, this man remains always the same abstract man who occupied the field in the philosophy of religion. For this man is not born of woman; he issues, as from a chrysalis, from the god of monotheistic religions. He therefore does not live in a real world historically come into being and historically determined. True, he has intercourse with other men; however, each one of them is just as much an abstraction as he himself. In his philosophy of religion we still had men and women, but in his ethics even this last distinction disappears. Feuerbach, to be sure, at long intervals makes such statements as: "Man thinks differently in a palace and in a hut." "If because of hunger, of misery, you have no stuff in your body, you likewise have no stuff for morality in your head, in your mind, or heart." "Politics must become our religion," etc.

But Feuerbach is absolutely incapable of achieving anything with these maxims. They remain mere phrases, and even Starcke has to admit that for Feuerbach politics constituted an impassable frontier and the "science of society, sociology, was terra incognita to him".

He appears just as shallow, in comparison with Hegel, in his treatment of the antithesis of good and evil.

"One believes one is saying something great," Hegel remarks, "if one says that 'man is naturally good'. But one forgets that one says something far greater when one says 'man is naturally evil'."

With Hegel, evil is the form in which the motive force of historical development presents itself. This contains the twofold meaning that, on the one hand, each new advance necessarily appears as a sacrilege against things hallowed, as a rebellion against condition, though old and moribund, yet sanctified by custom; and that, on the other hand, it is precisely the wicked passions of man — greed and lust for power — which, since the emergence of class antagonisms, serve as levers of historical development — a fact of which the history of feudalism and of the bourgeoisie, for example, constitutes a single continual proof. But it does not occur to Feuerbach to investigate the historical role of moral evil. To him, history is altogether an uncanny domain in which he feels ill at ease. Even his dictum: "Man as he sprang originally from nature was only a mere creature of nature, not a man. Man is a product of man, of culture, of history" — with him, even this dictum remains absolutely sterile.

What Feuerbach has to tell us about morals can, therefore, only be extremely meagre. The urge towards happiness is innate in man, and must therefore form the basis of all morality. But the urge towards happiness is subject to a double correction. First, by the natural consequences of our actions: after the debauch comes the "blues", and habitual excess is followed by illness. Secondly, by its social consequences: if we do not respect the similar urge of other people towards happiness they will defend themselves, and so interfere with our own urge toward happiness. Consequently, in order to satisfy our urge, we must be in a position to appreciate rightly the results of our conduct and must likewise allow others an equal right to seek happiness. Rational self-restraint with regard to ourselves, and love — again and again love! — in our intercourse with others — these are the basic laws of Feuerbach's morality; from them, all others are derived. And neither the most spirited utterances of Feuerbach nor the strongest eulogies of Starcke can hide the tenuity and banality of these few propositions.

Only very exceptionally, and by no means to this and other people's profit, can an individual satisfy his urge towards happiness by preoccupation with himself. Rather, it requires preoccupation with the outside world, with means to satisfy his needs — that is to say, food, an individual of the opposite sex, books, conversation, argument, activities, objects for use and working up. Feuerbach's morality either presupposes that these means and objects of satisfaction are given to every individual as a matter of course, or else it offers only inapplicable good advice and is, therefore, not worth a brass farthing to people who are without these means. And Feuerbach himself states this in plain terms:

"Man thinks differently in a palace and in a hut. If because of hunger, of misery, you have no stuff in your body, you likewise have no stuff for morality in your head, in your mind, or heart."

Do matters fare any better in regard to the equal right of others to satisfy their urge towards happiness? Feuerbach posed this claim as absolute, as holding good for all times and circumstances. But since when has it been valid? Was there ever in antiquity between slaves and masters, or in the Middle Ages between serfs and barons, any talk about an equal right to the urge towards happiness? Was not the urge towards happiness of the oppressed class sacrificed ruthlessly and "by the right of law" to that of the ruling class? Yes, that was indeed immoral; nowadays, however, equality of rights is recognized. Recognized in words ever since and inasmuch as the bourgeoisie, in its fight against feudalism and in the development of capitalist production, was compelled to abolish all privileges of estate, that is, personal privileges, and to introduce the equality of all individuals before law, first in the sphere in private law, then gradually also in the sphere of public law. But the urge towards happiness thrives only to a trivial extent on ideal rights. To the greatest extent of all it thrives on material means; and capitalist production takes care to ensure that the great majority of those equal rights shall get only what is essential for bare existence. Capitalist production has, therefore, little more respect, if indeed any more, for the equal right to the urge towards happiness of the majority than had slavery or serfdom. And are we better off in regard to the mental means of happiness, the educational means? Is not even "the schoolmaster of Sadowa" a mythical person?

More. According to Feuerbach's theory of morals, the Stock Exchange is the highest temple of moral conduct, provided only that one always speculates right. If my urge towards happiness leads me to the Stock Exchange, and if there I correctly gauge the consequences of my actions so that only agreeable results and no disadvantages ensue — that is, I always win — then I am fulfilling Feuerbach's precept. Moreover, I do not thereby interfere with the equal right of another person to pursue his happiness; for that other man went to the Exchange just as voluntarily as I did and in concluding the speculative transaction with me he has followed his urge towards happiness as I have followed mine. If he loses his money, his action is *ipso facto* proved to have been unethical, because of his bad reckoning, and since I have given him the punishment he deserves, I can even slap my chest proudly, like a modern Rhadamanthus. Love, too, rules on the Stock Exchange, in so far as it is not simply a sentimental figure of speech, for each finds in others the satisfaction of his own urge towards happiness, which is just what love ought to achieve and how it acts in practice. And if I gamble with correct prevision of the consequences of my operations, and therefore with success, I fulfill all the strictest injunctions of Feuerbachian morality — and become a rich man into the bargain. In other words, Feuerbach's morality is cut exactly to the pattern of modern capitalist society, little as Feuerbach himself might desire or imagine it.

But love! — yes, with Feuerbach, love is everywhere and at all times the wonder-working god who should help to surmount all difficulties of practical life — and at that in a society which is split into classes with diametrically opposite interests. At this point, the last relic of the revolutionary character disappears from his philosophy, leaving only the old cant: Love one another — fall into each other's arms regardless of distinctions of sex or estate — a universal orgy of reconciliation!

In short, the Feuerbachian theory of morals fares like all its predecessors. It is designed to suit all periods, all peoples and all conditions, and precisely for that reason it is never and nowhere applicable. It remains, as regards the real world, as powerless as Kant's categorical imperative. In reality every class, even every profession, has its own morality, and even this it violates whenever it can do so with impunity. And love, which is to unite all, manifests itself in wars, altercations, lawsuits, domestic broils, divorces, and every possible exploitation of one by another.

Now how was it possible that the powerful impetus given by Feuerbach turned out to be so unfruitful for himself? For the simple reason that Feuerbach himself never contrives to escape from the realm of abstraction — for which he has a deadly hatred — into that of living reality. He clings fiercely to nature and man; but nature and man remain mere words with him. He is incapable of telling us anything definite either about real nature or real men. But from the abstract man of Feuerbach, one arrives at real living men only when one considers them as participants in history. And that is what Feuerbach resisted, and therefore the year 1848, which he did not understand, meant to him merely the final break with the real world, retirement into solitude. The blame for this again falls chiefly on the conditions them obtaining in Germany, which condemned him to rot away miserably.

But the step which Feuerbach did not take nevertheless had to be taken. The cult of abstract man, which formed the kernel of Feuerbach's new religion, had to be replaced by the science of real men and of their historical development. This further development of Feuerbach's standpoint beyond Feuerbach was inaugurated by Marx in 1845 in *The Holy Family*.

Strauss, Bauer, Stirner, Feuerbach — these were the offshoots of Hegelian philosophy, in so far as they did not abandon the field of philosophy. Strauss, after his *Life of Jesus* and *Dogmatics*, produced only literary studies in philosophy and ecclesiastical history after the fashion of Renan. Bauer only achieved something in the field of the history of the origin of Christianity, though what he did here was important. Stirner remained a curiosity, even after Bakunin blended him with Proudhon and labeled the blend "anarchism". Feuerbach alone was of significance as a philosopher. But not only did philosophy — claimed to soar above all special sciences and to be the science of sciences connecting them — remain to him an impassable barrier, an inviolable holy thing, but as a philosopher, too, he stopped half-incapable of disposing of Hegel through criticism; he simply threw him aside as useless, while he himself, compared with the encyclopaedic wealth of the Hegelian system, achieved nothing positive beyond a turgid religion of love and a meagre, impotent morality.

Out of the dissolution of the Hegelian school, however, there developed still another tendency, the only one which has borne real fruit. And this tendency is essentially connected with the name of Marx.

The separation from Hegelian philosophy was here also the result of a return to the materialist standpoint. That means it was resolved to comprehend the real world — nature and history — just as it presents itself to everyone who approaches it free from preconceived idealist crotchets. It was decided mercilessly to sacrifice every idealist fancy which could not be brought into harmony with the facts conceived in their own and not in a fantastic interconnection. And materialism means nothing more than this. But here the materialistic world outlook was taken really seriously for the first time and was carried through consistently — at least in its basic features — in all domains of knowledge concerned.

Hegel was not simply put aside. On the contrary, a start was made from his revolutionary side, described above, from the dialectical method. But in its Hegelian form, this method was unusable. According to Hegel, dialectics is the self-development of the concept. The absolute concept does not only exist — unknown where — from eternity, it is also the actual living soul of the whole existing world. It develops into itself through all the preliminary stages which are treated at length in the Logic and which are all included in it. Then it "alienates" itself by changing into nature, where, unconscious of itself, disguised as a natural necessity, it goes through a new development and finally returns as man's consciousness of himself. This self-consciousness then elaborates itself again in history in the crude form until finally the absolute concept again comes to itself completely in the Hegelian philosophy. According to Hegel, therefore, the dialectical development apparent in nature and history — that is, the causal interconnection of the progressive movement from the lower to the higher, which asserts itself through all zigzag movements and temporary retrogression — is only a copy (*Abklatsch*) of the self-movement of the concept going on from eternity, no one knows where, but at all events independently of any thinking human brain. This ideological perversion had to be done away with. We again took a materialistic view of the thoughts in our heads, regarding them as images (*Abbilder*) of real things instead of regarding real things as images of this or that stage of the absolute concept. Thus dialectics reduced itself to the science of the general laws of motion, both of the external world and of human thought — two sets of laws which are identical in substance, but differ in their expression in so far as the human mind can apply them consciously, while in nature and also up to now for the most part in human history, these laws assert themselves unconsciously, in the form of external necessity, in the midst of an endless series of seeming accidents. Thereby the dialectic of concepts itself became merely the conscious reflex of the dialectical motion of the real world and thus the dialectic of Hegel was turned over; or rather, turned off its head, on which it was standing, and placed upon its feet. And this materialist dialectic, which for years has been our best working tool and our sharpest weapon, was, remarkably enough, discovered not only by us but also, independently of us and even of Hegel, by a German worker, Joseph Dietzgen.

In this way, however, the revolutionary side of Hegelian philosophy was again taken up and at the same time freed from the idealist trimmings which with Hegel had prevented its consistent execution. The great basic thought that the world is not to be comprehended as a complex of readymade things, but as a complex of processes, in which the things apparently stable no less than their mind images in our heads, the concepts, go through an uninterrupted change of coming into being and passing away, in which, in spite of all seeming accidentally and of all temporary retrogression, a progressive development asserts itself in the end — this great fundamental thought has, especially since the time of Hegel, so thoroughly permeated ordinary consciousness that in this generality it is now scarcely ever contradicted. But to acknowledge this fundamental thought in words and to apply it in reality in detail to each domain of investigation are two different things. If, however, investigation always proceeds from this standpoint, the demand for final solutions and eternal truths ceases once for all; one is always conscious of the necessary limitation of all acquired knowledge, of the fact that it is conditioned by the circumstances in which it was acquired. On the other hand, one no longer permits oneself to be imposed upon by the antithesis, insuperable for the still common old metaphysics, between true and false, good and bad, identical and different, necessary and accidental. One knows that these antitheses have only a relative validity; that that which is recognized now as true has also its latent false side which will later manifest itself, just as that which is now regarded as false has also its true side by virtue of which it could previously be regarded as true. One knows that what is maintained to be necessary is composed of sheer accidents and that the so-called accidental is the form behind which necessity hides itself — and so on.

The old method of investigation and thought which Hegel calls "metaphysical", which preferred to investigate things as given, as fixed and stable, a method the relics of which still strongly haunt people's minds, had a great deal of historical justification in its day. It was necessary first to examine things before it was possible to examine processes. One had first to know what a particular thing was before one could observe the changes it was undergoing. And such was the case with natural science. The old metaphysics, which accepted things as finished objects, arose from a natural science which investigated dead and living things as finished objects. But when this investigation had progressed so far that it became possible to take the decisive step forward, that is, to pass on the systematic investigation of the changes which these things undergo in nature itself, then the last hour of the old metaphysic struck in the realm of philosophy also. And in fact, while natural science up to the end of the last century was predominantly a collecting science, a science of finished things, in our century it is essentially a systematizing science, a science of the processes, of the origin and development of these things and of the interconnection which binds all these natural processes into one great whole. Physiology, which investigates the processes occurring in plant and animal organisms; embryology, which deals with the development of individual organisms from germs to maturity; geology, which investigates the gradual formation of the Earth's surface — all these are the offspring of our century.

But, above all, there are three great discoveries which have enabled our knowledge of the interconnection of natural processes to advance by leaps and bounds:

First, the discovery of the cell as the unit from whose multiplication and differentiation the whole plant and animal body develops. Not only is the development and growth of all higher organisms recognized to proceed according to a single general law, but the capacity of the cell to change indicates the way by which organisms can change their species and thus go through a more than individual development.

Second, the transformation of energy, which has demonstrated to us that all the so-called forces operative in the first instance in inorganic nature — mechanical force and its complement, so-called potential energy, heat, radiation (light, or radiant heat), electricity, magnetism, and chemical energy — are different forms of manifestation of universal motion, which pass into one another in definite proportions so that in place of a certain quantity of the one which disappears, a certain quantity of another makes its appearance and thus the whole motion of nature is reduced to this incessant process of transformation from one form into another.

Finally, the proof which Darwin first developed in connected form that the stock of organic products of nature environing us today, including man, is the result of a long process of evolution from a few originally unicellular germs, and that these again have arisen from protoplasm or albumen, which came into existence by chemical means.

Thanks to these three great discoveries, and the other immense advances in natural science, we have now arrived at the point where we can demonstrate the interconnection between the processes in nature not only in particular spheres but also the interconnection of these particular spheres on the whole, and so can present in an approximately systematic form a comprehensive view of the interconnection in nature by means of the facts provided by an empirical science itself. To furnish this comprehensive view was formerly the task of   so-called natural philosophy. It could do this only by putting in place of the real but as yet unknown interconnections ideal, fancied ones, filling in the missing facts by figments of the mind and bridging the actual gaps merely in imagination. In the course of this procedure it conceived many brilliant ideas and foreshadowed many later discoveries, but it also produced a considerable amount of nonsense, which indeed could not have been otherwise. Today, when one needs to comprehend the results of natural scientific investigation only dialetically, that is, in the sense of their own interconnection, in order to arrive at a "system of nature" sufficient for our time; when the dialectical character of this interconnection is forcing itself against their will even into the metaphysically-trained minds of the natural scientists, today natural philosophy is finally disposed of. Every attempt at resurrecting it would be not only superfluous but a step backwards.

But what is true of nature, which is hereby recognized also as a historical process of development, is likewise true of the history of society in all its branches and of the totality of all sciences which occupy themselves with things human (and divine). Here, too, the philosophy of history, of right, of religion, etc., has consisted in the substitution of an interconnection fabricated in the mind of the philosopher for the real interconnection to be demonstrated in the events; has consisted in the comprehension of history as a whole as well as in its separate parts, as the gradual realization of ideas — and naturally always only the pet ideas of the philosopher himself. According to this, history worked unconsciously but of necessity towards a certain ideal goal set in advance — as, for example, in Hegel, towards the realization of his absolute idea — and the unalterable trend towards this absolute idea formed the inner interconnection in the events of history. A new mysterious providence — unconscious or gradually coming into consciousness — was thus put in the place of the real, still unknown interconnection. Here, therefore, just as in the realm of nature, it was necessary to do away with these fabricated, artificial interconnections by the discovery of the real ones — a task which ultimately amounts to the discovery of the general laws of motion which assert themselves as the ruling ones in the history of human society.

In one point, however, the history of the development of society proves to be essentially different from that of nature. In nature — in so far as we ignore man's reaction upon nature — there are only blind, unconscious agencies acting upon one another, out of whose interplay the general law comes into operation. Nothing of all that happens — whether in the innumerable apparent accidents observable upon the surface, or in the ultimate results which confirm the regularity inherent in these accidents — happens as a consciously desired aim. In the history of society, on the contrary, the actors are all endowed with consciousness, are men acting with deliberation or passion, working towards definite goals; nothing happens without a conscious purpose, without an intended aim. But this distinction, important as it is for historical investigation, particularly of single epochs and events, cannot alter the fact that the course of history is governed by inner general laws. For here, also, on the whole, in spite of the consciously desired aims of all individuals, accident apparently reigns on the surface. That which is willed happens but rarely; in the majority of instances the numerous desired ends cross and conflict with one another, or these ends themselves are from the outset incapable of realization, or the means of attaining them are insufficient. thus the conflicts of innumerable individual wills and individual actions in the domain of history produce a state of affairs entirely analogous to that prevailing in the realm of unconscious nature. The ends of the actions are intended, but the results which actually follow from these actions are not intended; or when they do seem to correspond to the end intended, they ultimately have consequences quite other than those intended. Historical events thus appear on the whole to be likewise governed by chance. But where on the surface accident holds sway, there actually it is always governed by inner, hidden laws, and it is only a matter of discovering these laws.

Men make their own history, whatever its outcome may be, in that each person follows his own consciously desired end, and it is precisely the resultant of these many wills operating in different directions, and of their manifold effects upon the outer world, that constitutes history. Thus it is also a question of what the many individuals desire. The will is determined by passion or deliberation. But the levers which immediately determine passion or deliberation are of very different kinds. Partly they may be external objects, partly ideal motives, ambition, "enthusiasm for truth and justice", personal hatred, or even purely individual whims of all kinds. But, on the one hand, we have seen that the many individual wills active in history for the most part produce results quite other than those intended — often quite the opposite; that their motives, therefore, in relation to the total result are likewise of only secondary importance. On the other hand, the further question arises: What driving forces in turn stand behind these motives? What are the historical forces which transform themselves into these motives in the brains of the actors?

The old materialism never put this question to itself. Its conception of history, in so far as it has one at all, is therefore essentially pragmatic; it divides men who act in history into noble and ignoble and then finds that as a rule the noble are defrauded and the ignoble are victorious. Hence, it follows for the old materialism that nothing very edifying is to be got from the study of history, and for us that in the realm of history the old materialism becomes untrue to itself because it takes the ideal driving forces which operate there as ultimate causes, instead of investigating what is behind them, what are the driving forces of these driving forces. This inconsistency does not lie in the fact that ideal driving forces are recognized, but in the investigation not being carried further back behind these into their motive causes. On the other hand, the philosophy of history, particularly as represented by Hegel, recognizes that the ostensible and also the really operating motives of men who act in history are by no means the ultimate causes of historical events; that behind these motives are other motive powers, which have to be discovered. But it does not seek these powers in history itself, it imports them rather from outside, from philosophical ideology, into history. Hegel, for example, instead of explaining the history of ancient Greece out of its own inner interconnections, simply maintains that it is nothing more than the working out of "forms of beautiful individuality", the realization of a "work of art" as such. He says much in this connection about the old Greeks that is fine and profound, but that does not prevent us today from refusing to be put off with such an explanation, which is a mere manner of speech.

When, therefore, it is a question of investigating the driving powers which — consciously or unconsciously, and indeed very often unconsciously — lie behind the motives of men who act in history and which constitute the real ultimate driving forces of history, then it is not a question so much of the motives of single individuals, however eminent, as of those motives which set in motion great masses, whole people, and again whole classes of the people in each people; and this, too, not merely for an instant, like the transient flaring up of a straw-fire which quickly dies down, but as a lasting action resulting in a great historical transformation. To ascertain the driving causes which here in the minds of acting masses and their leaders — to so-called great men — are reflected as conscious motives, clearly or unclearly, directly or in an ideological, even glorified, form — is the only path which can put us on the track of the laws holding sway both in history as a whole, and at particular periods and in particular lands. Everything which sets men in motion must go through their minds; but what form it will take in the mind will depend very much upon the circumstances. The workers have by no means become reconciled to capitalist machine industry, even though they no longer simply break the machines to pieces, as they still did in 1848 on the Rhine.

But while in all earlier periods the investigation of these driving causes of history was almost impossible — on account of the complicated and concealed interconnections between them and their effects — our present period has so far simplified these interconnections that the riddle could be solved. Since the establishment of large-scale industry — that is, at least since the European peace of 1815 — it has been no longer a secret to any man in England that the whole political struggle there pivoted on the claims to supremacy of two classes: the landed aristocracy and the bourgeoisie (middle class). In France, with the return of the Bourbons, the same fact was perceived, the historians of the Restoration period, from Thierry to Guisot, Mignet, and Thiers, speak of it everywhere as the key to the understanding of all French history since the Middle Ages. And since 1830, the working class, the proletariat, has been recognized in both countries as a third competitor for power. Conditions had become so simplified that one would have had to close one's eyes deliberately not to see in the light of these three great classes and in the conflict of their interests the driving force of modern history — at least in the two most advanced countries.

But how did these classes come into existence? If it was possible at first glance still to ascribe the origin of the great, formerly feudal landed property — at least in the first instance — to political causes, to taking possession by force, this could not be done in regard to the bourgeoise and the proletariat. Here, the origin and development of two great classes was seen to lie clearly and palpably in purely economic causes. And it was just as clear that in the struggle between landed property and the bourgeoisie, no less than in the struggle between the bourgeoisie and the proletariat, it was a question, first and foremost, of economic interests, to the furtherance of which political power was intended to serve merely as a means. Bourgeoisie and proletariat both arose in consequences of a transformation of the economic conditions, more precisely, of the mode of production. The transition, first from guild handicrafts to manufacture, and then from manufacture to large-scale industry, with steam and mechanical power, had caused the development of these two classes. At a certain stage, the new productive forces set in motion by the bourgeoisie — in the first place the division of labor and the combination of many detail laborers (*Teilarbeiter*) in one general manufactory — and the conditions and requirements of exchange, developed through these productive forces, became incompatible with the existing order of production handed down by history and sanctified by law — that is to say, incompatible with the privileges of the guild and the numerous other personal and local privileges (which were only so many fetters to the unprivileged estates) of the feudal order to society. The productive forces represented by the bourgeoisie rebelled against the order of production represented by the feudal landlords and the guild-masters. The result is known, the feudal fetters were smashed, gradually in England, at one blow in France. In Germany, the process is not yet finished. But just as, at a definite stage of its development, manufacture came into conflict with the feudal order of production, so now large-scale industry has already come into conflict with the bourgeois order or production established in its place. Tied down by this order, by the narrow limits of the capitalist mode of production, this industry produces, on the one hand, an ever-increasingly proletarianization of the great mass of the people, and on the other hand, an ever greater mass of unsalable products. Overproduction and mass misery, each the cause of the other — that is the absurd contradiction which is its outcome, and which of necessity calls for the liberation of the productive forces by means of a change in the mode of production.

In modern history at least it is, therefore, proved that all political struggles are class struggles, and all class struggles for emancipation, despite their necessarily political form — for every class struggle is a political struggle — turn ultimately on the question of economic emancipation. Therefore, here at least, the state — the political order — is the subordination, and civil society — the realm of economic relations — the decisive element. The traditional conception, to which

Hegel, too, pays homage, saw in the state the determining element, and in civil society the element determined by it. Appearances correspond to this. As all the driving forces of the actions of any individual person must pass through his brain, and transform themselves into motives of his will in order to set him into action, so also all the needs of civil society — no matter which class happens to be the ruling one — must pass through the will of the state in order to secure general validity in the form of laws. That is the formal aspect of the matter — the one which is self-evident. The question arises, however, what is the content of this merely formal will — of the individual as well as of the state — and whence is this content derived? Why is just this willed and not something else? If we enquire into this, we discover that in modern history the will of the state is, on the whole, determined by the changing needs of civil society, but the supremacy of this or that class, in the last resort, by the development of the productive forces and relations of exchange.

But if even in our modern era, with its gigantic means of production and communication, the state is not an independent domain with an independent development, but one whose existence as well as development is to be explained in the last resort by the economic conditions of life of society, then this must be still more true of all earlier times when the production of the material life of man was not yet carried on with these abundant auxiliary means, and when, therefore, the necessity of such production must have exercised a still greater mastery over men. If the state even today, in the era of big industry and of railways, is on the whole only a reflection, in concentrated form, of the economic needs of the class controlling production, then this must have been much more so in an epoch when each generation of men was forced to spend a far greater part of its aggregate lifetime in satisfying material needs, and was therefore much more dependent on them than we are today. An examination of the history of earlier periods, as soon as it is seriously undertaken from this angle, most abundantly confirms this. But, of course, this cannot be gone into here.

If the state and public law are determined by economic relations, so, too, of course, is private law, which indeed in essence only sanctions the existing economic relations between individuals which are normal in the given circumstances. The form in which this happens can, however, vary considerably. It is possible, as happened in England, in harmony with the whole national development, to retain in the main the forms of the old feudal laws while giving them a bourgeois content; in fact, directly reading a bourgeois meaning into the feudal name. But, also, as happened in Western continental Europe, roman law, the first world law of a commodity-producing society, with its unsurpassably fine elaboration of all the essential legal relations of simple commodity owners (of buyers and sellers, debtors and creditors, contracts, obligations, etc.) can be taken as the foundation. In which case, for the benefit of a still petty-bourgeois and semi-feudal society, it can either be reduced to the level of such a society simply through judicial practice (common law) or, with the help of allegedly enlightened, moralizing jurists it can be worked into a special code of law to correspond with such social level — a code which in these circumstances will be a bad one also from the legal standpoint (for instance, Prussian Landrecht). But after a great bourgeois revolution it is, however, also possible for such a classic law code of bourgeois society as the French Code Civile to be worked out upon the basis of this same Roman Law. If, therefore, bourgeois legal rules merely express the economic life conditions of society in legal form, then they can do so well or ill according to circumstances.

The state presents itself to us as the first ideological power over man. Society creates for itself an organ for the safeguarding of its common interests against internal and external attacks. This organ is the state power. Hardly come into being, this organ makes itself independent vis-a-vis society; and, indeed, the more so, the more it becomes the organ of a particular class, the more it directly enforces the supremacy of that class. The fight of the oppressed class against the ruling class becomes necessarily a political fight, a fight first of all against the political dominance of this class. The consciousness of the interconnection between this political struggle and its economic basis becomes dulled and can be lost altogether. While this is not wholly the case with the participants, it almost always happens with the historians. Of the ancient sources on the struggles within the Roman Republic, only Appian tells us clearly and distinctly what was at issue in the last resort — namely, landed property.

But once the state has become an independent power vis-a-vis society, it produces forthwith a further ideology. It is indeed among professional politicians, theorists of public law, and jurists of private law, that the connection with economic facts gets lost for fair. Since in each particular case, the economic facts must assume the form of juristic motives in order to receive legal sanction; and since, in so doing, consideration of course has to be given to the whole legal system already in operation, the juristic form is, in consequence, made everything and the economic content nothing. Public law and private law are treated as independent spheres, each being capable of and needing a systematic presentation by the consistent elimination of all inner contradictions.

Still higher ideologies, that is, such as are still further removed from the material, economic basis, take the form of philosophy and religion. Here the interconnection between conceptions and their material conditions of existence becomes more and more complicated, more and more obscured by intermediate links. But the interconnection exists. Just as the whole Renaissance period, from the middle of the 15th century, was an essential product of the towns and, therefore, of the burghers, so also was the subsequently newly-awakened philosophy. Its content was in essence only the philosophical expression of the thoughts corresponding to the development of the small and middle burghers into a big bourgeoisie. Among last century's Englishmen and Frenchmen who in many cases were just as much political economists as philosophers, this is clearly evident; and we have proved it above in regard to the Hegelian school.

We will now in addition deal only briefly with religion, since the latter stands further away from material life and seems to be most alien to it. Religion arose in very primitive times from erroneous, primitive conceptions of men about their own nature and external nature surrounding them. Every ideology, however, once it has arisen, develops in connection with the given concept-material, and develops this material further; otherwise, it would not be an ideology, that is, occupation with thoughts as with independent entities, developing independently and subject only to their own laws. In the last analysis, the material life conditions of the persons inside whose heads this thought process goes on determine the course of the process, which of necessity remains unknown to these persons, for otherwise there would be an end to all ideology. These original religious notions, therefore, which in the main are common to each group of kindred peoples, develop, after the group separates, in a manner peculiar to each people, according to the conditions of life falling to their lot. For a number of groups of peoples, and particularly for the Aryans (so-called Indo-Europeans) this process has been shown in detail by comparative mythology. The gods thus fashioned within each people were national gods, whose domain extended no farther than the national territory which they were to protect; on the other side of its boundaries, other gods held undisputed sway. They could continue to exist, in imagination, only as long as the nation existed; they fell with its fall. The Roman world empire, the economic conditions of whose origin we do not need to examine here, brought about this downfall of the old nationalities. The old national gods decayed, even those of the Romans, which also were patterned to suit only the narrow confines of the city of Rome. The need to complement the world empire by means of a world religion was clearly revealed in the attempts made to recognize all foreign gods that were the least bit respectable and provide altars for them in Rome alongside the native gods. But a new world religion is not to be made in this fashion, by imperial decree. The new world religion, Christianity, had already quietly come into being, out of a mixture of generalized Oriental, particularly Jewish, theology, and vulgarized Greek, particularly Stoic, philosophy. What it originally looked like has to be first laboriously discovered, since its official form, as it has been handed down to us, is merely that in which it became the state religion to which purpose it was adapted by the Council of Nicaea. The fact that already after 250 years it became the state religion suffices to show that it was the religion in correspondence with the conditions of the time. In the Middle Ages, in the same measure as feudalism developed, Christianity grew into the religious counterpart to it, with a corresponding feudal hierarchy. And when the burghers began to thrive, there developed, in opposition to feudal Catholicism, the Protestant heresy, which first appeared in Southern France among the Albigenses, at the time the cities there reached the highest point of their florescence. The Middle Ages had attached to theology all the other forms of ideology — philosophy, politics, jurisprudence — and made them subdivision of theology. It thereby constrained every social and political movement to take on a theological form. The sentiments of the masses were fed with religion to the exclusion of all else; it was therefore necessary to put forward their own interests in a religious guise in order to produce a great tempest. And just as the burghers from the beginning brought into being an appendage of propertyless urban plebeians, day laborers and servants of all kinds, belonging to no recognized social estate, precursors of the later proletariat, so likewise heresy soon became divided into a burgher-moderate heresy and a plebeian-revolutionary one, the latter an abomination to the burgher heretics themselves.

The ineradicability of the Protestant heresy corresponded to the invincibility of the rising burghers. When these burghers had become sufficiently strengthened, their struggle against the feudal nobility, which till then had been predominantly local, began to assume national dimensions. The first great action occurred in Germany — the so-called reformation. The burghers were neither powerful enough nor sufficiently developed to be able to unite under their banner the remaining rebellious estates — the plebeians of the towns, the lower nobility, and the peasants on the land. At first, the nobles were defeated; the peasants rose in a revolt which formed the peak of the whole revolutionary struggle; the cities left them in the lurch, and thus the revolution succumbed to the armies of the secular princes who reaped the whole profit. Thenceforward, Germany disappears for three centuries from the ranks of countries playing an independent active part in history. But, beside the German Luther appeared the Frenchman Calvin. With true French acuity, he put the bourgeois character of the Reformation in the forefront, republicanized and democratized the Church. While the Lutheran Reformation in Germany degenerated and reduced the country to rack and ruin, the Calvinist Reformation served as a banner for the republicans in Geneva, in Holland, and in Scotland, freed Holland from Spain and from the German Empire, and provided the ideological costume for the second act of the bourgeois revolution, which was taking place in England. Here, Calvinism justified itself as the true religious disguise of the interests of the bourgeoisie of that time, and on this account did not attain full recognition when the revolution ended in 1689 in a compromise between one part of the nobility and the bourgeoisie. The English state Church was re-established; but not in its earlier form of a Catholicism which had the king for its pope, being, instead, strongly Calvinized. The old state Church had celebrated the merry Catholic Sunday and had fought against the dull Calvinist one. The new, bourgeoisified Church introduced the latter, which adorns England to this day.

In France, the Calvinist minority was suppressed in 1685 and either Catholized or driven out of the country. But what was the good? Already at that time the freethinker Pierre Bayle was at the height of his activity, and in 1694 Voltaire was born. The forcible measures of Louis XIV only made it easier for the French bourgeoisie to carry through its revolution in the irreligious, exclusively political form which alone was suited to a developed bourgeoisie. Instead of Protestants, freethinkers took their seats in the national assemblies. Thereby Christianity entered into its final stage. It was incapable of doing any future service to any progressive class as the ideological garb of its aspirations. It became more and more the exclusive possession of the ruling classes; they apply it as a mere means of government, to keep the lower classes within bounds. Moreover, each of the different classes uses its own appropriate religion: the landed nobility — Catholic Jesuitism, or Protestant orthodoxy; the liberal and radical bourgeoisie — rationalism; and it makes little difference whether these gentlemen themselves believe in their respective religions or not.

We see, therefore: religion, once formed, always contains traditional material, just as in all ideological domains tradition forms a great conservative force. But the transformations which this material undergoes spring from class relations — that is to say, out of the economic relations of the people who execute these transformations. And here that is sufficient.

In the above, it could only be a question of giving a general sketch of the Marxist conception of history, at most with a few illustrations, as well. The proof must be derived from history itself; and, in this regard, it may be permitted to say that is has been sufficiently furnished in other writings. This conception, however, puts an end to philosophy in the realm of history, just as the dialectical conception of nature makes all natural philosophy both unnecessary and impossible. It is no longer a question anywhere of inventing interconnections from out of our brains, but of discovering them in the facts. For philosophy, which has been expelled from nature and history, there remains only the realm of pure thought, so far as it is left: the theory of the laws of the thought process itself, logic and dialectics.

With the Revolution of 1848, "educated" Germany said farewell to theory and went over to the field of practice. Small production and manufacture, based upon manual labor, were superseded by real large-scale industry. Germany again appeared on the world market. The new little German Empire abolished at least the most crying of the abuses with which this development had been obstructed by the system of petty states, the relics of feudalism, and bureaucratic management. But to the same degree that speculation abandoned the philosopher's study in order to set up its temple in the Stock Exchange, educated Germany lost the great aptitude for theory which had been the glory of Germany in the days of its deepest political humiliation — the aptitude for purely scientific investigation, irrespective of whether the result obtained was practically applicable or not, whether likely to offend the police authorities or not. Official German natural science, it is true, maintained its position in the front rank, particularly in the field of specialized research. But even the American journal *Science* rightly remarks that the decisive advances in the sphere of the comprehensive correlation of particular facts and their generalization into laws are now being made much more in England, instead of, as formerly, in Germany. And in the sphere of the historical sciences, philosophy included, the old fearless zeal for theory has now disappeared completely, along with classical philosophy. Inane eclecticism and an anxious concern for career and income, descending to the most vulgar job-hunting, occupy its place. The official representatives of these sciences have become the undisguised ideologists of the bourgeoisie and the existing state — but at a time when both stand in open antagonism to the working class.

Only among the working class does the German aptitude for theory remain unimpaired. Here, it cannot be exterminated. Here, there is no concern for careers, for profit-making, or for gracious patronage from above. On the contrary, the more ruthlessly and disinterestedly science proceeds the more it finds itself in harmony with the interest and aspirations of the workers. The new tendency, which recognized that the key to the understanding of the whole history of society lies in the history of the development of labor, from the outset addressed itself by preference to the working class and here found the response which it neither sought nor expected from officially recognized science. The German working-class movement is the inheritor of German classical philosophy.

Origins of the Family, Private Property, and the State

Preface to the First Edition, 1884

The following chapters are, in a sense, the execution of a bequest. No less a man than Karl Marx had made it one of his future tasks to present the results of Morgan's researches in the light of the conclusions of his own — within certain limits, I may say our — materialistic examination of history, and thus to make clear their full significance. For Morgan in his own way had discovered afresh in America the materialistic conception of history discovered by Marx forty years ago, and in his comparison of barbarism and civilization it had led him, in the main points, to the same conclusions as Marx. And just as the professional economists in Germany were for years as busy in plagiarizing *Capital* as they were persistent in attempting to kill it by silence, so Morgan's *Ancient Society* received precisely the same treatment from the spokesmen of "prehistoric" science in England. My work can only provide a slight substitute for what my departed friend no longer had the time to do. But I have the critical notes which he made to his extensive extracts from Morgan, and as far as possible I reproduce them here.

According to the materialistic conception, the determining factor in history is, in the final instance, the production and reproduction of the immediate essentials of life. This, again, is of a twofold character. On the one side, the production of the means of existence, of articles of food and clothing, dwellings, and of the tools necessary for that production; on the other side, the production of human beings themselves, the propagation of the species. The social organization under which the people of a particular historical epoch and a particular country live is determined by both kinds of production: by the stage of development of labor on the one hand and of the family on the other.

The lower the development of labor and the more limited the amount of its products, and consequently, the more limited also the wealth of the society, the more the social order is found to be dominated by kinship groups. However, within this structure of society based on kinship groups the productivity of labor increasingly develops, and with it private property and exchange, differences of wealth, the possibility of utilizing the labor power of others, and hence the basis of class antagonisms: new social elements, which in the course of generations strive to adapt the old social order to the new conditions, until at last their incompatibility brings about a complete upheaval. In the collision of the newly-developed social classes, the old society founded on kinship groups is broken up; in its place appears a new society, with its control centered in the state, the subordinate units of which are no longer kinship associations, but local associations; a society in which the system of the family is completely dominated by the system of property, and in which there now freely develop those class antagonisms and class struggles that have hitherto formed the content of all written history.

It is Morgan's great merit that he has discovered and reconstructed in its main lines this prehistoric basis of our written history, and that in the kinship groups of the North American Indians he has found the key to the most important and hitherto insoluble riddles of earliest Greek, Roman and German history. His book is not the work of a day. For nearly forty years he wrestled with his material, until he was completely master of it. But that also makes his book one of the few epoch-making works of our time.

In the following presentation, the reader will in general easily distinguish what comes from Morgan and what I have added. In the historical sections on Greece and Rome I have not confined myself to Morgan's evidence, but have added what was available to me. The sections on the Celts and the Germans are in the main my work;

Morgan had to rely here almost entirely on secondary sources, and for German conditions—apart from Tacitus—on the worthless and liberalistic falsifications of Mr. Freeman. The treatment of the economic aspects, which in Morgan's book was sufficient for his purpose but quite inadequate for mine, has been done afresh by myself. And, finally, I am, of course, responsible for all the conclusions drawn, in so far as Morgan is not expressly cited.

Preface to the Fourth Edition, 1891

The earlier large editions of this work have been out of print now for almost half a year, and for some time the publisher has been asking me to prepare a new edition. Until now, more urgent work kept me from doing so. Since the appearance of the first edition seven years have elapsed, during which our knowledge of the primitive forms of the family has made important advances. There was, therefore, plenty to do in the way of improvements and additions; all the more so as the proposed stereotyping of the present text will make any further alterations impossible for some time.

I have accordingly submitted the whole text to a careful revision and made a number of additions which, I hope, take due account of the present state of knowledge. I also give in the course of this preface a short review of the development of the history of the family from Bachofen to Morgan; I do so chiefly because the chauvinistically inclined English anthropologists are still striving their utmost to kill by silence the revolution which Morgan's discoveries have effected in our conception of primitive history, while they appropriate his results without the slightest compunction. Elsewhere also the example of England is in some cases followed only too closely.

My work has been translated into a number of other languages. First, Italian: *L'origine delta famiglia, delta proprieta privata e dello stato, versions riveduta dall'autore, di Pasquale Martignetti, Benevento*, 1885. Then, Rumanian: *Origina famdei, proprietatei private si a statului, traducere de Joan Nadeide*, in the Yassy periodical *Contemporanul*, September, 1885, to May, 1886. Further, Danish: *Familjens, Privatejendommens og Statens Oprindelse, Dansk, af Forfattern gennemgaaet Udgave, besorget af Gerson Trier*, Kobenhavn, 1888. A French translation by Henri Rave, based on the present German edition, is on the press.

Before the beginning of the 'sixties, one cannot speak of a history of the family. In this field, the science of history was still completely under the influence of the five books of Moses. The patriarchal form of the family, which was there described in greater detail than anywhere else, was not only assumed without question to be the oldest form, but it was also identified – minus its polygamy – with the bourgeois family of today, so that the family had really experienced no historical development at all; at most it was admitted that in primitive times there might have been a period of sexual promiscuity. It is true that in addition to the monogamous form of the family, two other forms were known to exist – polygamy in the Orient and polyandry in India and Tibet; but these three forms could not be arranged in any historical order and merely appeared side by side without any connection. That among some peoples of ancient history, as well as among some savages still alive today, descent was reckoned, not from the father, but from the mother, and that the female line was therefore regarded as alone valid; that among many peoples of the present day in every continent marriage is forbidden within certain large groups which at that time had not been closely studied – these facts were indeed known and fresh instances of them were continually being collected. But nobody knew what to do with them, and even as late as E. B. Tylor's *Researches into the Early History of Mankind, etc.* (1865) they are listed as mere "curious customs," side by side with the prohibition among some savages against touching burning wood with an iron tool and similar religious mumbo-jumbo.

The history of the family dates from 1861, from the publication of Bachofen's *Mutterrecht*. In this work the author advances the following propositions:

(1) That originally man lived in a state of sexual promiscuity, to describe which Bachofen uses the mistaken term "hetaerism";

(2) that such promiscuity excludes any certainty of paternity, and that descent could therefore be reckoned only in the female line, according to mother-right, and that this was originally the case amongst all the peoples of antiquity;

(3) that since women, as mothers, were the only parents of the younger generation that were known with certainty, they held a position of such high respect and honor that it became the foundation, in Bachofen's conception, of a regular rule of women (gynaecocracy);

(4) that the transition to monogamy, where the woman belonged to one man exclusively, involved a violation of a primitive religious law (that is, actually a violation of the traditional right of the other

men to this woman), and that in order to expiate this violation or to purchase indulgence for it the woman had to surrender herself for a limited period.

Bachofen finds the proofs of these assertions in innumerable passages of ancient classical literature, which he collected with immense industry. According to him, the development from "hetaerism" to monogamy and from mother-right to father-right is accomplished, particularly among the Greeks, as the consequence of an advance in religious conceptions, introducing into the old hierarchy of the gods, representative of the old outlook, new divinities, representative of the new outlook, who push the former more and more into the background. Thus, according to Bachofen, it is not the development of men's actual conditions of life, but the religious reflection of these conditions inside their heads, which has brought about the historical changes in the social position of the sexes in relation to each other. In accordance with this view, Bachofen interprets the *Oresteia* of Aschylus as the dramatic representation of the conflict between declining mother-right and the new father-right that arose and triumphed in the heroic age. For the sake of her paramour, AEgisthus, Clytemnestra slays her husband, Agamemnon, on his return from the Trojan War; but Orestes, the son of Agamemnon and herself, avenges his father's murder by slaying his mother. For this act he is pursued by the Furies, the demonic guardians of mother-right, according to which matricide is the gravest and most inexpiable crime. But Apollo, who by the voice of his oracle had summoned Orestes to this deed, and Athena, who is called upon to give judgment – the two deities who here represent the new patriarchal order – take Orestes under their protection; Athena hears both sides. The whole matter of the dispute is briefly summed up in the debate which now takes place between Orestes and the Furies. Orestes contends that Clytemnestra has committed a double crime; she has slain her husband and thus she has also slain his father. Why should the Furies pursue him, and not her, seeing that she is by far the more guilty? The answer is striking: "She was not kin by blood to the man she slew."

The murder of a man not related by blood, even if he be the husband of the murderess, is expiable and does not concern the Furies; their office is solely to punish murder between blood relations, and of such murders the most grave and the most inexpiable, according to mother-right, is matricide. Apollo now comes forward in

Orestes' defense; Athena calls upon the Areopagites – the Athenian jurors – to vote; the votes for Orestes' condemnation and for his acquittal are equal; Athena, as president, gives her vote for Orestes and acquits him. Father-right has triumphed over mother-right, the "gods of young descent," as the Furies themselves call them, have triumphed over the Furies; the latter then finally allow themselves to be persuaded to take up a new office in the service of the new order.

This new but undoubtedly correct interpretation of the *Oresteia* is one of the best and finest passages in the whole book, but it proves at the same time that Bachofen believes at least as much as AEschylus did in the Furies, Apollo, and Athena; for, at bottom, he believes that the overthrow of mother-right by father-right was a miracle wrought during the Greek heroic age by these divinities. That such a conception, which makes religion the lever of world history, must finally end in pure mysticism, is clear. It is therefore a tough and by no means always a grateful task to plow through Bachofen's solid tome. But all that does not lessen his importance as a pioneer. He was the first to replace the vague phrases about some unknown primitive state of sexual promiscuity by proofs of the following facts: that abundant traces survive in old classical literature of a state prior to monogamy among the Greeks and Asiatics when not only did a man have sexual intercourse with several women, but a woman with several men, without offending against morality; that this custom did not disappear without leaving its traces in the limited surrender which was the price women had to pay for the right to monogamy; that therefore descent could originally be reckoned only in the female line, from mother to mother; that far into the period of monogamy, with its certain or at least acknowledged paternity, the female line was still alone recognized; and that the original position of the mothers, as the only certain parents of their children, secured for them, and thus for their whole sex, a higher social position than women have ever enjoyed since. Bachofen did not put these statements as clearly as this, for he was hindered by his mysticism. But he proved them; and in 1861 that was a real revolution.

Bachofen's massive volume was written in German, the language of the nation which at that time interested itself less than any other in the prehistory of the modern family. Consequently, he remained unknown. His first successor in the same field appeared in 1865, without ever having heard of Bachofen.

This successor was J. F. McLennan, the exact opposite of his predecessor. Instead of a mystic of genius, we have the dry-as-dust jurist; instead of the exuberant imagination of a poet, the plausible arguments of a barrister defending his brief. McLennan finds among many savage, barbarian, and even civilized peoples of ancient and modern times a form of marriage in which the bridegroom, alone or with his friends, must carry off the bride from her relations by a show of force. This custom must be the survival of an earlier custom when the men of one tribe did in fact carry off their wives by force from other tribes. What was the origin of this "marriage by capture"? So long as men could find enough women in their own tribe, there was no reason whatever for it. We find, however, no less frequently that among undeveloped peoples there are certain groups (which in 1865 were still often identified with the tribes themselves) within which marriage is forbidden, so that the men are obliged to take their wives, and women their husbands, from outside the group; whereas among other peoples the custom is that the men of one group must take their wives only from within their own group. McLennan calls the first peoples "exogamous" and the second "endogamous"; he then promptly proceeds to construct a rigid opposition between exogamous and endogamous "tribes." And although his own investigations into exogamy force the fact under his nose that in many, if not in most or even in all, cases, this opposition exists only in his own imagination, he nevertheless makes it the basis of his whole theory. According to this theory, exogamous tribes can only obtain their wives from other tribes; and since in savagery there is a permanent state of war between tribe and tribe, these wives could only be obtained by capture. McLennan then goes on to ask: Whence this custom of exogamy? The conception of consanguinity and incest could not have anything to do with it, for these things only came much later. But there was another common custom among savages-the custom of killing female children immediately after birth. This would cause a surplus of men in each individual tribe, of which the inevitable and immediate consequence would be that several men possessed a wife in common: polyandry. And this would have the further consequence that it would be known who was the mother of a child, but not who its father was: hence relationship only in the female line, with exclusion of the male line – mother-right. And a second consequence of the scarcity of women within a tribe – a scarcity which polyandry mitigated, but did not remove – was precisely this systematic, forcible abduction of women from other tribes.

As exogamy and polyandry are referable to one and the same cause – a want of balance between the sexes-we are forced to regard all the exogamous races as- having originally been polyandrous.... Therefore we must hold it to be beyond dispute that among exogamous races the first system of kinship was that which recognized blood-ties through mothers only. (McLennan, *Studies in Ancient History*, 1886. Primitive Marriage, p. 124)

It is McLennan's merit to have directed attention to the general occurrence and great importance of what he calls exogamy. He did not by any means discover the existence of exogamous groups; still less did he understand them. Besides the early, scattered notes of many observers (these were McLennan's sources), Latham (*Descriptive Ethnology*, 1859) had given a detailed and accurate description of this institution among the Indian Magars, and had said that it was very widespread and occurred in all parts of the world – a passage which McLennan himself cites. Morgan, in 1847, in his letters on the Iroquois (*American Review*) and in 1851 in *The League of the Iroquois*, had already demonstrated the existence of exogamous groups among this tribe and had given an accurate account of them; whereas McLennan, as we shall see, wrought greater confusion here with his legalistic mind than Bachofen wrought in the field of mother-right with his mystical fancies. It is also a merit of McLennan that he recognized matrilineal descent as the earlier system, though he was here anticipated by Bachofen, as he later acknowledged. But McLennan is not clear on this either; he always speaks of "kinship through females only," and this term, which is correct for an earlier stage, he continually applies to later stages of development when descent and inheritance were indeed still traced exclusively through the female line, but when kinship on the male side was also recognized and expressed. There you have the pedantic mind of the jurist, who fixes on a rigid legal term and goes on applying it unchanged when changed conditions have made it applicable no longer.

Apparently McLennan's theory, plausible though it was, did not seem any too well established even to its author. At any rate, he himself is struck by the fact that "it is observable that the form of capture is now most distinctly marked and impressive just among those races which have male kinship" (should be "descent in the male line"). (Ibid., p. 140) And again: "It is a curious fact that nowhere now, that we are aware of, is infanticide a system where exogamy and the earliest form of kinship co-exist." (Ibid., p. 146.) Both these facts flatly contradict his method of explanation, and he can only meet them with new and still more complicated hypotheses.

Nevertheless, his theory found great applause and support in England. McLennan was here generally regarded as the founder of the history of the family and the leading authority on the subject. However many exceptions and variations might be found in individual cases, his opposition of exogamous and endogamous tribes continued to stand as the recognized foundation of the accepted view, and to act as blinkers, obstructing any free survey of the field under investigation and so making any decisive advance impossible. Against McLennan's exaggerated reputation in England – and the English fashion is copied elsewhere – it becomes a duty to set down the fact that be has done more harm with his completely mistaken antithesis between exogamous and endogamous "tribes" than he has done good by his research.

Facts were now already coming to light in increasing number which did not fit into his neat framework. McLennan knew only three forms of marriage: polygyny, polyandry and monogamy. But once attention had been directed to the question, more and more proofs were found that there existed among undeveloped peoples forms of marriage in which a number of men possessed a number of women in common, and Lubbock (*The Origin of Civilization*, 1870) recognized this group marriage ("communal marriage") as a historical fact.

Immediately afterwards, in 1871, Morgan came forward with new and in many ways decisive evidence. He had convinced himself that the peculiar system of consanguinity in force among the Iroquois was common to all the aboriginal inhabitants of the United States and therefore extended over a whole continent, although it directly contradicted the degrees of relationship arising out of the system of marriage as actually practiced by these peoples. He then induced the Federal government to collect information about the systems of consanguinity among the other peoples of the world and to send out for this purpose tables and lists of questions prepared by himself. He discovered from the replies: (1) that the system of consanguinity of the American Indians was also in force among numerous peoples in Asia and, in a somewhat modified form, in Africa and Australia; (2) that its complete explanation was to be found in a form of group marriage which was just dying out in Hawaii and other Australasian islands; and (3) that side by side with this form of marriage a system of consanguinity was in force in the same islands which could only be explained through a still more primitive, now extinct, form of group marriage. He published the collected evidence, together with the conclusions he drew from it, in his *Systems of Consanguinity and Affinity,* 1871, and thus carried the debate on to an infinitely wider field. By starting from the systems of consanguinity and reconstructing from them the corresponding forms of family, he opened a new line of research and extended our range of vision into the prehistory of man. If this method proved to be sound, McLennan's pretty theories would be completely demolished.

McLennan defended his theory in a new edition of *Primitive Marriage (Studies in Ancient History*, 1876). Whilst he himself constructs a highly artificial history of the family out of pure hypotheses, he demands from Lubbock and Morgan not merely proofs for every one of their statements, but proofs as indisputably valid as if they were to be submitted in evidence in a Scottish court of law. And this is the man who, from Tacitus' report on the close relationship between maternal uncle and sister's son among the Germans (*Germania*, Chap. 20), from Caesar's report that the Britons in groups of ten or twelve possessed their wives in common, from all the other reports of classical authors on community of wives among barbarians, calmly draws the conclusion that all these peoples lived in a state of polyandry! One might be listening to a prosecuting counsel who can allow himself every liberty in arguing his own case, but demands from defending counsel the most formal, legally valid proof for his every word.

He maintains that group marriage is pure imagination, and by so doing falls far behind Bachofen. He declares that Morgan's systems of consanguinity are mere codes of conventional politeness, the proof being that the Indians also address a stranger or a white man as brother or father. One might as well say that the terms "father," "mother," "brother," "sister" are mere meaningless forms of address because Catholic priests and abbesses are addressed as "father" and "mother," and because monks and nuns, and even freemasons and members of English trade unions and associations at their full sessions are addressed as "brother" and "sister." In a word, McLennan's defense was miserably feeble.

But on one point he had still not been assailed. The opposition of exogamous and endogamous "tribes" on which his whole system rested not only remained unshaken, but was even universally acknowledged as the keystone of the whole history of the family. McLennan's attempt to explain this opposition might be inadequate and in contradiction with his own facts. But the antithesis itself, the existence of two mutually exclusive types of self-sufficient and independent tribes, of which the one type took their wives from within the tribe, while the other type absolutely forbade it – that was sacred gospel. Compare, for example, Giraud-Teulon's *Origines de la famille* (1874) and even Lubbock's *Origin of Civilization* (fourth edition, 1882).

Here Morgan takes the field with his main work, *Ancient Society* (1877), the work that underlies the present study. What Morgan had only dimly guessed in 1871 is now developed in full consciousness. There is no antithesis between endogamy and exogamy; up to the present, the existence of exogamous "tribes" has not been demonstrated anywhere. But at the time when group marriage still prevailed – and in all probability it prevailed everywhere at some time – the tribe was subdivided into a number of groups related by blood on the mother's side, gentes, within which it was strictly forbidden to marry, so that the men of a gens, though they could take their wives from within the tribe and generally did so, were compelled to take them from outside their gens. Thus while each gens was strictly exogamous, the tribe embracing all the gentes was no less endogamous. Which finally disposed of the last remains of McLennan's artificial constructions.

But Morgan did not rest here. Through the gens of the American Indians, he was enabled to make his second great advance in his field of research. In this gens, organized according to mother-right, he discovered the primitive form out of which had developed the later gens organized according to father-right, the gens as we find it among the ancient civilized peoples. The Greek and Roman gens, the old riddle of all historians, now found its explanation in the Indian gens, and a new foundation was thus laid for the whole of primitive history.

This rediscovery of the primitive matriarchal gens as the earlier stage of the patriarchal gens of civilized peoples has the same importance for anthropology as Darwin's theory of evolution has for biology and Marx's theory of surplus value for political economy. It enabled Morgan to outline for the first time a history of the family in which for the present, so far as the material now available permits, at least the classic stages of development in their main outlines are now determined. That this opens a new epoch in the treatment of primitive history must be clear to everyone. The matriarchal gens has become the pivot on which the whole science turns; since its discovery we know where to look and what to look for in our research, and how to arrange the results. And, consequently, since Morgan's book, progress in this field has been made at a far more rapid speed.

Anthropologists, even in England, now generally appreciate, or rather appropriate, Morgan's discoveries. But hardly one of them has the honesty to admit that it is to Morgan that we owe this revolution in our ideas. In England they try to kill his book by silence, and dispose of its author with condescending praise for his earlier achievements; they niggle endlessly over details and remain obstinately silent about his really great discoveries. The original edition of *Ancient Society* is out of print; in America there is no sale for such things; in England, it seems, the book was systematically suppressed, and the only edition of this epochmaking work still circulating in the book trade is – the German translation.

Why this reserve? It is difficult not to see in it a conspiracy of silence; for politeness' sake, our recognized anthropologists generally pack their writings with quotations and other tokens of camaraderie. Is it, perhaps, because Morgan is an American, and for the English anthropologists it goes sorely against the grain that, despite their highly creditable industry in collecting material, they should be dependent for their general points of view in the arrangement and grouping of this material, for their ideas in fact, on two foreigners of genius, Bachofen and Morgan? They might put up with the German – but the American? Every Englishman turns patriotic when he comes up against an American, and of this I saw highly entertaining instances in the United States. Moreover, McLennan was, so to speak, the officially appointed founder and leader of the English school of anthropology. It was almost a principle of anthropological etiquette to speak of his artificially constructed historical series – child-murder, polygyny, marriage by capture, matriarchal family – in tones only of profoundest respect. The slightest doubt in the existence of exogamous and endogamous "tribes" of absolute mutual exclusiveness was considered rank heresy. Morgan had committed a kind of sacrilege in dissolving all these hallowed dogmas into thin air. Into the bargain, he had done it in such a way that it only needed saying to carry immediate conviction; so that the McLennanites, who had hitherto been helplessly reeling to and fro between exogamy and endogamy, could only beat their brows and exclaim: "How could we be such fools as not to think of that for ourselves long ago?"

As if these crimes had not already left the official school with the option only of coldly ignoring him, Morgan filled the measure to overflowing by not merely criticizing civilization, the society of commodity production, the basic form of present-day society, in a manner reminiscent of Fourier, but also by speaking of a future transformation of this society in words which Karl Marx might have used. He had therefore amply merited McLennan's indignant reproach that "the historical method is antipathetical to Mr. Morgan's mind," and its echo as late as 1884 from Mr. Professor Giraud-Teulon of Geneva. In 1874 (*Origines de la famille*) this same gentleman was still groping helplessly in the maze of the McLennanite exogamy, from which Morgan had to come and rescue him!

Of the other advances which primitive anthropology owes to Morgan, I do not need to speak here; they are sufficiently discussed in the course of this study. The fourteen years which have elapsed since the publication of his chief work have greatly enriched the material available for the study of the history of primitive human societies. The anthropologists, travelers and primitive historians by profession have now been joined by the comparative jurists, who have contributed either new material or new points of view. As a result, some of Morgan's minor hypotheses have been shaken or even disproved. But not one of the great leading ideas of his work has been ousted by this new material. The order which he introduced into primitive history still holds in its main lines today. It is, in fact, winning recognition to the same degree in which Morgan's responsibility for the great advance is carefully concealed.

Frederick Engels
London, June 16, 1891

I. Stages of Prehistoric Culture

Morgan is the first man who, with expert knowledge, has attempted to introduce a definite order into the history of primitive man; so long as no important additional material makes changes necessary, his classification will undoubtedly remain in force.

Of the three main epochs – savagery, barbarism, and civilization – he is concerned, of course, only with the first two and the transition to the third. He divides both savagery and barbarism into lower, middle, and upper stages according to the progress made in the production of food; for, he says:

Upon their skill in this direction, the whole question of human supremacy on the earth depended. Mankind are the only beings who may be said to have gained an absolute control over the production of food.... It is accordingly probable that the great epochs of human progress have been identified, more or less directly, with the enlargement of the sources of subsistence.

The development of the family takes a parallel course, but here the periods have not such striking marks of differentiation.

I. Savagery

(a.) Lower Stage. Childhood of the human race. Man still lived in his original habitat, in tropical or subtropical forests, and was partially at least a tree-dweller, for otherwise his survival among huge beasts of prey cannot be explained. Fruit, nuts and roots served him for food. The development of articulate speech is the main result of this period. Of all the peoples known to history none was still at this primitive level. Though this period may have lasted thousands of years, we have no direct evidence to prove its existence; but once the evolution of man from the animal kingdom is admitted, such a transitional stage must necessarily be assumed.

(b.) Middle Stage. Begins with the utilization of fish for food (including crabs, mussels, and other aquatic animals), and with the use of fire. The two are complementary, since fish becomes edible only by the use of fire. With this new source of nourishment, men now became independent of climate and locality; even as savages, they could, by following the rivers and coasts, spread over most of the earth. Proof of these migrations is the distribution over every continent of the crudely worked, unsharpened flint tools of the earlier Stone Age, known as "palaeoliths," all or most of which date from this period. New environments, ceaseless exercise of his inventive faculty, and the ability to produce fire by friction, led man to discover new kinds of food: farinaceous roots and tubers, for instance, were baked in hot ashes or in ground ovens. With the invention of the first weapons, club and spear, game could sometimes be added to the fare. But the tribes which figure in books as living entirely, that is, exclusively, by hunting never existed in reality; the yield of the hunt was far too precarious. At this stage, owing to the continual uncertainty of food supplies, cannibalism seems to have arisen, and was practiced from now onwards for a long time. The Australian aborigines and many of the Polynesians are still in this middle stage of savagery today.

(c.) Upper Stage. Begins with the invention of the bow and arrow, whereby game became a regular source of food, and hunting a normal form of work. Bow, string, and arrow already constitute a very complex instrument, whose invention implies long, accumulated experience and sharpened intelligence, and therefore knowledge of many other inventions as well. We find, in fact, that the peoples acquainted with the bow and arrow but not yet with pottery (from which Morgan dates the transition to barbarism) are already making some beginnings towards settlement in villages and have gained some control over the production of means of subsistence; we find wooden vessels and utensils, finger-weaving (without looms) with filaments of bark; plaited baskets of bast or osier; sharpened (neolithic) stone tools. With the discovery of fire and the stone ax, dug-out canoes now become common; beams and planks arc also sometimes used for building houses. We find all these advances, for instance, among the Indians of northwest America, who are acquainted with the bow and arrow but not with pottery. The bow and arrow was for savagery what the iron sword was for barbarism and fire-arms for civilization – the decisive weapon.

2. Barbarism

(a.) Lower Stage. Dates from the introduction of pottery. In many cases it has been proved, and in all it is probable, that the first pots originated from the habit of covering baskets or wooden vessels with clay to make them fireproof; in this way it was soon discovered that the clay mold answered the purpose without any inner vessel.

Thus far we have been able to follow a general line of development applicable to all peoples at a given period without distinction of place. With the beginning of barbarism, however, we have reached a stage when the difference in the natural endowments of the two hemispheres of the earth comes into play. The characteristic feature of the period of barbarism is the domestication and breeding of animals and the cultivation of plants. Now, the Eastern Hemisphere, the so-called Old World, possessed nearly all the animals adaptable to domestication, and all the varieties of cultivable cereals except one; the Western Hemisphere, America, had no mammals that could be domesticated except the llama, which, moreover, was only found in one part of South America, and of all the cultivable cereals only one, though that was the best, namely, maize. Owing to these differences in natural conditions, the population of each hemisphere now goes on its own way, and different landmarks divide the particular stages in each of the two cases.

(b.) Middle Stage. Begins in the Eastern Hemisphere with domestication of animals; in the Western, with the cultivation, by means of irrigation, of plants for food, and with the use of adobe (sun-dried) bricks and stone for building.

We will begin with the Western Hemisphere, as here this stage was never superseded before the European conquest.

At the time when they were discovered, the Indians at the lower stage of barbarism (comprising all the tribes living east of the Mississippi) were already practicing some horticulture of maize, and possibly also of gourds, melons, and other garden plants, from which they obtained a very considerable part of their food. They lived in wooden houses in villages protected by palisades. The tribes in the northwest, particularly those in the region of the Columbia River, were still at the upper stage of savagery and acquainted neither with pottery nor with any form of horticulture. The so-called Pueblo Indians of New Mexico, however, and the Mexicans, Central Americans, and Peruvians at the time of their conquest were at the middle stage of barbarism. They lived in houses like fortresses, made of adobe brick or of stone, and cultivated maize and other plants, varying according to locality and climate, in artificially irrigated plots of ground, which supplied their main source of food; some animals even had also been domesticated – the turkey and other birds by the Mexicans, the llama by the Peruvians. They could also work metals, but not iron; hence they were still unable to dispense with stone weapons and tools. The Spanish conquest then cut short any further independent development.

In the Eastern Hemisphere the middle stage of barbarism began with the domestication of animals providing milk and meat, but horticulture seems to have remained unknown far into this period. It was, apparently, the domestication and breeding of animals and the formation of herds of considerable size that led to the differentiation of the Aryans and Semites from the mass of barbarians. The European and Asiatic Aryans still have the same names for cattle, but those for most of the cultivated plants are already different.

In suitable localities, the keeping of herds led to a pastoral life: the Semites lived upon the grassy plains of the Euphrates and Tigris, and the Aryans upon those of India and of the Oxus and Jaxartes, of the Don and the Dnieper. It must have been on the borders of such pasture lands that animals were first domesticated. To later generations, consequently, the pastoral tribes appear to have come from regions which, so far from being the cradle of mankind, were almost uninhabitable for their savage ancestors and even for man at the lower stages of barbarism. But having once accustomed themselves to pastoral life in the grassy plains of the rivers, these barbarians of the middle period would never have dreamed of returning willingly to the native forests of their ancestors. Even when they were forced further to the north and west, the Semites and Aryans could not move into the forest regions of western Asia and of Europe until by cultivation of grain they had made it possible to pasture and especially to winter their herds on this less favorable land. It is more than probable that among these tribes the cultivation of grain originated from the need for cattle fodder and only later became important as a human food supply.

The plentiful supply of milk and meat and especially the beneficial effect of these foods on the growth of the children account perhaps for the superior development of the Aryan and Semitic races. It is a fact that the Pueblo Indians of New Mexico, who are reduced to an almost entirely vegetarian diet, have a smaller brain than the Indians at the lower stage of barbarism, who eat more meat and fish. In any case, cannibalism now gradually dies out, surviving only as a religious act or as a means of working magic, which is here almost the same thing.

(c.) Upper Stage. Begins with the smelting of iron ore, and passes into civilization with the invention of alphabetic writing and its use for literary records. This stage (as we have seen, only the Eastern Hemisphere passed through it independently) is richer in advances in production than all the preceding stages together. To it belong the Greeks of the heroic age, the tribes of Italy shortly before the foundation of Rome, the Germans of Tacitus and the Norsemen of the Viking age.

Above all, we now first meet the iron plowshare drawn by cattle, which made large-scale agriculture, the cultivation of fields, possible, and thus created a practically unrestricted food supply in comparison with previous conditions. This led to the clearance of forest land for tillage and pasture, which in turn was impossible on a large scale without the iron ax and the iron spade. Population rapidly increased in number, and in small areas became dense. Prior to field agriculture, conditions must have been very exceptional if they allowed half a million people to be united under a central organization; probably such a thing never occurred.

We find the upper stage of barbarism at its highest in the Homeric poems, particularly in the Iliad. Fully developed iron tools, the bellows, the hand-mill, the potter's wheel, the making of oil and wine, metal work developing almost into a fine art, the wagon and the war-chariot, ship-building with beams and planks, the beginnings of architecture as art, walled cities with towers and battlements, the Homeric epic and a complete mythology – these are the chief legacy brought by the Greeks from barbarism into civilization. When we compare the descriptions which Caesar and even Tacitus give of the Germans, who stood at the beginning of the cultural stage from which the Homeric Greeks were just preparing to make the next advance, we realize how rich was the development of production within the upper stage of barbarism.

The sketch which I have given here, following Morgan, of the development of mankind through savagery and barbarism to the beginnings of civilization, is already rich enough in new features; what is more, they cannot be disputed, since they are drawn directly from the process of production. Yet my sketch will seem flat and feeble compared with the picture to be unrolled at the end of our travels; only then will the transition from barbarism to civilization stand out in full light and in all its striking contrasts. For the time being, Morgan's division may be summarized thus:

Savagery – the period in which man's appropriation of products in their natural state predominates; the products of human art are chiefly instruments which assist this appropriation.

Barbarism – the period during which man learns to breed domestic animals and to practice agriculture, and acquires methods of increasing the supply of natural products by human activity.

Civilization – the period in which man learns a more advanced application of work to the products of nature, the period of industry proper and of art.

II. The Family

The Consanguine Family, The First Stage of the Family
The Punaluan Family
The Pairing Family
The Monogamous Family

Morgan, who spent a great part of his life among the Iroquois Indians—settled to this day in New York State—and was adopted into one of their tribes (the Senecas), found in use among them a system of consanguinity which was in contradiction to their actual family relationships. There prevailed among them a form of monogamy easily terminable on both sides, which Morgan calls the "pairing family." The issue of the married pair was therefore known and recognized by everybody: there could be no doubt about whom to call father, mother, son, daughter, brother, sister. But these names were actually used quite differently. The Iroquois calls not only his own children his sons and daughters, but also the children of his brothers; and they call him father. The children of his sisters, however, he calls his nephews and nieces, and they call him their uncle. The Iroquois woman, on the other hand, calls her sisters' children, as well as her own, her sons and daughters, and they call her mother. But her brothers' children she calls her nephews and nieces, and she is known as their aunt. Similarly, the children of brothers call one another brother and sister, and so do the children of sisters. A woman's own children and the children of her brother, on the other hand, call one another cousins.

And these are not mere empty names, but expressions of actual conceptions of nearness and remoteness, of equality and difference in the degrees of consanguinity: these conceptions serve as the foundation of a fully elaborated system of consanguinity through which several hundred different relationships of one individual can be expressed. What is more, this system is not only in full force among all American Indians (no exception has been found up to the present), but also retains its validity almost unchanged among the aborigines of India, the Dravidian tribes in the Deccan and the Gaura tribes in Hindustan. To this day the Tamils of southern India and the Iroquois Seneca Indians in New York State still express more than two hundred degrees of consanguinity in the same manner. And among these tribes of India, as among all the American Indians, the actual relationships arising out of the existing form of the family contradict the system of consanguinity.

How is this to be explained? In view of the decisive part played by consanguinity in the social structure of all savage and barbarian peoples, the importance of a system so widespread cannot be dismissed with phrases. When a system is general throughout America and also exists in Asia among peoples of a quite different race, when numerous instances of it are found with greater or less variation in every part of Africa and Australia, then that system has to be historically explained, not talked out of existence, as McLennan, for example, tried to do. The names of father, child, brother, sister are no mere complimentary forms of address; they involve quite definite and very serious mutual obligations which together make up an essential part of the social constitution of the peoples in question.

The explanation was found. In the Sandwich Islands (Hawaii) there still existed in the first half of the nineteenth century a form of family in which the fathers and mothers, brothers and sisters, sons and daughters, uncles and aunts, nephews and nieces were exactly what is required by the American and old Indian system of consanguinity. But now comes a strange thing. Once again, the system of consanguinity in force in Hawaii did not correspond to the actual form of the Hawaiian family. For according to the Hawaiian system of consanguinity all children of brothers and sisters are without exception brothers and sisters of one another and are considered to be the common children not only of their mother and her sisters or of their father and his brothers, but of all the brothers and sisters of both their parents without distinction. While, therefore, the American system of consanguinity presupposes a more primitive form of the family which has disappeared in America, but still actually exists in Hawaii, the Hawaiian system of consanguinity, on the other hand, points to a still earlier form of the family which, though we can nowhere prove it to be still in existence, nevertheless must have existed; for otherwise the corresponding system of consanguinity could never have arisen.

The family (says Morgan) represents an active principle. It is never stationary, but advances from a lower to a higher form as society advances from a lower to a higher condition.... Systems of consanguinity, on the contrary, are passive; recording the progress made by the family at long intervals apart, and only changing radically when the family has radically changed.

"And," adds Marx, "the same is true of the political, juridical, religious, and philosophical systems in general." While the family undergoes living changes, the system of consanguinity ossifies; while the system survives by force of custom, the family outgrows it. But just as Cuvier could deduce from the marsupial bone of an animal skeleton found near Paris that it belonged to a marsupial animal and that extinct marsupial animals once lived there, so with the same certainty we can deduce from the historical survival of a system of consanguinity that an extinct form of family once existed which corresponded to it.

The systems of consanguinity and the forms of the family we have just mentioned differ from those of today in the fact that every child has more than one father and mother. In the American system of consanguinity, to which the Hawaiian family corresponds, brother and sister cannot be the father and mother of the same child; but the Hawaiian system of consanguinity, on the contrary, presupposes a family in which this was the rule. Here we find ourselves among forms of family which directly contradict those hitherto generally assumed to be alone valid. The traditional view recognizes only monogamy, with, in addition, polygamy on the part of individual men, and at the very most polyandry on the part of individual women; being the view of moralizing philistines, it conceals the fact that in practice these barriers raised by official society are quietly and calmly ignored. The study of primitive history, however, reveals conditions where the men live in polygamy and their wives in polyandry at the same time, and their common children are therefore considered common to them all—and these conditions in their turn undergo a long series of changes before they finally end in monogamy. The trend of these changes is to narrow more and more the circle of people comprised within the common bond of marriage, which was originally very wide, until at last it includes only the single pair, the dominant form of marriage today.

Reconstructing thus the past history of the family, Morgan, in agreement with most of his colleagues, arrives at a primitive stage when unrestricted sexual freedom prevailed within the tribe, every woman belonging equally to every man and every man to every woman. Since the eighteenth century there had been talk of such a primitive state, but only in general phrases. Bachofen—and this is one of his great merits—was the first to take the existence of such a state seriously and to search for its traces in historical and religious survivals. Today we know that the traces he found do not lead back to a social stage of promiscuous sexual intercourse, but to a much later form—namely, group marriage. The primitive social stage of promiscuity, if it ever existed, belongs to such a remote epoch that we can hardly expect to prove its existence directly by discovering its social fossils among backward savages. Bachofen's merit consists in having brought this question to the forefront for examination.

Lately it has become fashionable to deny the existence of this initial stage in human sexual life. Humanity must be spared this "shame." It is pointed out that all direct proof of such a stage is lacking, and particular appeal is made to the evidence from the rest of the animal world; for, even among animals, according to the numerous facts collected by Letourneau (*Evolution du manage et de la faults*, 1888), complete promiscuity in sexual intercourse marks a low stage of development.

But the only conclusion I can draw from all these facts, so far as man and his primitive conditions of life are concerned, is that they prove nothing whatever. That vertebrates mate together for a considerable period is sufficiently explained by physiological causes-in the case of birds, for example, by the female's need of help during the brooding period; examples of faithful monogamy among birds prove nothing about man, for the simple reason that men are not descended from birds. And if strict monogamy is the height of all virtue, then the palm must go to the tapeworm, which has a complete set of male and female sexual organs in each of its 50-200 proglottides, or sections, and spends its whole life copulating in all its sections with itself. Confining ourselves to mammals, however, we find all forms of sexual life—promiscuity, indications of group marriage, polygyny, monogamy. Polyandry alone is lacking-it took human beings to achieve that. Even our nearest relations, the quadrumana, exhibit every possible variation in the grouping of males and females; and if we narrow it down still more and consider only the four anthropoid apes, all that Letourneau has to say about them is that they are sometimes monogamous, sometimes polygamous, while Saussure, quoted by Giraud-Teulon, maintains that they are monogamous. The more recent assertions of the monogamous habits of the anthropoid apes which are cited by Westermarck (*The History of Human Marriage*, London, 1891), are also very far from proving anything. In short, our evidence is such that honest Letourneau admits: "Among mammals there is no strict relation between the degree of intellectual development and the form of sexual life." And Espinas (*Des societes animates*, 1877), says in so many words:

"The herd is the highest social group which we can observe among animals. It is composed, so it appears, of families, but from the start the family and the herd are in conflict with one another and develop in inverse proportion."

As the above shows, we know practically nothing definite about the family and other social groupings of the anthropoid apes; the evidence is flatly contradictory. Which is not to be wondered at. The evidence with regard to savage human tribes is contradictory enough, requiring very critical examination and sifting; and ape societies are far more difficult to observe than human. For the present, therefore, we must reject any conclusion drawn from such completely unreliable reports.

The sentence quoted from Espinas, however, provides a better starting point. Among the higher animals the herd and the family are not complementary to one another, but antagonistic. Espinas shows very well how the jealousy of the males during the mating season loosens the ties of every social herd or temporarily breaks it up.

"When the family bond is close and exclusive, herds form only in exceptional cases. When on the other hand free sexual intercourse or polygamy prevails, the herd comes into being almost spontaneously.... Before a herd can be formed, family ties must be loosened and the individual must have become free again. This is the reason why organized flocks are so rarely found among birds.... We find more or less organized societies among mammals, however, precisely because here the individual is not merged in the family.... In its first growth, therefore, the common feeling of the herd has no greater enemy than the common feeling of the family. We state it without hesitation: only by absorbing families which had undergone a radical change could a social form higher than the family have developed; at the same time, these families were thereby enabled later to constitute themselves afresh under infinitely more favorable circumstances." (Espinas, op. cit., quoted by Giraud-Teulon, *Origines du mariage et de la famille*, 1884, pp. 518-20)

Here we see that animal societies are, after all, of some value for drawing conclusions about human societies; but the value is only negative. So far as our evidence goes, the higher vertebrates know only two forms of family — polygyny or separate couples; each form allows only one adult male, only one husband. The jealousy of the male, which both consolidates and isolates the family, sets the animal family in opposition to the herd. The jealousy of the males prevents the herd, the higher social form, from coming into existence, or weakens its cohesion, or breaks it up during the mating period; at best, it attests its development. This alone is sufficient proof that animal families and primitive human society are incompatible, and that when primitive men were working their way up from the animal creation, they either had no family at all or a form that does not occur among animals. In small numbers, an animal so defenseless as evolving man might struggle along even in conditions of isolation, with no higher social grouping than the single male and female pair, such as Westermarck, following the reports of hunters, attributes to the gorillas and the chimpanzees. For man's development beyond the level of the animals, for the achievement of the greatest advance nature can show, something more was needed: the power of defense lacking to the individual had to be made good by the united strength and co-operation of the herd. To explain the transition to humanity from conditions such as those in which the anthropoid apes live today would be quite impossible; it looks much more as if these apes had strayed off the line of evolution and were gradually dying out or at least degenerating. That alone is sufficient ground for rejecting all attempts based on parallels drawn between forms of family and those of primitive man. Mutual toleration among the adult males, freedom from jealousy, was the first condition for the formation of those larger, permanent groups in which alone animals could become men. And what, in fact, do we find to be the oldest and most primitive form of family whose historical existence we can indisputably prove and which in one or two parts of the world we can still study today? Group marriage, the form of family in which whole groups of men and whole groups of women mutually possess one another, and which leaves little room for jealousy. And at a later stage of development we find the exceptional form of polyandry, which positively revolts every jealous instinct and is therefore unknown among animals. But as all known forms of group marriage are accompanied by such peculiarly complicated regulations that they necessarily point to earlier and simpler forms of sexual relations, and therefore in the last resort to a period of promiscuous intercourse corresponding to the transition from the animal to the human, the references to animal marriages only bring us back to the very point from which we were to be led away for good and all.

What, then, does promiscuous sexual intercourse really mean? It means the absence of prohibitions and restrictions which are or have been in force. We have already seen the barrier of jealousy go down. If there is one thing certain, it is that the feeling of jealousy develops relatively late. The same is true of the conception of incest. Not only were brother and sister originally man and wife; sexual intercourse between parents and children is still permitted among many peoples today. Bancroft (*The Native Races of the Pacific States of North America,* 1875, Vol. I), testifies to it among the Kadiaks on the Behring Straits, the Kadiaks near Alaska, and the Tinneh in the interior of British North America; Letourneau compiled reports of it among the Chippewa Indians, the Cucus in Chile, the Caribs, the Karens in Burma; to say nothing of the stories told by the old Greeks and Romans about the Parthians, Persians, Scythians, Huns, and so on. Before incest was invented — for incest is an invention, and a very valuable one, too — sexual intercourse between parents and children did not arouse any more repulsion than sexual intercourse between other persons of different generations, and that occurs today even in the most philistine countries without exciting any great horror; even "old maids" of over sixty, if they are rich enough, sometimes marry young men in their thirties. But if we consider the most primitive known forms of family apart from their conceptions of incest — conceptions which are totally different from ours and frequently in direct contradiction to them-then the form of sexual intercourse can only be described as promiscuous — promiscuous in so far as the restrictions later established by custom did not yet exist. But in everyday practice that by no means necessarily implies general mixed mating. Temporary pairings of one man with one woman were not in any way excluded, just as in the cases of group marriages today the majority of relationships are of this character. And when Westermarck, the latest writer to deny the existence of such a primitive state, applies the term "marriage" to every relationship in which the two sexes remain mated until the birth of the offspring, we must point out that this kind of marriage can very well occur under the conditions of promiscuous intercourse without contradicting the principle of promiscuity — the absence of any restriction imposed by custom on sexual intercourse. Westermarck, however, takes the standpoint that promiscuity "involves a suppression of individual inclinations," and that therefore "the most genuine form of it is prostitution." In my opinion, any understanding of primitive society is impossible to people who only see it as a brothel. We will return to this point when discussing group marriage.

According to Morgan, from this primitive state of promiscuous intercourse there developed, probably very early:

1. The Consanguine Family, The First Stage of the Family

Here the marriage groups are separated according to generations: all the grandfathers and grandmothers within the limits of the family are all husbands and wives of one another; so are also their children, the fathers and mothers; the latter's children will form a third circle of common husbands and wives; and their children, the great-grandchildren of the first group, will form a fourth. In this form of marriage, therefore, only ancestors and progeny, and parents and children, are excluded from the rights and duties (as we should say) of marriage with one another. Brothers and sisters, male and female cousins of the first, second, and more remote degrees, are all brothers and sisters of one another, and precisely for that reason they are all husbands and wives of one another. At this stage the relationship of brother and sister also includes as a matter of course the practice of sexual intercourse with one another. In its typical form, such a family would consist of the descendants of a single pair, the descendants of these descendants in each generation being again brothers and sisters, and therefore husbands and wives, of one another.

The consanguine family is extinct. Even the most primitive peoples known to history provide no demonstrable instance of it. But that it must have existed, we are compelled to admit: for the Hawaiian system of consanguinity still prevalent today throughout the whole of Polynesia expresses degrees of consanguinity which could only arise in this form of family; and the whole subsequent development of the family presupposes the existence of the consanguine family as a necessary preparatory stage.

III. The Iroquois Gens

We now come to another discovery made by Morgan, which is at least as important as the reconstruction of the family in its primitive form from the systems of consanguinity. The proof that the kinship organizations designated by animal names in a tribe of American Indians are essentially identical with the genea of the Greeks and the gentes of the Romans; that the American is the original form and the Greek and Roman forms are later and derivative; that the whole social organization of the primitive Greeks and Romans into gens, phratry, and tribe finds its faithful parallel in that of the American Indians; that the gens is an institution common to all barbarians until their entry into civilization and even afterwards (so far as our sources go up to the present) -- this proof has cleared up at one stroke the most difficult questions in the most ancient periods of Greek and Roman history, providing us at the same time with an unsuspected wealth of information about the fundamental features of social constitution in primitive times—before the introduction of the state. Simple as the matter seems once it is understood, Morgan only made his discovery quite recently. In his previous work, published in 1871, he had not yet penetrated this secret, at whose subsequent revelation the English anthropologists, usually so self-confident, became for a time as quiet as mice.

The Latin word gens, which Morgan uses as a general term for such kinship organizations, comes, like its Greek equivalent, genos, from the common Aryan root gan (in German, where, following the law Aryan g is regularly replaced by k, kan), which means to beget. Gens, Genos, Sanscrit janas, Gothic kuni (following the same law as above), Old Norse and Anglo-Saxon kyn, English kin, Middle High German kunne., all signify lineage, descent. Gens in Latin and genos in Greek are, however, used specifically to denote the form of kinship organization which prides itself on its common descent (in this case from a common ancestral father) and is bound together by social and religious institutions into a distinct community, though to all our historians its origin and character have hitherto remained obscure.

We have already seen, in connection with the punaluan family (P-33), what is the composition of a gens in its original form. It consists of all the persons who in punaluan marriage, according to the conceptions necessarily prevailing under it, form the recognized descendants of one particular ancestral mother, the founder of the gens. In this form of family, as paternity is uncertain, only the female line counts. Since brothers may not marry their sisters but only women of different descent, the children begotten by them with these alien women cannot, according to mother-right, belong to the father's gens. Therefore only the offspring of the daughters in each generation remain within the kinship organization; the offspring of the sons go into the gentes of their mothers. What becomes of this consanguine group when it has constituted itself a separate group, distinct from similar groups within the tribe?

As the classic form of this original gens, Morgan takes the gens among the Iroquois, and especially in the Seneca tribe. In this tribe there are eight gentes, named after animals: (1) Wolf, (2) Bear, (3) Turtle, (4) Beaver, (5) Deer, (6) Snipe, (7) Heron, (8) Hawk. In every gens the following customs are observed:

1. The gens elects its sachem (head of the gens in peace) and its chief (leader in war). The sachem had to be chosen from among the members of the gens, and his office was hereditary within the gens, in the sense that it had to be filled immediately as often as a vacancy occurred; the military leader could be chosen from outside the gens, and for a time the office might even be vacant. A son was never chosen to succeed his father as sachem, since mother- right prevailed among the Iroquois and the son consequently belonged to a different gens; but the office might and often did pass to a brother of the previous sachem or to his sister's son. All voted in the elections, both men and women. The election, however, still required the confirmation of the seven remaining gentes, and only then was the new sachem ceremonially invested with his office by the common council of the whole Iroquois confederacy. The significance of this will appear later. The authority of the sachem within the gens was paternal, and purely moral in character; he had no means of coercion. By virtue of his office he was also a member of the tribal council of the Senecas and also of the federal council of all the Iroquois. The war-chief could only give orders on military expeditions.

2. The gens deposes the sachem and war-chief at will. This also is done by men and women jointly. After a sachem or chief had been deposed, they became simple braves, private persons, like the other members. The tribal council also had the power to depose sachems, even against the will of the gens.

3. No member is permitted to marry within the gens. This is the fundamental law of the gens, the bond which holds it together. It is the negative expression of the very positive blood relationship, by virtue of which the individuals it comprises become a gens. By his discovery of this simple fact Morgan has revealed for the first time the nature of the gens. How little the gens was understood before is obvious from the earlier reports about savages and barbarians, in which the various bodies out of which the gentile organization is composed are ignorantly and indiscriminately referred to as tribe, clan, thum, and so forth, and then sometimes designated as bodies within which marriage is prohibited. Thus was created the hopeless

confusion which gave Mr. McLennan his chance to appear as Napoleon, establishing order by his decree: All tribes are divided into those within which marriage is prohibited (exogamous) and those within which it is permitted (endogamous). Having now made the muddle complete, he could give himself up to the profoundest inquiries as to which of his two absurd classes was the older exogamy or endogamy. All this nonsense promptly stopped of itself with the discovery of the gens and of its basis in consanguinity, involving the exclusion of its members from intermarriage with one another. It goes without saying that at the stage at which we find the Iroquois the prohibition of marriage within the gens was stringently observed.

4. The property of deceased persons passed to the other members of the gens; it had to remain in the gens. As an Iroquois had only things of little value to leave, the inheritance was shared by his nearest gentile relations; in the case of a man, by his own brothers and sisters and maternal uncle; in the case of a woman, by her children and own sisters, but not by her brothers. For this reason man and wife could not inherit from one another, nor children from their father.

5. The members of the gens owed each other help, protection, and especially assistance in avenging injury by strangers. The individual looked for his security to the protection of the gens, and could rely upon receiving it; to wrong him was to wrong his whole gens. From the bonds of blood uniting the gens sprang the obligation of blood revenge, which the Iroquois unconditionally recognized. If any person from outside the gens killed a gentile member, the obligation of blood revenge rested on the entire gens of the slain man. First, mediation was tried; the gens of the slayer sat in council, and made proposals of settlement to the council of the gens of the slain, usually offering expressions of regret and presents of considerable value. If these were accepted, the matter was disposed of. In the contrary case, the wronged gens appointed one or more avengers, whose duty it was to pursue and kill the slayer. If this was accomplished, the gens of the slayer had no ground of complaint; accounts were even and closed.

6. The gens has special names or classes of names, which may not be used by any other gens in the whole tribe, so that the name of the individual indicates the gens to which he belongs. A gentile name confers of itself gentile rights.

7. The gens can adopt strangers and thereby admit them into the whole tribe. Thus among the Senecas the prisoners of war who were

not killed became through adoption into a gens members of the tribe, receiving full gentile and tribal rights. The adoption took place on the proposal of individual members of the gens; if a man adopted, he accepted the stranger as brother or sister; if a woman, as son or daughter. The adoption had to be confirmed by ceremonial acceptance into the tribe. Frequently a gens which was exceptionally reduced in numbers was replenished by mass adoption from another gens, with its consent. Among the Iroquois the ceremony of adoption into the gens was performed at a public council of the tribe, and therefore was actually a religious rite.

8. Special religious ceremonies can hardly be found among the Indian gentes; the religious rites of the Indians are, however, more or less connected with the gens. At the six yearly religious festivals of the Iroquois the sachems and war-chiefs of the different gentes were included ex officio among the "Keepers of the Faith" and had priestly functions.

9. The gens has a common burial place. Among the Iroquois of New York State, who are hedged in on all sides by white people, this has disappeared, but it existed formerly. It exists still among other Indians - for example, among the Tuscaroras, who are closely related to the Iroquois; although they are Christians, each gens has a separate row in the cemetery; the mother is therefore buried in the same row as her children, but not the father. And among the Iroquois also the whole gens of the deceased attends the burial, prepares the grave, the funeral addresses, etc.

10. The gens has a council: the democratic assembly of all male and female adult gentiles, all with equal votes. This council elected sachems, war-chiefs and also the other "Keepers of the Faith," and deposed them; it took decisions regarding blood revenge or payment of atonement for murdered gentiles; it adopted strangers into the gens. In short, it was the sovereign power in the gens. Such were the rights and privileges of a typical Indian gens.

All the members of an Iroquois gens were personally free, and they were bound to defend each other's freedom; they were equal in privileges and in personal rights, the sachem and chiefs claiming no superiority; and they were a brotherhood bound together by the ties of kin. Liberty, equality, and fraternity, though never formulated, were cardinal principles of the gens. These facts are material, because the gens was the unit of a social and governmental system, the foundation upon which Indian society was organized.... It serves to explain that sense of independence and personal dignity universally an attribute of Indian character.

The Indians of the whole of North America at the time of its discovery were organized in gentes under mother-right. The gentes had disappeared only in some tribes, as among the Dakotas; in others, as among the Ojibwas and the Omahas, they were organized according to father-right.

Among very many Indian tribes with more than five or six gentes, we find every three, four, or more gentes united in a special group, which Morgan, rendering the Indian name faithfully by its Greek equivalent, calls a "phratry" (brotherhood). Thus the Senecas have two phratries: the first comprises gentes 1 to 4, the second gentes 5 to 8. Closer investigation shows that these phratries generally represent the original gentes into which the tribe first split up; for since marriage was prohibited within the gens, there had to be at least two gentes in any tribe to enable it to exist independently.

In the measure in which the tribe increased, each gens divided again into two or more gentes, each of which now appears as a separate gens, while the original gens, which includes all the daughter gentes, continues as the phratry. Among the Senecas and most other Indians, the gentes within one phratry are brother gentes to one another, while those in the other phratry are their cousin gentes-terms which in the American system of consanguinity have, as we have seen, a very real and expressive meaning. Originally no Seneca was allowed to marry within his phratry, but this restriction has long since become obsolete and is now confined to the gens. According to Senecan tradition, the Bear and the Deer were the two original gentes, from which the others branched off. After this new institution had once taken firm root, it was modified as required; if the gentes in one phratry died out, entire gentes were sometimes transferred into it from other phratries to make the numbers even. Hence we find gentes of the same name grouped in different phratries in different tribes.

Among the Iroquois, the functions of the phratry are partly social, partly religious.

(1) In the ball game one phratry plays against another. Each phratry puts forward its best players, while the other members, grouped according to phratries, look on and bet against one another on the victory of their players.

(2) In the tribal council the sachems and the war-chiefs of each phratry sit together, the two groups facing one another; each speaker addresses the representatives of each phratry as a separate body.

(3) If a murder had been committed in the tribe, and the slayer and the slain belonged to different phratries, the injured gens often appealed to its brother gentes; these held a council of the phratry and appealed in a body to the other phratry that it also should assemble its council to effect a settlement. Here the phratry reappears as the original gens, and with greater prospect of success than the weaker single gens, its offspring.

(4) At the death of prominent persons the opposite phratry saw to the interment and the burial ceremonies, while the phratry of the dead person attended as mourners. If a sachem died, the opposite phratry reported to the federal council of the Iroquois that the office was vacant.

(5) The council of the phratry also played a part in the election of a sachem. That the election would be confirmed by the brother gentes was more or less taken for granted, but the gentes of the opposite phratry might raise an objection. In this case the council of the opposite phratry was assembled; if it maintained the objection, the election was void.

(6) The Iroquois formerly had special religious mysteries, called medicine lodges by the white men. Among the Senecas, these mysteries were celebrated by two religious brotherhoods, into which new members were admitted by formal initiation; there was one such brotherhood in each of the two phratries.

(7) If, as is almost certain, the four lineages occupying the four quarters of Tlascala at the time of the conquest were four phratries, we here have proof that the phratries were also military units, like the phratries among the Greeks and similar kinship organizations among the Germans; these four lineages went into battle as separate groups, each with its own uniform and flag, and under its own leader.

As several gentes make up a phratry, so in the classic form several phratries make up a tribe; in some cases, when tribes have been much weakened, the intermediate form, the phratry, is absent. What distinguishes an Indian tribe in America?

1. Its own territory and name. In addition to its actual place of settlement, every tribe further possessed considerable territory for hunting and lashing. Beyond that lay a broad strip of neutral land reaching to the territory of the neighboring tribe; it was smaller

between tribes related in language, larger between tribes not so related. It is the same as the boundary forest of the Germans, the waste made by Caesar's Suevi around their territory, the isarnholt (in Danish, jarnved, limes Danicus) between Danes and Germans, the Sachsenwald (Saxon wood) and branibor (Slav, "protecting wood") between Germans and Slavs, from which Brandenburg takes its name. The territory delimited by these uncertain boundaries was the common land of the tribe, recognized as such by neighboring tribes and defended by the tribe itself against attacks. In most cases the uncertainty of the boundaries only became a practical disadvantage when there had been a great increase in population. The names of the tribes seem generally to have arisen by chance rather than to have been deliberately chosen; in the course of time it often happened that a tribe was called by another name among the neighboring tribes than that which it used itself, just as the Germans were first called Germans by the Celts.

2. A distinct dialect peculiar to the tribe alone. Tribe and dialect are substantially coextensive; the formation through segmentation of new tribes and dialects was still proceeding in America until quite recently, and most probably has not entirely stopped even today. When two weakened tribes have merged into one, the exceptional case occurs of two closely related dialects being spoken in the same tribe. The average strength of American tribes is under 2,000 members; the Cherokees, however, number about 26,000, the greatest number of Indians in the United States speaking the same dialect.

3. The right to install into office the Sachems and war-chiefs elected by the Gentes and the right to depose them, even against the will of their gens. As these sachems and war-chiefs are members of the council of the tribe, these rights of the tribe in regard to them explain themselves. Where a confederacy of tribes had been formed, with all the tribes represented in a federal council, these rights were transferred to the latter.

4. The possession of common religious conceptions (Mythology) and ceremonies. "After the fashion of barbarians the American Indians were a religious people." Their mythology has not yet been studied at all critically. They already embodied their religious ideas-spirits of every kind-in human form; but the lower stage of barbarism, which they had reached, still knows no plastic representations, so-called idols. Their religion is a cult of nature and of elemental forces, in process of development to polytheism. The various tribes had their

regular festivals, with definite rites, especially dances and games. Dancing particularly was an essential part of all religious ceremonies; each tribe held its own celebration separately.

5. A tribal council for the common affairs of the tribe. It was composed of all the sachems and war-chiefs of the different gentes, who were genuinely representative because they could be deposed at any time. It held its deliberations in public, surrounded by the other members of the tribe, who had the right to join freely in the discussion and to make their views heard. The decision rested with the council. As a rule, everyone was given a hearing who asked for it; the women could also have their views expressed by a speaker of their own choice. Among the Iroquois the final decision had to be unanimous, as was also the case in regard to many decisions of the German mark communities. The tribal council was responsible especially for the handling of relations with other tribes; it received and sent embassies, declared war and made peace. If war broke out, it was generally carried on by volunteers. In principle, every tribe was considered to be in a state of war with every other tribe with which it had not expressly concluded a treaty of peace. Military expeditions against such enemies were generally organized by prominent individual warriors; they held a war-dance, and whoever joined in the dance announced thereby his participation in the expedition. The column was at once formed, and started off. The defense of the tribal territory when attacked was also generally carried out by volunteers. The departure and return of such columns were always an occasion of public festivities. The consent of the tribal council was not required f or such expeditions, and was neither asked nor given. They find their exact counterpart in the private war expeditions of the German retinues described by Tacitus, only with the difference that among the Germans the retinues have already acquired a more permanent character, forming a firm core already organized in peacetime to which the other volunteers are attached in event of war. These war parties are seldom large; the most important expeditions of the Indians, even to great distances, were undertaken with insignificant forces. If several such parties united for operations on a large scale, each was under the orders only of its own leader. Unity in the plan of campaign was secured well or ill by a council of these leaders. It is the same manner of warfare as we find described by Ammianus Marcellinus among the Alemanni on the Upper Rhine in the fourth century.

6. Among some tribes we find a head chief, whose powers, however, are very slight. He is one of the sachems, and in situations demanding swift action he has to take provisional measures, until the council can assemble and make a definite decision. His function represents the first feeble attempt at the creation of an official with executive power, though generally nothing more came of it; as we shall see, the executive official developed in most cases, if not in all, out of the chief military commander.

The great majority of the American Indians did not advance to any higher form of association than the tribe. Living in small tribes, separated from one another by wide tracts between their frontiers, weakened by incessant wars, they occupied an immense territory with few people. Here and there alliances between related tribes came into being in the emergency of the moment and broke up when the emergency had passed. But in certain districts tribes which were originally related and had then been dispersed, joined together again in permanent federations, thus taking the first step towards the formation of nations. In the United States we find the most developed form of such a federation among the Iroquois. Emigrating from their homes west of the Mississippi, where they probably formed a branch of the great Dakota family, they settled after long wanderings in what is now the State of New York. They were divided into five tribes: Senecas, Cayugas, Onondagas, Oneidas and Mohawks. They subsisted on fish, game, and the products of a crude horticulture, and lived in villages, which were generally protected by a stockade. Never more than twenty thousand strong, they had a number of gentes common to all the five tribes, spoke closely related dialects of the same language, and occupied a continuous stretch of territory which was divided up among the five tribes. As they had newly conquered this territory, these tribes were naturally accustomed to stand together against the Inhabitants they had driven out. From this developed, at the beginning of the fifteenth century at latest, a regular C(everlasting league," a sworn confederacy, which in the consciousness of its new strength immediately assumed an aggressive character, and at the height of its power, about 1675, conquered wide stretches of the surrounding country, either expelling the inhabitants or making them pay tribute. The Iroquois confederacy represents the most advanced social organization achieved by any Indians still at the lower stage of barbarism (excluding, therefore, the Mexicans, New Mexicans and Peruvians).

The main provisions of the confederacy were as follows:

1. Perpetual federation of the five consanguineous tribes on the basis of complete equality and independence in all internal matters of the tribe. This bond of kin represented the real basis of the confederacy. Of the five tribes, three were known as father tribes and were brother tribes to one another; the other two were known as son tribes, and were likewise brother tribes to one another. Three gentes, the oldest, still had their living representatives in all five tribes, and another three in three tribes; the members of each of these gentes were all brothers of one another throughout all the five tribes. Their common language, in which there were only variations of dialect, was the expression and the proof of their common descent.

2. The organ of the confederacy was federal council of fifty sachems, all equal in rank and authority; the decisions of this council were final in all matters relating to the confederacy.

3. The fifty sachems were distributed among the tribes and gentes at the foundation of the confederacy to hold the new offices specially created for federal purposes. They were elected by the respective gentes whenever a vacancy occurred and could be deposed by the gentes at any time; but the right of investing them with their office belonged to the federal council.

4. These federal sachems were also sachems in their respective tribes, and had a seat and a vote in the tribal council.

5. All decisions of the federal council had to be unanimous.

6. Voting was by tribes, so that for a decision to be valid every tribe and all members of the council in every tribe had to signify their agreement.

7. Each of the five tribal councils could convene the federal council, but it could not convene itself.

8. The meetings of the council were held in the presence of the assembled people; every Iroquois could speak; the council alone decided.

9. The confederacy had no official head or chief executive officer.

10. On the other hand, the council had two principal war-chiefs, with equal powers and equal authority (the two "kings" of the Spartans, the two consuls in Rome).

That was the whole public constitution under which the Iroquois lived for over four hundred years and are still living today. I have described it fully, following Morgan, because here we have the opportunity of studying the organization of a society which still has no state. The state presupposes a special public power separated from the body of the people, and Maurer, who with a true instinct recognizes that the constitution of the German mark is a purely social institution, differing essentially from the state, though later providing a great part of its basis, consequently investigates in all his writings the gradual growth of the public power out of, and side by side with, the primitive constitutions of marks, villages, homesteads, and towns. Among the North American Indians we see how an originally homogeneous tribe gradually spreads over a huge continent; how through division tribes become nations, entire groups of tribes; how the languages change until they not only become unintelligible to other tribes, but also lose almost every trace of their original identity; how at the same time within the tribes each gens splits up into several gentes, how the old mother gentes are preserved as phratries, while the names of these oldest gentes nevertheless remain the same in widely distant tribes that have long been separated-the Wolf and the Bear are still gentile names among a majority of all Indian tribes. And the constitution described above applies in the main to them all, except that many of them never advanced as far as the confederacy of related tribes.

But once the gens is given as the social unit, we also see how the whole constitution of gentes, phratries, and tribes is almost necessarily bound to develop from this unit, because the development is natural. Gens, phratry, and tribe are all groups of different degrees of consanguinity, each self-contained and ordering its own affairs, but each supplementing the other. And the affairs which fall within their sphere comprise all the public affairs of barbarians of the lower stage. When we find a people with the gens as their social unit, we may therefore also look for an organization of the tribe similar to that here described; and when there are adequate sources, as in the case of the Greeks and the Romans, we shall not only find it, but we shall also be able to convince ourselves that where the sources fail us, comparison with the American social constitution helps us over the most difficult doubts and riddles.

And a wonderful constitution it is, this gentile constitution, in all its childlike simplicity! No soldiers, no gendarmes or police, no nobles, kings, regents, prefects, or judges, no prisons, no lawsuits - and everything takes its orderly course. All quarrels and disputes are settled by the whole of the community affected, by the gens or the tribe, or by the gentes among themselves; only as an extreme and exceptional measure is blood revenge threatened-and our capital punishment is nothing but blood revenge in a civilized form, with all the advantages and drawbacks of civilization. Although there were many more matters to be settled in common than today - the household is maintained by a number of families in common, and is communistic, the land belongs to the tribe, only the small gardens are allotted provisionally to the households - yet there is no need for even a trace of our complicated administrative apparatus with all its ramifications. The decisions are taken by those concerned, and in most cases everything has been already settled by the custom of centuries. There cannot be any poor or needy - the communal household and the gens know their responsibilities towards the old, the sick, and those disabled in war. All are equal and free - the women included. There is no place yet for slaves, nor, as a rule, for the subjugation of other tribes. When, about the year 1651, the Iroquois had conquered the Eries and the "Neutral Nation," they offered to accept them into the confederacy on equal terms; it was only after the defeated tribes had refused that they were driven from their territory. And what men and women such a society breeds is proved by the admiration inspired in all white people who have come into contact with unspoiled Indians, by the personal dignity, uprightness, strength of character, and courage of these barbarians.

We have seen examples of this courage quite recently in Africa. The Zulus a few years ago and the Nubians a few months ago—both of them tribes in which gentile institutions have not yet died out—did what no European army can do. Armed only with lances and spears, without firearms, under a hail of bullets from the breech-loaders of the English infantry - acknowledged the best in the world at fighting in close order—they advanced right up to the bayonets and more than once threw the lines into disorder and even broke them, in spite of the enormous inequality of weapons and in spite of the fact that they have no military service and know nothing of drill. Their powers of endurance and performance are shown by the complaint of the English that a Kaffir travels farther and faster in twenty-four hours than a horse. His smallest muscle stands out hard and firm like whipcord, says an English painter.

That is what men and society were before the division into classes. And when we compare their position with that of the overwhelming majority of civilized men today, an enormous gulf separates the present-day proletarian and small peasant from the free member of the old gentile society.

That is the one side. But we must not forget that this organization was doomed. It did not go beyond the tribe. The confederacy of tribes already marks the beginning of its collapse, as will soon be apparent, and was already apparent in the attempts at subjugation by the Iroquois. Outside the tribe was outside the law. Wherever there was not an explicit treaty of peace, tribe was at war with tribe, and wars were waged with the cruelty which distinguishes man from other animals, and which was only mitigated later by self-interest. The gentile constitution in its best days, as we saw it in America, presupposed an extremely undeveloped state of production and therefore an extremely sparse population over a wide area. Man's attitude to nature was therefore one of almost complete subjection to a strange incomprehensible power, as is reflected in his childish religious conceptions. Man was bounded by his tribe, both in relation to strangers from outside the tribe and to himself; the tribe, the gens, and their institutions were sacred and inviolable, a higher power established by nature, to which the individual subjected himself unconditionally in feeling, thought, and action. However impressive the people of this epoch appear to us, they are completely undifferentiated from one another; as Marx says, they are still attached to the navel string of the primitive community. The power of this primitive community had to be broken, and it was broken. But it was broken by influences which from the very start appear as a degradation, a fall from the simple moral greatness of the old gentile society. The lowest interests — base greed, brutal appetites, sordid avarice, selfish robbery of the common wealth — inaugurate the new, civilized, class society. It is by the vilest means — theft, violence, fraud, treason — that the old classless gentile society is undermined and overthrown. And the new society itself, during all the two and a half thousand years of its existence, has never been anything else but the development of the small minority at the expense of the great exploited and oppressed majority; today it is so more than ever before.

Chapter IV. The Greek Gens

From prehistoric times Greeks and Pelasgians alike, and other peoples of kindred stock, had been organized in the same organic series as the

Americans: gens, phratry, tribe, confederacy of tribes. The phratry might be absent, as among the Dorians, and the confederacy of tribes was not necessarily fully developed everywhere as yet; but in every case the gens was the unit. At the time of their entry into history, the Greeks are on the threshold of civilization; between them and the American tribes, of whom we spoke above, lie almost two entire great periods of development, by which the Greeks of the heroic age are ahead of the Iroquois. The gens of the Greeks is therefore no longer the archaic gens of the Iroquois; the impress of group marriage is beginning to be a good deal blurred. Mother-right has given way to father-right; increasing private wealth has thus made its first breach in the gentile constitution. A second breach followed naturally from the first. After the introduction of father-right the property of a rich heiress would have passed to her husband and thus into another gens on her marriage, but the foundation of all gentile law was now violated and in such a case the girl was not only permitted but ordered to marry within the gens, in order that her property should be retained for the gens.

According to Grote's *History of Greece*, the Athenian gens, in particular, was held together by the following institutions and customs:

1. Common religious rites, and the exclusive privilege of priesthood in honor of a particular god, the supposed ancestral father of the gens, who in this attribute was designated by a special surname.

2. A common burial place (cf. Demosthenes' Eubulides).

3. Mutual right of inheritance.

4. Mutual obligations of help, protection, and assistance in case of violence.

5. Mutual right and obligation to marry within the gens in certain cases, especially for orphan girls and heiresses.

6. Possession, at least in some cases, of common property, with a special archon (head man or president) and treasurer.

Next, several gentes were united in the phratry, but less closely; though here also we find mutual rights and obligations of a similar kind, particularly the common celebration of certain religious ceremonies and the right to avenge the death of a phrator. Similarly, all the phratries of a tribe held regularly recurring religious festivals in common, at which a leader of the tribe (phylobasileus), elected from the nobility (Eupatridai), officiated.

Thus far Grote. And Marx adds:

"In the Greek gens, the savage (e.g. Iroquois) shows through unmistakably." He becomes still more unmistakable when we investigate further.

For the Greek gens has also the following characteristics:

7. Descent in the male line.

8. Prohibition of marriage within the gens except in the case of heiresses. This exception, and its formulation as an ordinance, prove the old rule to be valid. This is further substantiated by the universally accepted principle that at her marriage the woman renounced the religious rites of her gens and went over to those of her husband, being also inscribed in his phratry. This custom and a famous passage in Diccarchus both show that marriage outside the gens was the rule, and Becker in Charicles directly assumes that nobody might marry within his own gens.

9. The right of adoption into the gens. This was exercised through adoption into the family, but required public formalities and was exceptional.

10. The right to elect chieftains and to depose them. We know that every gens had its archon; but it is nowhere stated that the office was hereditary in certain families. Until the end of barbarism the probability is always against strict heredity, which is quite incompatible with conditions in which rich and poor had completely equal rights within the gens.

Not only Grote, but also Niebuhr, Mommsen and all the other historians of classical antiquity, have come to grief over the gens. Though they correctly noted many of its characteristics, they always took it to be a group of families, thus making it impossible for themselves to understand the nature and origin of the gens. Under the gentile constitution, the family was never an organizational unit, and could not be so, for man and wife necessarily belonged to two different gentes. The whole gens was incorporated within the phratry, and the whole phratry within the tribe; but the family belonged half to the gens of the man and half to the gens of the woman. In public law the state also does not recognize the family; up to this day, the family only exists for private law. And yet all our histories have hitherto started from the absurd assumption, which, since the eighteenth century in particular, has become inviolable, that the monogamous single family, which is hardly older than civilization, is the core around which society and state have gradually crystallized.

Mr. Grote will also please note (Marx throws in) that though the Greeks derive their gentes from mythology, the gentes are older than the mythology which they themselves created with all its gods and demigods.

Morgan prefers to quote Grote because he is not only an impressive but also a trustworthy witness. Grote goes on to say that every Athenian gens had a name derived from its supposed ancestor; that it was the general custom before Solon, and even after Solon, in the absence of a will, for the property of a deceased person to pass to the members of his gens (gennetai), and that in the case of a murder it was the light and the duty, first of the relatives of the murdered man, then of the members of his gens, and lastly of his phratry, to prosecute the criminal before the tribunals: "All that we hear of the most ancient Athenian laws is based upon the gentile and phratric divisions." (Grote.)

The descent of the gentes from common ancestors has caused the "pedantic philistines," as Marx calls them, a lot of brain-racking. As they of course declare the common ancestors to be pure myths, they are at an utter loss to explain how the gens originated out of a number of separate and originally quite unrelated families; yet they have to perform this feat in order to explain how the gentes exist at all. So they argue in circles, with floods of words, never getting any further than the statement: the ancestral tree is a fairy tale, but the gens is a reality. And finally Grote declares (interpolations by Marx):

We hear of this genealogy but rarely, because it is only brought before the public in certain cases pre-eminent and venerable. But the humbler gentes had their common rites (this is strange, Mr. Grote!), and common superhuman ancestor and genealogy, as well as the more celebrated (this is most strange, Mr. Grote, among humbler gentes!): the scheme and ideal basis (my good sir, not ideal, but carnal, germanice fleishlich!) was the same in all.

Marx summarizes Morgan's reply to this as follows:

"The system of consanguinity corresponding to the original form of the gens and the Greeks, like other mortals, once possessed such a gens - preserved the knowledge of the mutual relations between all members of a gens to each other. They learned this, for them decisively important, fact by practice from early childhood. This fell into desuetude with the rise of the monogamian family. The gentile name created a pedigree beside which that of the individual family was insignificant. This name was now to preserve the fact of the common descent of those who bore it; but the lineage of the gens went so far that its members could no longer prove teh actual relationship existing between them, except in a limited number of cases through recent common ancestors. The name itself was the evidence of a common descent, and conclusive proof, except in cases of adoptin. The actual denial of all kinship between gentiles à la Grote and Neibuhr, which transforms teh gens into a purely fictitious, fanciful creation of the brain, is, on the other hand, worthy of 'ideal' scientists, that is, of cloistered bookworms. Because concatention of the generations, especially withthe incipience of monogamy, is removed into the distance, and the reality of the past seems reflected in mythological fantasy, the good old Philistines concluded, and still conclude, that the fancied genealogy created real gentes!"

As among the Americans, the phratry was a mother gens, split up into several daughter gentes, and uniting them, often tracing them all to a common ancestor. Thus, according to Grote, "all the ciontemporary members of the phratry of Hekataeus had a common god for their ancestor at the sixteenth degree."

Hence, all the gentes of this phratry were literally brother gentes. The phratry still occurs in Homer as a military unit in that famous passage where Nestos advises Aagamemnon: Draw up people by tribes and by phratries so that phratry may support phratry, and tribe tribe. The phratry has further the right and the duty of prosecuting for blood-guilt incurred against a phrator; hence in earlier times it also had the obligation of blood revenge. Further, it had common shrines and festivals; in fact the elaboration of the whole Greek mythology out of the traditional old Aryan nature-cult was essentially conditioned by the phratries and gentes, and took place within them. The phratry also had a chief (the phratriarchos) and, according to de Coulanges, assemblies. It could pass binding resolutions, and act as a judicial and administrative body. Even the later state, while it ignored the gens, left certain public offices in the hands of the phratry.

Several related phratries form a tribe. In Attica there were four tribes, each consisting of three phratries, each phratry numbering thirty gentes. Such a rounded symmetry of groups presupposes conscious, purposeful interference with the naturally developed order. As to how, when, and why this occurred,. Greek history is silent; the historical memory of the Greeks only went back to the heroic age.

As the Greeks were crowded together in a relatively small territory, differences of dialect were less developed than in the wide American forests; yet in Greece also it was only tribes of the same main dialect that united in a larger organization, and even Attica, small as it was, had a dialect of its own, which later, through its general use as the language of prose, became the dominant dialect.

In the Homeric poems we find most of the Greek tribes already united into small nations, within which, however, gentes, phratries, and tribes retained their full independence. They already lived in towns fortified with walls; the population increased with the increase of the herds, the extension of agriculture and the beginnings of handicraft. The differences in wealth thus became more pronounced, and with them the aristocratic element within the old primitive democracy. The various small nations waged incessant wars for the possession of the best land and doubtless also for booty; the use of prisoners of war as slaves was already a recognized institution.

The constitution of these tribes and small nations was as follows:

(1) The permanent authority was the council (boule), probably composed originally of all the chiefs of the gentes; later, when their number became too large, of a selection, whose choice provided an opportunity of extending and strengthening the aristocratic element. Dionysius actually speaks of the council in the heroic age as composed of nobles (kratistoi). The ultimate decision in important matters rested with the council. Thus in AEschylus the council of Thebes makes what is in the circumstances the vital decision to give Eteocles an honorable burial, but to throw out the corpse of Polynices to be devoured by dogs. When the state was established, this council was merged into the senate.

(2) The assembly of the people (agora). We saw among the Iroquois how the people, men and women, stood round the council when it was holding its meetings, intervening in an orderly manner in its deliberations and thus influencing its decisions. Among the Homeric Greeks, this Umstand (standing round), to use an old German legal expression, had already developed into a regular assembly of the people, as was also the case among the Germans in primitive times. It was convened by the council to decide important questions; every man bad the right to speak. The decision was given by a show of hands (AEschylus, *The Suppliants*) or by acclamation. The decision of the assembly was supreme and final, for, says Schomann, in *Griechische Altertumer*, "if the matter was one requiring

the co-operation of the people for its execution, Homer does not indicate any means by which the people could be forced to co-operate against their will."

For at this time, when every adult male member of the tribe was a warrior, there was as yet no public power separate from the people which could have been used against the people. Primitive democracy was still in its full strength, and it is in relation to that fact that the power and the position both of the council and of the basileus must first be judged.

(3) The leader of the army (basileus). Marx makes the following comment:

European scholars, born lackeys most of them, make the basileus into a monarch in the modern sense. Morgan, the Yankee republican, protests. Very ironically, but truly, he says of the oily-tongued Gladstone and his *Juventus Mundi*: "Mr. Gladstone, who presents to his readers the Grecian chiefs of the heroic age as kings and princes, with the superadded qualities of gentlemen, is forced to admit that 'on the whole we seem to have the custom or law of primogeniture sufficiently, but not oversharply defined.'"

Mr. Gladstone will probably agree that such an ambiguous law of primogeniture may be "sufficiently, but not oversharply defined" as being just as good as none at all.

In what sense the offices of sachem and chieftain were hereditary among the Iroquois and other Indians, we have already seen. All offices were elective, generally within a gens, and to that extent hereditary to the gens. In the course of time, preference when filling vacancies was given to the nearest gentile relation-brother or sister's son- unless there were reasons for passing him over. The fact that among the Greeks, under father-right, the office of basileus generally passed to the son, or one of the sons, only proves that the probabilities were in favor of the sons succeeding to the office by popular election; it is no proof at all of legal hereditary succession without popular election. All that we have here is the first beginnings among the Iroquois and Greeks of distinct noble families within the gentes and, in the case of the Greeks, the first beginnings also of a future hereditary leadership or monarchy. The probability is, therefore, that among the Greeks the basileus had either to be elected by the people or at least confirmed in his office by the recognized organs of the people, the council or agora, as was the case with the Roman "king" (rex).

In the Iliad, Agamemnon, the ruler of men, does not appear as the supreme king of the Greeks, but as supreme commander of a federal army before a besieged town. It is to this supremacy of command that Odysseus, after disputes had broken out among the Greeks, refers in a famous passage: "Evil is the rule of many; let one be commander," etc. (The favorite line about the scepter is a later addition.)

Odysseus is here not giving a lecture on a form of government, but demanding obedience to the supreme commander in war. Since they are appearing before Troy only as an army, the proceedings in the agora secure to the Greeks all necessary democracy. When Achilles speaks of presents—that is, the division of the booty—he always leaves the division, not to Agamemnon or any other basileus, but to the "sons of the Achacans," that is, the people. Such epithets as "descended from Zeus," "nourished by Zeus," prove nothing, for every gens is descended from a god, that of the leader of the tribe being already descended from a "superior" god, in this case Zeus. Even those without personal freedom, such as the swineherd Eumaecus and others, are "divine" (dioi and theioi), and that too in the Odyssey, which is much later than the Iliad; and again in the Odyssey the name Heros is given to the herald Mulius as well as to the blind bard Demodocus. Since, in short, council and assembly of the people function together with the basileus, the word basileia, which Greek writers employ to denote the so-called Homeric kingship (chief command in the army being the principal characteristic of the office), only means—military democracy. (Marx.)

In addition to his military functions, the basileus also held those of priest and judge, the latter not clearly defined, the former exercised in his capacity as supreme representative of the tribe or confederacy of tribes. There is never any mention of civil administrative powers; he seems, however, to be a member of the council ex officio. It is there fore quite correct etymologically to translate basileus as king, since king (kuning) is derived from kuni, kunne, and means head of a gens. But the old Greek basileus does not correspond in any way to the present meaning of the word "king." Thucydides expressly refers to the old basileia as patrike, i.e. derived from gentes, and says it had strictly defined, and therefore limited, functions. And Aristotle says that the basileia of the heroic age was a leadership over free men and that the basileus was military leader, judge and high priest; he thus had no governmental power in the later sense.

Thus in the Greek constitution of the heroic age we see the old gentile order as still a living force. But we also see the beginnings of its disintegration: father-right, with transmission of the property to the children, by which accumulation of wealth within the family was favored and the family itself became a power as against the gens; reaction of the inequality of wealth on the constitution by the formation of the first rudiments of hereditary nobility and monarchy; slavery, at first only of prisoners of war, but already preparing the way for the enslavement of fellow-members of the tribe and even of the gens; the old wars between tribe and tribe already degenerating into systematic pillage by land and sea for the acquisition of cattle, slaves and treasure, and becoming a regular source of wealth; in short, riches praised and respected as the highest good and the old gentile order misused to justify the violent seizure of riches. Only one thing was wanting: an institution which not only secured the newly acquired riches of individuals against the communistic traditions of the gentile order, which not only sanctified the private property formerly so little valued, and declared this sanctification to be the highest purpose of all human society; but an institution which set the seal of general social recognition on each new method of acquiring property and thus amassing wealth at continually increasing speed; an institution which perpetuated, not only this growing cleavage of society into classes, but also the right of the possessing class to exploit the non-possessing, and the rule of the former over the latter.

And this institution came. The state was invented.

Chapter V. The Rise of the Athenian State

How the state developed, how the organs of the gentile constitution were partly transformed in this development, partly pushed aside by the introduction of new organs, and at last superseded entirely by real state authorities, while the true "people in arms," organized for its self-defense in its gentes, phratries, and tribes, was replaced by an armed "public force" in the service of these state authorities and therefore at their command for use also against the people—this process, at least in its first stages, can be followed nowhere better than in ancient Athens. The changes in form have been outlined by Morgan, but their economic content and cause must largely be added by myself.

In the Heroic age the four tribes of the Athenians were still settled in Attica in separate territories; even the twelve phratries composing them seem still to have had distinct seats in the twelve towns of Cecrops. The constitution was that of the heroic age: assembly of the people, council of the people, basileus. As far as written history takes us back, we find the land already divided up and privately owned, which is in accordance with the relatively advanced commodity production and the corresponding trade in commodities developed towards the end of the upper stage of barbarism. In addition to grain, wine and oil were produced; to a continually increasing extent, the sea trade in the Agean was captured from the Phoenicians, and most of it passed into Athenian hands. Through the sale and purchase of land, and the progressive division of labor between agriculture and handicraft, trade, and shipping, it was inevitable that the members of the different gentes, phratries, and tribes very soon became intermixed, and that into the districts of the phratry and tribe moved inhabitants, who, although fellow countrymen, did not belong to these bodies and were therefore strangers in their own place of domicile. For when times were quiet, each tribe and each phratry administered its own affairs without sending to Athens to consult the council of the people or the basileus. But anyone not a member of the phratry or tribe was, of course, excluded from taking any part in this administration, even though living in the district.

The smooth functioning of the organs of the gentile constitution was thus thrown so much out of gear that even in the heroic age remedies had to be found. The constitution ascribed to Theseus was introduced. The principal change which it made was to set up a central authority in Athens—that is, part of the affairs hitherto administered by the tribes independently were declared common affairs and entrusted to the common council sitting in Athens. In taking this step, the Athenians went further than any native people of America had ever done: instead of neighboring tribes forming a simple confederacy, they fused together into one single nation. Hence arose a common Athenian civil law, which stood above the legal customs of the tribes and gentes.

The Athenian citizen, as such, acquired definite rights and new protection in law even on territory which was not that of his tribe. The first step had been taken towards undermining the gentile constitution; for this was the first step to the later admission of citizens who did not belong to any tribe in all Attica, but were, and remained, completely outside the Athenian gentile constitution. By a second measure ascribed to Theseus, the entire people, regardless of gens, phratry or tribe, was divided into three classes: eupatridai, or nobles, geomoroi, or farmers, and demiourgoi, or artisans, and the right to hold office was vested exclusively in the nobility. Apart from the tenure of offices by the nobility, this division remained inoperative, as it did not create any other legal distinctions between the classes. It is, however, important because it reveals the new social elements which had been developing unobserved. It shows that the customary appointment of members of certain families to the offices of the gens had already grown into an almost uncontested right of these families to office; it shows that these families, already powerful through their wealth, were beginning to form groupings outside their gentes as a separate, privileged class, and that the state now taking form sanctioned this presumption. It shows further that the division of labor between peasants and artisans was now firmly enough established in its social importance to challenge the old grouping of gentes and tribes. And, finally, it proclaims the irreconcilable opposition between gentile society and the state; the first attempt at forming a state consists in breaking up the gentes by dividing their members into those with privileges and those with none, and by further separating the latter into two productive classes and thus setting them one against the other.

The further political history of Athens up to the time of Solon is only imperfectly known. The office of basileus fell into disuse; the positions at the head of the state were occupied by archons elected from the nobility. The power of the nobility continuously increased, until about the year 600 B.C. it became insupportable. And the principal means for suppressing the common liberty were—money and usury. The nobility had their chief seat in and around Athens, whose maritime trade, with occasional piracy still thrown in, enriched them and concentrated in their hands the wealth existing in the form of money. From here the growing money economy penetrated like corrosive acid into the old traditional life of the rural communities founded on natural economy. The gentile constitution is absolutely irreconcilable with money economy; the ruin of the Attic small farmers coincided with the loosening of the old gentile bonds which embraced and protected them. The debtor's bond and the lien on property (for already the Athenians had invented the mortgage also) respected neither gens nor phratry, while the old gentile constitution, for its part, knew neither money nor advances of money nor debts in money. Hence the money rule of the aristocracy now in full flood of expansion also created a new customary law to secure the creditor against the debtor and to sanction the exploitation of the small peasant by the possessor of money. All the fields of Attica were thick with mortgage columns bearing inscriptions stating that the land on which they stood was mortgaged to such and such for so and so much. The fields not so marked had for the most part already been sold on account of unpaid mortgages or interest, and had passed into the ownership of the noble usurer; the peasant could count himself lucky if he was allowed to remain on the land as a tenant and live on one-sixth of the produce of his labor, while he paid five-sixths to his new master as rent. And that was not all. If the sale of the land did not cover the debt, or if the debt had been contracted without any security, the debtor, in order to meet his creditor's claims, had to sell his children into slavery abroad. Children sold by their father—such was the first fruit of father-right and monogamy! And if the blood-sucker was still not satisfied, he could sell the debtor himself as a slave. Thus the pleasant dawn of civilization began for the Athenian people.

Formerly, when the conditions of the people still corresponded to the gentile constitution, such an upheaval was impossible; now it had happened—nobody knew how. Let us go back for a moment to our Iroquois, amongst whom the situation now confronting the Athenians, without their own doing, so to speak, and certainly against their will, was inconceivable. Their mode of producing the necessities of life, unvarying from year to year, could never generate such conflicts as were apparently forced on the Athenians from without; it could never create an opposition of rich and poor, of exploiters and exploited. The Iroquois were still very far from controlling nature, but within the limits imposed on them by natural forces they did control their own production. Apart from bad harvests in their small gardens, the exhaustion of the stocks of fish in their lakes and rivers or of the game in their woods, they knew what results they could expect, making their living as they did. The certain result was a livelihood, plentiful or scanty; but one result there could never be—social upheavals that no one had ever intended, sundering of the gentile bonds, division of gens and tribe into two opposing and warring classes. Production was limited in the extreme, but—the producers controlled their product. That was the immense advantage of barbarian production, which was lost with the coming of civilization; to reconquer it, but on the basis of the gigantic control of nature now achieved by man and of the free association now made possible, will be the task of the next generations.

Not so among the Greeks. The rise of private property in herds and articles of luxury led to exchange between individuals, to the transformation of products into commodities. And here lie the seeds of the whole subsequent upheaval. When the producers no longer directly consumed their product themselves, but let it pass out of their hands in the act of exchange, they lost control of it. They no longer knew what became of it; the possibility was there that one day it would be used against the producer to exploit and oppress him. For this reason no society can permanently retain the mastery of its own production and the control over the social effects of its process of production unless it abolishes exchange between individuals.

But the Athenians were soon to learn how rapidly the product asserts its mastery over the producer when once exchange between individuals has begun and products have been transformed into commodities. With the coming of commodity production, individuals began to cultivate the soil on their own account, which soon led to individual ownership of land. Money followed, the general commodity with which all others 101 were exchangeable. But when men invented money, they did not think that they were again creating a new social power, the one general power before which the whole of society must bow. And it was this new power, suddenly sprung to life without knowledge or will of its creators, which now, in all the brutality of its youth, gave the Athenians the first taste of its might.

What was to be done? The old gentile constitution had not only shown itself powerless before the triumphal march of money; it was absolutely incapable of finding any place within its framework for such things as money, creditors, debtors, and forcible collection of debts. But the new social power was there; pious wishes, and yearning for the return of the good old days would not drive money and usury out of the world. Further, a number of minor breaches had also been made in the gentile constitution. All over Attica, and especially in Athens itself, the members of the different gentes and phratries became still more indiscriminately mixed with every generation, although even now an Athenian was only allowed to sell land outside his gens, not the house in which he lived. The division of labor between the different branches of production—agriculture, handicrafts (in which there were again innumerable subdivisions), trade, shipping, and so forth—had been carried further with every advance of industry and commerce; the population was now divided according to occupation into fairly permanent groups, each with its new common interests; and since the gens and the phratry made no provision for dealing with them, new offices had to be created. The number of slaves had increased considerably, and even at that time must have far exceeded the number of free Athenians; the gentile constitution originally knew nothing of slavery and therefore had no means of keeping these masses of bondsmen in order. Finally, trade had brought to Athens a number of foreigners who settled there on account of the greater facilities of making money; they also could claim no rights or protection under the old constitution; and, though they were received with traditional tolerance, they remained a disturbing and alien body among the people.

In short, the end of the gentile constitution was approaching. Society was outgrowing it more every day; even the worst evils that had grown up under its eyes were beyond its power to check or remove. But in the meantime the state had quietly been developing. The new groups formed by the division of labor, first between town and country, then between the different branches of town labor, had created new organs to look after their interests; official posts of all kinds had been set up. And above everything else the young state needed a power of its own, which in the case of the seafaring Athenians could at first only be a naval power, for the purpose of carrying on small wars and protecting its merchant ships. At some unknown date before Solon, the naukrariai were set up, small territorial districts, twelve to each tribe; each naukratia had to provide, equip and man a warship and also contribute two horsemen. This institution was a twofold attack on the gentile constitution. In the first place, it created a public force which was now no longer simply identical with the whole body of the armed people; secondly, for the first time it divided the people for public purposes, not by groups of kinship, but by common place of residence. We shall see the significance of this.

The gentile constitution being incapable of bringing help to the exploited people, there remained only the growing state. And the state brought them its help in the form of the constitution of Solon, thereby strengthening itself again at the expense of the old constitution. Solon — the manner in which his reform, which belongs to the year 594 B.C., was carried through does not concern us here — opened the series of so-called political revolutions; and he did so with an attack on property. All revolutions hitherto have been revolutions to protect one kind of property against another kind of property. They cannot protect the one without violating the other. In the great French Revolution feudal property was sacrificed to save bourgeois property; in that of Solon, the property of the creditors had to suffer for the benefit of the property of the debtors. The debts were simply declared void. We do not know the exact details, but in his poems Solon boasts of having removed the mortgage columns from the fields and brought back all the people who had fled or been sold abroad on account of debt. This was only possible by open violation of property. And, in fact, from the first to the last, all so-called political revolutions have been made to protect property — of one kind; and they have been carried out by confiscating, also called stealing, property — of another kind. The plain truth is that for two and a half thousand years it has been possible to preserve private property only by violating property.

But now the need was to protect the free Athenians against the return of such slavery. The first step was the introduction of general measures — for example, the prohibition of debt contracts pledging the person of the debtor. Further, in order to place at least some check on the nobles' ravening hunger for the land of the peasants, a maximum limit was fixed for the amount of land that could be owned by one individual. Then changes were made in the constitution, of which the most important for us are the following:

The council was raised to four hundred members, one hundred for each tribe; here, therefore, the tribe was still taken as basis. But that was the one and only feature of the new state incorporating anything from the old constitution. For all other purposes Solon divided the citizens into four classes according to their property in land and the amount of its yield: five hundred, three hundred and one hundred fifty medimni of grain (one medimnus equals about 1.16 bushels) were the minimum yields for the first three classes; those who owned less land or none at all were placed in the fourth class. All offices could be filled only from the three upper classes, and the highest offices only from the first. The fourth class only had the right to speak and vote in the assembly of the people; but it was in this assembly that all officers were elected, here they had to render their account, here all laws were made; and here the fourth class formed the majority. The privileges of the aristocracy were partially renewed in the form of privileges of wealth, but the people retained the decisive power. Further, the four classes formed the basis of a new military organization. The first two classes provided the cavalry; the third had to serve as heavy infantry; the fourth served either as light infantry without armor or in the fleet, for which they probably received wages.

A completely new element is thus introduced into the constitution: private ownership. According to the size of their property in land, the rights and duties of the citizens of the state are now assessed, and in the same degree to which the classes based on property gain influence, the old groups of blood relationship lose it; the gentile constitution had suffered a new defeat.

However, the assessment of political rights on a property basis was not an institution indispensable to the existence of the state. In spite of the great part it has played in the constitutional history of states, very many states, and precisely those most highly developed, have not required it. In Athens also its role was only temporary; from the time of Aristides all offices were open to every citizen.

During the next eighty years Athenian society gradually shaped the course along which it developed in the following centuries. Usury on the security of mortgaged land, which had been rampant in the period before Solon, had been curbed, as had also the inordinate concentration of property in land. Commerce and handicrafts, including artistic handicrafts, which were being increasingly developed on a large scale by the use of slave labor, became the main occupations. Athenians were growing more enlightened. Instead of exploiting their fellow citizens in the old brutal way, they exploited chiefly the slaves and the non-Athenian customers. Movable property, wealth in the form of money, of slaves and ships, continually increased, but it was no longer a mere means to the acquisition of landed property, as in the old slow days: it had become an end in itself. On the one hand the old power of the aristocracy now had to contend with successful competition from the new class of rich industrialists and merchants; but, on the other hand, the ground was also cut away from beneath the last remains of the old gentile constitution. The gentes, phratries, and tribes, whose members were now scattered over all Attica and thoroughly intermixed, had thus become useless as political bodies; numbers of Athenian citizens did not belong to any gens at all; they were immigrants, who had indeed acquired rights of citizenship, but had not been adopted into any of the old kinship organizations; in addition, there was the steadily increasing number of foreign immigrants who only had rights of protection.

Meanwhile, the fights went on between parties; the nobility tried to win back their former privileges and for a moment regained the upper hand, until the revolution of Cleisthenes (509 B.C.) overthrew them finally, but with them also the last remnants of the gentile constitution.

In his new constitution, Cleisthenes ignored the four old tribes founded on gentes and phratries. In their place appeared a completely new organization on the basis of division of the citizens merely according to their place of residence, such as had been already attempted in the naukrariai. Only domicile was now decisive, not membership of a kinship group. Not the people, but the territory was now divided: the inhabitants became a mere political appendage of the territory.

The whole of Attica was divided into one hundred communal districts, called "demes," each of which was self-governing. The citizens resident in each deme (demotes) elected their president (demarch) and treasurer, as well as thirty judges with jurisdiction in minor disputes. They were also given their own temple and patron divinity or hero, whose priests they elected. Supreme power in the deme was vested in the assembly of the demotes. As Morgan rightly observes, here is the prototype of the self-governing American township. The modern state, in its highest development, ends in the same unit with which the rising state in Athens began.

Ten of these units (demes) formed a tribe, which, however, is now known as a local tribe to distinguish it from the old tribe of kinship. The local tribe was not only a self -governing political body, but also a military body; it elected its phylarch, or tribal chief, who commanded the cavalry, the taxiarch commanding the infantry, and the strategos, who was in command over all the forces raised in the tribal area. It further provided five warships with their crews and commanders, and received as patron deity an Attic hero, after whom it was named. Lastly, it elected fifty councilors to the Athenian council.

At the summit was the Athenian state, governed by the council composed of the five hundred councilors elected by the ten tribes, and in the last instance by the assembly of the people, at which every Athenian citizen had the right to attend and to vote; archons and other officials managed the various departments of administration and justice. In Athens there was no supreme official with executive power.

Through this new constitution and the admission to civil rights of a very large number of protected persons, partly immigrants, partly freed slaves, the organs of the gentile constitution were forced out of public affairs; they sank to the level of private associations and religious bodies. But the moral influence of the old gentile period and its traditional ways of thought were still handed down for a long time to come, and only died out gradually. We find evidence of this in another state institution.

We saw that an essential characteristic of the state is the existence of a public force differentiated from the mass of the people. At this time, Athens still had only a people's army and a fleet provided directly by the people; army and fleet gave protection against external enemies and kept in check the slaves, who already formed the great majority of the population. In relation to the citizens, the public power at first existed only in the form of the police force, which is as old as the state itself; for which reason the naive French of the eighteenth century did not speak of civilized peoples, but of policed peoples (nations policees). The Athenians then instituted a police force simultaneously with their state, a veritable gendarmerie of bowmen, foot and mounted Landidger (the country's hunters) as they call them in South Germany and Switzerland. But this gendarmerie consisted of slaves. The free Athenian considered police duty so degrading that he would rather be arrested by an armed slave than himself have any hand in such despicable work. That was still the old gentile spirit. The state could not exist without police, but the state was still young and could not yet inspire enough moral respect to make honorable an occupation which, to the older members of the gens, necessarily appeared infamous.

Now complete in its main features, the state was perfectly adapted to the new social conditions of the Athenians, as is shown by the rapid growth of wealth, commerce, and industry. The class opposition on which the social and political institutions rested was no longer that of nobility and common people, but of slaves and free men, of protected persons and citizens. At the time of their greatest prosperity, the entire free-citizen population of Athens, women and children included, numbered about ninety thousand; besides them there were three hundred and sixty-five thousand slaves of both sexes and forty-five thousand protected persons - aliens and freedmen.

There were therefore at least eighteen slaves and more than two protected persons to every adult male citizen. The reason for the large number of slaves was that many of them worked together in manufactories, in large rooms, under overseers. But with the development of commerce and industry wealth was accumulated and concentrated in a few hands, and the mass of the free citizens were impoverished. Their only alternatives were to compete against slave labor with their own labor as handicraftsman, which was considered base and vulgar and also offered very little prospect of success, or to become social scrap. Necessarily, in the circumstances, they did the latter, and, as they formed the majority, they thereby brought about the downfall of the whole Athenian state. The downfall of Athens was not caused by democracy, as the European lickspittle historians assert to flatter their princes, but by slavery, which banned the labor of free citizens.

The rise of the state among the Athenians is a particularly typical example of the formation of a state; first, the process takes place in a pure form, without any interference through use of violent force, either from without or from within (the usurpation by Pisistratus left no trace of its short duration); second, it shows a very highly developed form of state, the democratic republic, arising directly out of gentile society; and lastly we are sufficiently acquainted with all the essential details.

Chapter VI: The Gens and the State in Rome

According to the legendary account of the foundation of Rome, the first settlement was established by a number of Latin gentes (one hundred, says the legend), who were united in a tribe; these were soon joined by a Sabellian tribe, also said to have numbered a hundred gentes, and lastly by a third tribe of mixed elements, again said to have been composed of a hundred gentes. The whole account reveals at the first glance that very little was still primitive here except the gens, and that even it was in some cases only an offshoot from a mother gens still existing in its original home. The tribes clearly bear the mark of their artificial composition, even though they are generally composed out of related elements and after the pattern of the old tribe, which was not made but grew; it is, however, not an impossibility that the core of each of the three tribes was a genuine old tribe. The intermediate group, the phratry, consisted of ten gentes and was called a curia; there were therefore thirty curiae.

The Roman gens is recognized to be the same institution as the Greek gens; and since the Greek gens is a further development of the social unit whose original form is found among the American Indians, this, of course, holds true of the Roman gens also. Here therefore we can be more brief.

The Roman gens, at least in the earliest times of Rome, had the following constitution:

1. Mutual right of inheritance among gentile members; the property remained within the gens. Since father-right already prevailed in the Roman gens as in the Greek, descendants in the female line were excluded. According to the Law of the Twelve Tables, the oldest written Roman law known to us, the children, as natural heirs, had the first title to the estate; in default of children, then the agnates (descendants in the male line); in default of agnates, the gentiles. In all cases the property remained within the gens. Here we see gentile custom gradually being penetrated by the new legal provisions springing from increased wealth and monogamy: the original equal right of inheritance of all members of the gens is first restricted in practice to the agnates-probably very early, as already mentioned — finally, to the children and their issue in the male line; in the Twelve Tables this appears, of course, in the reverse order.

2. Possession of a common burial place. On their immigration to Rome from Regilli, the patrician gens of the Claudii received a piece of land for their own use and also a common burial place in the town. Even in the time of Augustus, the head of Varus, who had fallen in the battle of the Teutoburg Forest, was brought to Rome and interred in the gentilitius tumulusi the gens (Quinctilia) therefore still had its own burial mound.

3. Common religious rites. These, the sacra gentilitia, are well known.

4. Obligation not to marry within the gens. This seems never to have become written law in Rome, but the custom persisted. Of all the countless Roman married couples whose names have been preserved, there is not one where husband and wife have the same gentile name. The law of inheritance also proves the observance of this rule. The woman loses her agnatic rights on marriage and leaves her gens; neither she nor her children can inherit from her father or his brothers, because otherwise the inheritance would be lost to the father's gens. There is no sense in this rule unless a woman may not marry a member of her own gens.

5. Common land. In primitive times the gens had always owned common land, ever since the tribal land began to be divided up. Among the Latin tribes, we find the land partly in the possession of the tribe, partly of the gens, and partly of the households, which at that time can hardly have been single families. Romulus is said to have made the first allotments of land to individuals, about two and one-half acres (two jugera) to a person. But later we still find land owned by the gentes, to say nothing of the state land, round which the whole internal history of the republic centers.

6. Obligation of mutual protection and help among members of the gens. Only vestiges remain in written history; from the very start the Roman state made its superior power so manifest that the right of protection against injury passed into its hands. When Appius Claudius was arrested, the whole of his gens, even those who were his personal enemies, put on mourning. At the time of the second Punic war the gentes joined together to ransom their members who had been taken prisoner; the senate prohibited them from doing so.

7. Right to bear the gentile name. Persisted till the time of the emperors; freedmen were allowed to use the gentile name of their former master, but without gentile rights.

8. Right to adopt strangers into the gens. This was done through adoption into a family (as among the Indians), which carried with it acceptance into the gens.

9. The right to elect the chief and to depose him is nowhere mentioned. But since in the earliest days of Rome all offices were filled by election or nomination, from the elected king downwards, and since the priests of the curiae were also elected by the curiae themselves, we may assume the same procedure for the presidents (Incises) of the gentes however firmly established the election from one and the same family within the gens may have already become.

Such were the rights of a Roman gens. Apart from the already completed transition to father-right, they are the perfect counterpart of the rights and duties in an Iroquois gens; here again "the Iroquois shows through unmistakably" (p. 90).

The confusion that still exists today, even among our leading historians, on the subject of the Roman gens, may be illustrated by one example. In his paper on Roman family names in the period of the Republic and of Augustus (*Romische Forschungen*, Berlin, 1864, Vol. I, pp. 8-11) Mommsen writes:

"The gentile name belongs to all the male members of the gens, excluding, of course, the slaves, but including adopted and protected persons; it belongs also to the women.... The tribe (as Mommsen here translates gens) is... a communal entity, derived from common lineage (real, supposed or even pretended) and united by communal festivities, burial rites and laws of inheritance; to it all personally free individuals, and therefore all women also, may and must belong. But it is difficult to determine what gentile name was borne by married women. So long as the woman may only marry a member of her own gens, this problem does not arise; and there is evidence that for a long period it was more difficult for women to marry outside than inside the gens; for instance, so late as the sixth century B.C. the right of gentis enuptio (marriage outside the gens) was a personal privilege, conceded as a reward.... But when such marriages outside the tribe took place, the wife, in earliest times, must thereby have gone over to her husband's tribe. Nothing is more certain than that the woman, in the old religious marriage, enters completely into the legal and sacramental bonds of her husband's community and leaves her own. Everyone knows that the married woman forfeits the right of inheritance and bequest in relation to members of her own gens but shares rights of inheritance with her husband and children and the members of their gens. And if she is adopted by her husband and taken into his family, how can she remain apart from his gens?"

Mommsen therefore maintains that the Roman women who belonged to a gens had originally been permitted to marry only within the gens, that the gens had therefore been endogamous, not exogamous. This view, which is in contradiction to all the evidence from other peoples, rests chiefly, if not exclusively, on one much disputed passage from Livy (Book XXXIX, Ch. 19), according to which the senate in the year 568 after the foundation of the city, or 186 B.C., decreed: *"Uti Feceniae Hispalae datio deminutio gentis enuptio tutoris optio item esset, quasi ei vir testaments dedisset; utique ei ingenuo nubere liceret, neu quid ei qui eam duxisset ob id fraudi ignominiave essee"* — that Fecenia Hispala shall have the right to dispose of her property, to decrease it, to marry outside the gens, and to choose for herself a guardian, exactly as if her (deceased) husband had conferred this right on her by testament; that she may marry a freeman, and that the man who takes her to wife shall not be considered to have committed a wrongful or shameful act thereby.

Without a doubt, Fecenia, a freedwoman, is here granted the right to marry outside the gens. And equally without a doubt the husband possessed the right, according to this passage, to bequeath to his wife by will the right to marry outside the gens after his death. But outside which gens?

If the woman had to marry within her gens, as Mommsen assumes, she remained within this gens also after her marriage. But in the first place the endogamous character of the gens which is here asserted is precisely what has to be proved. And, secondly, if the wife had to marry within the gens, then, of course, so had the man, for otherwise he could not get a wife. So we reach the position that the man could bequeath to his wife by will a right which he himself, and for himself, did not possess; we arrive at a legal absurdity. Mommsen also feels this, and hence makes the assumption: "For a lawful marriage outside the gens, it was probably necessary to have the consent, not only of the chief, but of all members of the gens." That is a very bold assumption in the first place, and, secondly, it contradicts the clear wording of the passage. The senate grants her this right in the place of her husband; it grants her expressly neither more nor less than her husband could have granted her, but what it grants her is an absolute right, conditional upon no other restriction. Thus it is provided that if she makes use of this right, her new husband also shall not suffer any disability. The senate even directs the present and future consuls and praetors to see to it that no injurious consequences to her follow. Mommsen's assumption therefore seems to be completely inadmissible.

Or assume that the woman married a man from another gens, but herself remained in the gens into which she had been born. Then, according to the above passage, the man would have had the right to allow his wife to marry outside her own gens. That is, he would have had the right to make dispositions in the affairs of a gens to which he did not even belong. The thing is so patently absurd that we need waste no more words on it.

Hence there only remains the assumption that in her first marriage the woman married a man from another gens, and thereby immediately entered the gens of her husband, which Mommsen himself actually admits to have been the practice when the woman married outside her gens. Then everything at once becomes clear. Severed from her old gens by her marriage and accepted into the gentile group of her husband, the woman occupies a peculiar position in her new gens. She is, indeed, a member of the gens, but not related by blood. By the mere manner of her acceptance as a gentile member, she is entirely excluded from the prohibition against marrying within the gens, for she has just married into it; further, she is accepted as one of the married members of the gens, and on her husband's death inherits from his property, the property of a gentile member. What is more natural than that this property should remain within the gens and that she should therefore be obliged to marry a member of her husband's gens and nobody else? And if an exception is to be made, who is so competent to give her the necessary authorization as the man who has bequeathed her this property, her first husband? At the moment when he bequeaths to her a part of his property and at the same time allows her to transfer it into another gens through marriage or in consequence of marriage, this property still belongs to him and he is therefore literally disposing of his own property. As regards the woman herself and her relation to her husband's gens, it was he who brought her into the gens by a free act of will- the marriage; hence it also seems natural that he should be the proper person to authorize her to leave this gens by a second marriage. In a word, the matter appears simple and natural as soon as we abandon the extraordinary conception of the endogamous Roman gens and regard it, with Morgan, as originally exogamous.

There still remains one last assumption which has also found adherents, and probably the most numerous. On this view, the passage only means that "freed servants (liberty) could not without special permission *e gente enubere* (marry out of the gens) or perform any of the acts, which, involving loss of rights (*capitis deminutio minima*), would have resulted in the liberta leaving the gens." (Lange, Romische Altertumer, Berlin 1856, I, 195, where Huschke is cited in connection with our passage from Livy.) If this supposition is correct, the passage then proves nothing at all about the position of free Roman women, and there can be even less question of any obligation resting on them to marry within the gens.

The expression *enuptio gentis* only occurs in this one passage and nowhere else in the whole of Latin literature; the word enubere, to marry outside, only occurs three times, also in Livy, and then not in reference to the gens. The fantastic notion that Roman women were only allowed to marry within their gens owes its existence solely to this one passage. But it cannot possibly be maintained. For either the passage refers to special restrictions for freedwomen, in which case it proves nothing about free women (ingenue,); or it applies also to free women; and then it proves, on the contrary, that the woman married as a rule outside her gens, but on her marriage entered into the gens of her husband; which contradicts Mommsen and supports Morgan.

Almost three centuries after the foundation of Rome, the gentile groups were still so strong that a patrician gens, that of the Fabii, was able to undertake an independent campaign, with the permission of the senate, against the neighboring town of Veii; three hundred and six Fabii are said to have set out and to have been killed to a man, in an ambush; according to the story, only one boy who had remained behind survived to propagate the gens.

As we have said, ten gentes formed a phratry, which among the Romans was called a curia and had more important public functions than the Greek phratry. Every curia had its own religious rites, shrines and priests; the latter, as a body, formed one of the Roman priestly colleges. Ten curiae formed a tribe, which probably, like the rest of the Latin tribes, originally had an elected president-military leader and high priest. The three tribes together formed the Roman people, the Populus Romanus.

Thus no one could belong to the Roman people unless he was a member of a gens and through it of a curia and a tribe. The first constitution of the Roman people was as follows: Public affairs were managed in the first instance by the senate, which, as Niebuhr first rightly saw, was composed of the presidents of the three hundred gentes; it was because they were the elders of the gens that they were called fathers, patres, and their body, the senate (council of the elders, from *senex*, old). Here again the custom of electing always from the same family in the gens brought into being the first hereditary nobility; these families called themselves "patricians," and claimed for themselves exclusive right of entry into the senate and tenure of all other offices. The acquiescence of the people in this claim, in course of time, and its transformation into an actual right, appear in legend as the story that Romulus conferred the patriciate and its privileges on the first senators and their descendants. The senate, like the Athenian boule, made final decisions in many matters and held preparatory discussions on those of greater importance, particularly new laws. With regard to these, the decision rested with the assembly of the people, called the *comitia curiata* (assembly of the curiae). The people assembled together, grouped in curiae, each curia probably grouped in gentes; each of the thirty curiae, had one vote in the final decision.

The assembly of the curiae accepted or rejected all laws, elected all higher officials, including the rex (so-called king), declared war (the senate, however, concluded peace), and, as supreme court, decided, on the appeal of the parties concerned, all cases involving death sentence on a Roman citizen. Lastly, besides the senate and the assembly of the people, there was the rex, who corresponded exactly to the Greek basileus and was not at all the almost absolute king which Mommsen made him out to be. He also was military leader, high priest, and president of certain courts. He had no civil authority whatever, nor any power over the life, liberty, or property of citizens, except such as derived from his disciplinary powers as military leader or his executive powers as president of a court. The office of rex was not hereditary; on the contrary, he was first elected by the assembly of the curiae, probably on the nomination of his predecessor, and then at a second meeting solemnly installed in office. That he could also be deposed is shown by the fate of Tarquinius Superbus.

Like the Greeks of the heroic age, the Romans in the age of the so-called kings lived in a military democracy founded on gentes, phratries, and tribes and developed out of them. Even if the curiae and tribes were to a certain extent artificial groups, they were formed after the genuine, primitive models of the society out of which they had arisen and by which they were still surrounded on all sides. Even if the primitive patrician nobility had already gained ground, even if the reges were endeavoring gradually to extend their power, it does not change the original, fundamental character of the constitution, and that alone matters.

Meanwhile, Rome and the Roman territory, which had been enlarged by conquest, increased in population, partly through immigration, partly through the addition of inhabitants of the subjugated, chiefly Latin, districts. All these new citizens of the state (we leave aside the question of the clients) stood outside the old gentes, curiae, and tribes, and therefore formed no part of the populus Romanus, the real Roman people. They were personally free, could own property in land, and had to pay taxes and do military service. But they could not hold any office, nor take part in the assembly of the curiae, nor share in the allotment of conquered state lands. They formed the class that was excluded from all public rights, the plebs. Owing to their continually increasing numbers, their military training and their possession of arms, they became a powerful threat to the old populus, which now rigidly barred any addition to its own ranks from outside. Further, landed property seems to have been fairly equally divided between populus and plebs, while the commercial and industrial wealth, though not as yet much developed, was probably for the most part in the hands of the plebs.

The great obscurity which envelops the completely legendary primitive history of Rome - an obscurity considerably deepened by the rationalistically pragmatical interpretations and accounts given of the subject by later authors with legalistic minds - makes it impossible to say anything definite about the time, course, or occasion of the revolution which made an end of the old gentile constitution. All that is certain is that its cause lay in the struggles between plebs and populus.

The new constitution, which was attributed to the rex Servius Tullius and followed the Greek model, particularly that of Solon, created a new assembly of the people, in which populus and plebeian without distinction were included or excluded according to whether they performed military service or not. The whole male population liable to bear arms was divided on a property basis into six classes. The lower limit in each of the five classes was: (1) 100,000 asses; (2) 75,000 asses; (3) 50,000 asses; (4) 25,000 asses; (5) 11,000 asses; according to Dureau de la Malle, the equivalent to about 14,000; 10,500; 7,000; 3,600; and 1,570 marks respectively. The sixth class, the proletarians, consisted of those with less property than the lower class and those exempt from military service and taxes. In the new popular assembly of the centuries (*comitia centuriata*) the citizens appeared in military formation, arranged by companies in their centuries of a hundred men, each century having one vote. Now the first class put eighty centuries in the field, the second twenty-two, the third twenty, the fourth twenty-two, the fifth thirty, and the sixth also on century for the sake of appearances. In addition, there was the cavalry, drawn from the wealthiest men, with eighteen centuries; total, 193; ninety-seven votes were thus required for a clear majority. But the cavalry and the first class alone had together ninety-eight votes, an therefore the majority; if they were agreed, they did not ask the others; they made their decision, and it stood.

This new assembly of the centuries now took over all political rights of the former assembly of the curiae, with the exception of a few nominal privileges. The curiae and the gentes of which they were composed were thus degraded, as in Athens, to mere private and religious associations and continued to vegetate as such for a long period while the assembly of the curiae soon became completely dormant. In order that the three old tribes of kinship should also be excluded from the state, four local tribes were instituted, each of which inhabited one quarter of the city and possessed a number of political rights.

Thus in Rome also, even before the abolition of the so-called monarchy, the old order of society based on personal ties of blood was destroyed and in its place was set up a new and complete state constitution based on territorial division and difference of wealth. Here the public power consisted of the body of citizens liable to military service, in opposition not only to the slaves, but also to those excluded from service in the army and from possession of arms, the so-called proletarians.

The banishment of the last rex, Tarquinius Superbus, who usurped real monarchic power, and the replacement of the office of rex by two military leaders (consuls) with equal powers (as among the Iroquois) was simply a further development of this new constitution. Within this new constitution, the whole history of the Roman Republic runs its course, with all the struggles between patricians and plebeians for admission to office and share in the state lands, and the final merging of the patrician nobility in the new class of the great land and money owners, who, gradually swallowing up all the land of the peasants ruined by military service, employed slave labor to cultivate the enormous estates thus formed, depopulated Italy and so threw open the door, not only to the emperors, but also to their successors, the German barbarians.

Chapter VII: The Gens among Celts and Germans

Space does not allow us to consider the gentile institutions still existing in greater or lesser degree of purity among the most various savage and barbarian peoples, nor the traces of these institutions in the ancient history of the civilized peoples of Asia. The institutions or their traces are found everywhere. A few examples will be enough. Before the gens had been recognized, the man who took the greatest pains to misunderstand it, McLennan himself, proved its existence, and in the main accurately described it, among the Kalmucks, Circassians, Samoyeds and three Indian peoples: the Warali, Magars and Munniporees. Recently it has been discovered and described by M. Kovalevsky among the Pshavs, Shevsurs, Svanets and other

Caucasian tribes. Here we will only give some short notes on the occurrence of the gens among Celts and Germans.

The oldest Celtic laws which have been preserved show the gens still fully alive: in Ireland, after being forcibly broken up by the English, it still lives today in the consciousness of the people, as an instinct at any rate; in Scotland it was still in full strength in the middle of the eighteenth century, and here again it succumbed only to the weapons, laws, and courts of the English.

The old Welsh laws, which were recorded in writing several centuries before the English conquest, at the latest in the eleventh century, still show common tillage of the soil by whole villages, even if only as an exceptional relic of a once general custom; each family had five acres for its own cultivation; a piece of land was cultivated collectively as well and the yield shared. In view of the analogy of Ireland and Scotland, it cannot be doubted that these village communities represent gentes or subdivisions of gentes, even though further examination of the Welsh laws, which I cannot undertake for lack of time (my notes date from 1869), should not provide direct proof. But what is directly proved by the Welsh sources and by the Irish is that among the Celts in the eleventh century pairing marriage had not by any means been displaced by monogamy.

In Wales a marriage only became indissoluble, or rather it only ceased to be terminable by notification, after seven years had elapsed. If the time was short of seven years by only three nights, husband and wife could separate. They then shared out their property between them; the woman divided and the man chose. The furniture was divided according to fixed and very humorous rules. If it was the man who dissolved the marriage, he had to give the woman back her dowry and some other things; if it was the woman, she received less. Of the children the man took two and the woman one, the middle child. If after the separation the woman took another husband and the first husband came to fetch her back again, she had to follow him even if she had already one foot in her new marriage bed. If, on the other hand, the man and woman had been together for seven years, they were husband and wife, even without any previous formal marriage. Chastity of girls before marriage was not at all strictly observed, nor was it demanded; the provisions in this respect are of an extremely frivolous character and not at all in keeping with bourgeois morality. If a woman committed adultery, the husband had the right to beat her (this was one of the three occasions when he was allowed to do so; otherwise he was punished), but not then to demand any other satisfaction, since "for the one offense there shall be either atonement or vengeance, but not both." The grounds on which the wife could demand divorce without losing any of her claims in the subsequent settlement were very comprehensive; if the husband had bad breath, it was enough. The money which had to be paid to the chief of the tribe or king to buy off his right of the first night (*gobr merch*, whence the medieval name, *marcheta*; French Marquette), plays a large part in the code of laws. The women had the right to vote in the assemblies of the people. When we add that the evidence shows similar conditions in Ireland; that there, also, temporary marriages were quite usual and that at the separation very favorable and exactly defined conditions were assured to the woman, including even compensation for her domestic services; that in Ireland there was a "first wife" as well as other wives, and that in the division of an inheritance no distinction was made between children born in wedlock or outside it—we then have a picture of pairing marriage in comparison with which the form of marriage observed in North America appears strict. This is not 120 surprising in the eleventh century among a people who even so late as Caesar's time were still living in group marriage.

The existence of the Irish gens (sept; the tribe was called clann, clan) is confirmed and described not only by the old legal codes, but also by the English jurists of the seventeenth century who were sent over to transform the clan lands into domains of the English crown. Until then, the land had been the common property of the clan or gens, in so far as the chieftains had not already converted it into their private domains. When a member of the gens died and a household consequently came to an end, the gentile chief (the English jurists called him *capiat cognationis*) made a new division of the whole territory among the remaining households. This must have been done, broadly speaking, according to the rules in force in Germany. Forty or fifty years ago village fields were very numerous, and even today a few of these rundales, as they are called, may still be found. The peasants of a rundale, now individual tenants on the soil that had been the common property of the gens till it was seized by the English conquerors, pay rent for their respective piece of land, but put all their shares in arable and meadowland together, which they then divide according to position and quality into Gewanne, as they are called on the Moselle, each receiving a share in each Gewann; moorland and pasture-land are used in common. Only fifty years ago new divisions were still made from time to time, sometimes annually. The field-map of such a village looks exactly like that of a German Gehoferschaft (peasant community) on the Moselle or in the Mittelwald. The gens also lives on in the "factions." The Irish peasants often divide themselves into parties based apparently on perfectly absurd or meaningless distinctions; to the English they are quite incomprehensible and seem to have no other purpose than the favorite ceremony of two factions hammering one another. They are artificial revivals, modern substitutes for the dispersed gentes, manifesting in their own peculiar manner the persistence of the inherited gentile instinct. In some districts the members of the gens still live pretty much together on the old territory; in the 'thirties the great majority of the inhabitants of County Monaghan still had only four family names, that is, they were descended from four gentes or clans.

In Scotland the decay of the gentile organization dates from the suppression of the rising of 1745. The precise function of the Scottish clan in this organization still awaits investigation; but that the clan is a gentile body is beyond doubt. In Walter Scott's novels the Highland clan lives before our eyes. It is, says Morgan:

"... an excellent type of the gens in organization and in spirit, and an extraordinary illustration of the power of the gentile life over its members.... We find in their feuds and blood revenge, in their localization by gentes, in their use of lands in common, in the fidelity of the clansman to his chief and of the members of the clan to each other, the usual and persistent features of gentile society.... Descent was in the male line, the children of the males remaining members of the clan, while the children of its female members belonged to the clans of their respective fathers."

But that formerly mother-right prevailed in Scotland is proved by the fact that, according to Bede, in the royal family of the Picts succession was in the female line. Among the Scots, as among the Welsh, a relic even of the punaluan family persisted into the Middle Ages in the form of the right of the first night, which the head of the clan or the king, as last representative of the former community of husbands, had the right to exercise with every bride, unless it was compounded for money.

That the Germans were organized in gentes until the time of the migrations is beyond all doubt. They can have occupied the territory between the Danube, Rhine, Vistula, and the northern seas only a few centuries before our era; the Cimbri and Teutons were then still in full migration, and the Suevi did not find any permanent habitation until Caesar's time. Caesar expressly states of them that they had settled in gentes and kindreds (*gentibus cognationtbusque*), and in the mouth of a Roman of the Julian gens the word gentibus has a definite meaning which cannot be argued away. The same was true of all the Germans; they seem still to have settled by gentes even in the provinces they conquered from the Romans. The code of laws of the Alemanni confirms that the people settled by kindreds (genealogiae) in the conquered territory south of the Danube; genealogia is used in exactly the same sense as Markgenossenschaft or Dorfgenossenschaft later. Kovalevsky has recently put forward the view that these genealogia- are the large household communities among which the land was divided, and from which the village community only developed later. This would then probably also apply to the fara, with which expression the Burgundians and the Lombards—that is, a Gothic and a Herminonian or High German tribe—designated nearly, if not exactly, the same thing as the genealogiae in the Alemannian code of laws. Whether it is really a gens or a household community must be settled by further research.

The records of language leave us in doubt whether all the Germans had a common expression for gens, and what that expression was. Etymologically, the Gothic kuni, Middle High German kunne, corresponds to the Greek genos and the Latin gens, and is used in the same sense. The fact that the term for woman comes from the same root—Greek gyne, Slav zena, Gothic qvino, Old Norse kona, kuna—points back to the time of mother-right. Among the Lombards and Burgundians we find, as already mentioned, the term fara, which Grimm derives from an imaginary root *fisan*, to beget. I should prefer to go back to the more obvious derivation from *faran*, to travel or wander; *fara* would then denote a section of the migrating people which remained permanently together and almost as a matter of course would be composed of relatives. In the several centuries of migration, first to the east and then to the west, the expression came to be transferred to the kinship group itself. There are, further, the Gothic sibia, Anglo-Saxon sib, Old High German sippia, sima, kindred. Old Norse only has the plural sifiar, relatives; the singular only occurs as the name of a goddess, Sif. Lastly, still another expression occurs in the Hildebrandslied, where Hildebrand asks

Hadubrand: "Who is thy father among the men of the people... or of what kin art thou?" (*eddo huilihes cnuosies du sis*). In as far as there was a common German name for the gens, it was probably the Gothic huni that was used; this is rendered probable, not only by its identity with the corresponding expression in the related languages, but also by the fact that from it is derived the word kuning, Konig (king), which originally denotes the head of a gens or of a tribe. Sibia, kindred, does not seem to call for consideration; at any rate, sifiar in Old Norse denotes not only blood relations, but also relations by marriage; thus it includes the members of at least two gentes, and hence sif itself cannot have been the term for the gens.

As among the Mexicans and Greeks, so also among the Germans, the order of battle, both the cavalry squadrons and the wedge formations of the infantry, was drawn up by gentes. Tacitus' use of the vague expression "by families and kindreds" is to be explained through the fact that in his time the gens in Rome had long ceased to be a living body.

A further passage in Tacitus is decisive. It states that the maternal uncle looks upon his nephew as his own son, and that some even regard the bond of blood between the maternal uncle and the nephew as more sacred and close than that between father and son, so that when hostages are demanded the sister's son is considered a better security than the natural son of the man whom it is desired to bind. Here we have living evidence, described as particularly characteristic of the Germans, of the matriarchal, and therefore primitive, gens. If a member of such a gens gave his own son as a pledge of his oath and the son then paid the penalty of death for his father's breach of faith, the father had to answer for that to himself. But if it was a sister's son who was sacrificed, then the most sacred law of the gens was violated. The member of the gens who was nearest of kin to the boy or youth, and more than all others was bound to protect him, was guilty of his death; either he should not have pledged him or he should have kept the agreement. Even if we had no other trace of gentile organization among the Germans, this one passage would suffice.

Still more decisive, because it comes about eight hundred years later, is a passage from the Old Norse poem of the twilight of the gods and the end of the world, the Voluspa. In this "vision of the seeress," into which Christian elements are also interwoven, as Bang and Bugge have now proved, the description of the period of universal degeneration and corruption leading up to the great catastrophe contains the following passage:

Broedhr munu berjask ok at bonum verdask, munu systrungar sifjum spilla.

"Brothers will make war upon one another and become one another's murderers, the children of sisters will break kinship." Systrungar means the son of the mother's sister, and that these sisters' sons should betray the blood-bond between them is regarded by the poet as an even greater crime than that of fratricide. The force of the climax is in the word systrungar, which emphasizes the kinship on the mother's side; if the word had been syskina-born, brothers' or sisters' children, or syskinasynir, brothers' or sisters' sons, the second line would not have been a climax to the first, but would merely have weakened the effect. Hence even in the time of the Vikings, when the Voluspa was composed, the memory of mother-right had not yet been obliterated in Scandinavia.

In the time of Tacitus, however, mother-right had already given way to father-right, at least among the Germans with whose customs he was more familiar. The children inherited from the father; if there were no children, the brothers, and the uncles on the father's and the mother's side. The fact that the mother's brother was allowed to inherit is connected with the survivals of mother-right already mentioned, and again proves how new father-right still was among the Germans at that time. Traces of mother-right are also found until late in the Middle Ages. Apparently even at that time people still did not have any great trust in fatherhood, especially in the case of serfs. When, therefore, a feudal lord demanded from a town the return of a fugitive serf, it was required—for example, in Augsburg, Basle and Kaiserslautern—that the accused person's status as serf should be sworn to by six of his nearest blood relations, and that they should all be relations on the mother's side. (Maurer, *Stadteverfassung*, I, p. 381.)

Another relic of mother-right, which was still only in process of dying out, was the respect of the Germans for the female sex, which to the Romans was almost incomprehensible. Young girls of noble family were considered the most binding hostages in treaties with the Germans. The thought that their wives and daughters might be taken captive and carried into slavery was terrible to them and more than anything else fired their courage in battle; they saw in a woman something holy and prophetic, and listened to her advice even in the most important matters. Veleda, the priestess of the Bructerians on the River Lippe, was the very soul of the whole Batavian rising in which Civilis, at the head of the Germans and Belgae, shook the foundations of Roman rule in Gaul. In the home, the woman seems to have held undisputed sway, though, together with the old people and the children, she also had to do all the work, while the man hunted, drank, or idled about. That, at least, is what Tacitus says; but as he does not say who tilled the fields, and definitely declares that the serfs only paid tribute, but did not have to render labor dues, the bulk of the adult men must have had to do what little work the cultivation of the land required. The form of marriage, as already said, was a pairing marriage which was gradually approaching monogamy. It was not yet strict monogamy, as polygamy was permitted for the leading members of the tribe. In general, strict chastity was required of the girls (in contrast to the Celts), and Tacitus also speaks with special warmth of the sacredness of the marriage tie among the Germans. Adultery by the woman is the only ground for divorce mentioned by him. But there are many gaps here in his report, and it is also only too apparent that he is holding up a mirror of virtue before the dissipated Romans. One thing is certain: if the Germans were such paragons of virtue in their forests, it only required slight contact with the outside world to bring them down to the level of the average man in the rest of Europe. Amidst the Roman world, the last trace of moral austerity disappeared far more rapidly even than the German language. For proof, it is enough to read Gregory of Tours. That in the German primeval forests there could be no such voluptuous abandonment to all the refinements of sensuality as in Rome is obvious; the superiority of the Germans to the Roman world in this respect also is sufficiently great, and there is no need to endow them with an ideal continence in things of the flesh, such as has never yet been practiced by an entire nation.

Also derived from the gentile organization is the obligation to inherit the enmities as well as the friendships of the father or the relatives; likewise the wergeld, the fine for idling or injuring, in place of blood revenge. The wergeld, which only a generation ago was regarded as a specifically German institution, has now been shown to be general among hundreds of peoples as a milder form of the blood revenge originating out of the gentile organization. We find it, for example, among the American Indians, who also regard hospitality as an obligation. Tacitus' description of hospitality as practiced among the Germans (*Germania*, Ch. XXI) is identical almost to the details with that given by Morgan of his Indians.

The endless, burning controversy as to whether the Germans of Tacitus' time had already definitely divided the land or not, and how the relevant passages are to be interpreted, now belongs to the past. No more words need be wasted in this dispute, since it has been established that among almost all peoples the cultivated land was tilled collectively by the gens, and later by communistic household communities such as were still found by Caesar among the Suevi, and that after this stage the land was allotted to individual families with periodical repartitions, which are shown to have survived as a local custom in Germany down to our day. If in the one hundred and fifty years between Caesar and Tacitus the Germans had changed from the collective cultivation of the land expressly attributed by Caesar to the Suevi (they had no divided or private fields whatever, he says) to individual cultivation with annual repartition of the land, that is surely progress enough. The transition from that stage to complete private property in land during such a short period and without any outside interference is a sheer impossibility. What I read in Tacitus is simply what he says in his own dry words: they change (or divide afresh) the cultivated land every year, and there is enough common land left over. It is the stage of agriculture and property relations in regard to the land which exactly corresponds to the gentile constitution of the Germans at that time.

I leave the preceding paragraph unchanged as it stood in the former editions. Meanwhile the question has taken another turn. Since Kovalevsky has shown (cf. pages 51-52) that the patriarchal household community was a very common, if not universal, intermediate form between the matriarchal communistic family and the modern isolated family, it is no longer a question of whether property in land is communal or private, which was the point at issue between Maurer and Waitz, but a question of the form of the communal property. There is no doubt at all that the Suevi in Caesar's time not only owned the land in common, but also cultivated it in common for the common benefit. Whether the economic unit was the gens or the household community or a communistic kinship group intermediate between the two; or whether all three groups occurred according to the conditions of the soil—these questions will be in dispute for a long time to come. Kovalevsky maintains, however, that the conditions described by Tacitus presuppose the existence, not of the mark or village community, but of the household community and that the village community only develops out of the latter much later, as a result of the increase in population.

According to this view, the settlements of the Germans in the territory of which they were already in possession at the time of the Romans, and also in the territory which they later took from the Romans, were not composed of villages but of large household communities, which included several generations, cultivated an amount of land proportionate to the number of their members, and had common use with their neighbors of the surrounding waste. The passage in Tacitus about changing the cultivated land would then have to be taken in an agronomic sense: the community cultivated a different piece of land every year, and allowed the land cultivated the previous year to lie fallow or run completely to waste; the population being scanty, there was always enough waste left over to make any disputes about land unnecessary. Only in the course of centuries, when the number of members in the household communities had increased so much that a common economy was no longer possible under the existing conditions of production did the communities dissolve. The arable and meadow lands which had hitherto been common were divided in the manner familiar to us, first temporarily and then permanently, among the single households which were now coming into being, while forest, pasture land, and water remained common.

In the case of Russia this development seems to be a proved historical fact. With regard to Germany, and, secondarily, the other Germanic countries, it cannot be denied that in many ways this view provides a better explanation of the sources and an easier solution to difficulties than that held hitherto, which takes the village community back to the time of Tacitus. On the whole, the oldest documents, such as the *Codex Laureshamensis*, can be explained much better in terms of the household community than of the village community. On the other hand, this view raises new difficulties and new questions, which have still to be solved. They can only be settled by new investigations; but I cannot deny that in the case also of Germany, Scandinavia and England there is very great probability in favor of the intermediate form of the household community.

While in Caesar's time the Germans had only just taken up or were still looking for settled abodes, in Tacitus' time they already had a full century of settled life behind them; correspondingly, the progress in the production of the necessities of life is unmistakable. They live in log-houses; their clothing is still very much that of primitive people of the forests: coarse woolen mantles, skins; for women and notable people underclothing of linen. Their food is milk, meat, wild fruits, and, as Pliny adds, oatmeal porridge (still the Celtic national food in Ireland and Scotland). Their wealth consists in cattle and horses, but of inferior breed; the cows are small, poor in build and without horns; the horses are ponies, with very little speed. Money was used rarely and in small amounts; it was exclusively Roman. They did not work gold or silver, nor did they value it. Iron was rare, and, at least, among the tribes on the Rhine and the Danube, seems to have been almost entirely imported, not mined. Runic writing (imitated from the Greek or Latin letters) was a purely secret form of writing, used only for religious magic. Human sacrifices were still offered. In short, we here see a people which had just raised itself from the middle to the upper stage of barbarism. But whereas the tribes living immediately on the Roman frontiers were hindered in the development of an independent metal and textile industry by the facility with which Roman products could be imported, such industry undoubtedly did develop in the northeast, on the Baltic. The fragments of weapons found in the Schleswig marshes—long iron sword, coat of mail, silver helmet, and so forth, together with Roman coins of the end of the second century—and the German metal objects distributed by the migrations, show quite a pronounced character of their own, even when they derive from an originally Roman model. Emigration into the civilized Roman world put an end to this native industry everywhere except in England. With what uniformity this industry arose and developed, can be seen, for example, in the bronze brooches; those found in Burgundy, Rumania and on the Sea of Azov might have come out of the same workshop as those found in England and Sweden, and are just as certainly of Germanic origin.

The constitution also corresponds to the upper stage of barbarism. According to Tacitus, there was generally a council of chiefs (principes), which decided minor matters, but prepared more important questions for decision by the assembly of the people; at the lower stage of barbarism, so far as we have knowledge of it, as among the Americans, this assembly of the people still comprises only the members of the gens, not yet of the tribe or of the confederacy of tribes. The chiefs (principes) are still sharply distinguished from the military leaders (duces) just as they are among the Iroquois; they already subsist partially on gifts of cattle, corn, etc., from the members of the tribe; as in America, they are generally elected from the same family. The transition to father-right favored, as in Greece and Rome, the gradual transformation of election into hereditary succession, and hence the rise of a noble family in each gens. This old so-called tribal nobility disappeared for the most part during the migrations or soon afterwards. The military leaders were chosen without regard to their descent, solely according to their ability. They had little power and had to rely on the force of example. Tacitus expressly states that the actual disciplinary authority in the army lay with the priests. The real power was in the hands of the assembly of the people. The king or the chief of the tribe presides; the people decide: "No" by murmurs; "Yes" by acclamation and clash of weapons. The assembly of the people is at the same time an assembly of justice; here complaints are brought forward and decided and sentences of death passed, the only capital crimes being cowardice, treason against the people, and unnatural lust. Also in the gentes and other subdivisions of the tribe all the members sit in judgment under the presidency of the chief, who, as in all the early German courts, can only have guided the proceedings and put questions; the actual verdict was always given among Germans everywhere by the whole community.

Confederacies of tribes had grown up since the time of Caesar; some of them already had kings; the supreme military commander was already aiming at the position of tyrant, as among the Greeks and Romans, and sometimes secured it. But these fortunate usurpers were not by any means absolute rulers; they were, however, already beginning to break the fetters of the gentile constitution. Whereas freed slaves usually occupied a subordinate position, since they could not belong to any gens, as favorites of the new kings they often won rank, riches and honors. The same thing happened after the conquest of the Roman Empire by these military leaders, who now became kings of great countries. Among the Franks, slaves and freedmen of the king played a leading part first at the court and then in the state; the new nobility was to a great extent descended from them.

One institution particularly favored the rise of kingship: the retinues. We have already seen among the American Indians how, side by side with the gentile constitution, private associations were formed to carry on wars independently. Among the Germans, these private associations had already become permanent. A military leader who had made himself a name gathered around him a band of young men eager for booty, whom he pledged to personal loyalty, giving the same pledge to them. The leader provided their keep, gave them gifts, and organized them on a hierarchic basis; a bodyguard and a standing troop for smaller expeditions and a regular corps of officers for operations on a larger scale. Weak as these retinues must have been, and as we in fact find them to be later—for example, under Odoacer in Italy—they were nevertheless the beginnings of the decay of the old freedom of the people and showed themselves to be such during and after the migrations. For in the first place they favored the rise of monarchic power. In the second place, as Tacitus already notes, they could only be kept together by continual wars and plundering expeditions. Plunder became an end in itself. If the leader of the retinue found nothing to do in the neighborhood, he set out with his men to other peoples where there was war and the prospect of booty. The German mercenaries who fought in great numbers under the Roman standard even against Germans were partly mobilized through these retinues. They already represent the first form of the system of Landsknechte, the shame and curse of the Germans. When the Roman Empire had been conquered, these retinues of the kings formed the second main stock, after the unfree and the Roman courtiers, from which the later nobility was drawn.

In general, then, the constitution of those German tribes which had combined into peoples was the same as had developed among the Greeks of the Heroic Age and the Romans of the so-called time of the kings: assembly of the people, council of the chiefs of the gentes, military leader, who is already striving for real monarchic power. It was the highest form of constitution which the gentile order could achieve; it was the model constitution of the upper stage of barbarism. If society passed beyond the limits within which this constitution was adequate, that meant the end of the gentile order; it was broken up and the state took its place.

Chapter VIII: The Formation of the State among Germans
According to Tacitus, the Germans were a very numerous people. Caesar gives us an approximate idea of the strength of the separate German peoples; he places the number of the Usipetans and the Tencterans who appeared on the left bank of the Rhine at 180,000, women and children included. That is about 100,000 to one people, already considerably more than, for instance, the total number of the Iroquois in their prime, when, no more than 20,000 strong, they were

the terror of the whole country from the Great Lakes to the Ohio and the Potomac. On the map, if we try to group the better known peoples settled near the Rhine according to the evidence of the reports, a single people occupies the space of a Prussian government districtthat is, about 10,000 square kilometers or 182 geographical square miles. Now, the Germania Magna of the Romans, which reached as far as the Vistula, had an area of 500,000 square kilometers in round figures. Reckoning the average number of each people at 100,000, the total population of Germania Magna would work out at 5,000,000 - a considerable figure for a barbarian group of peoples, but, compared with our conditions ten persons to the square kilometer, or about 550 to the geographical square mile - extremely low. But that by no means exhausts the number of the Germans then living. We know that all along the Carpathians and down to the south of the Danube there were German peoples descended from Gothic tribes, such as the Bastarnians, Peucinians and others, who were so numerous that Pliny classes them together as the fifth main tribe of the Germans. As early as 180 B.C. they make their appearance as mercenaries in the service of the Macedonian King Perseus, and in the first years of Augustus, still advancing, they almost reached Adrianople. If we estimate these at only 1,000,000, the probable total number of the Germans at the beginning of our era must have been at least 6,000,000.

After permanent settlements had been founded in Germany, the population must have grown with increasing rapidity; the advances in industry we mentioned are in themselves proof of this. The objects found in the Schleswig marshes date from the third century, according to the Roman coins discovered with them. At this time, therefore, there was already a developed metal and textile industry on the Baltic, brisk traffic with the Roman Empire and a certain degree of luxury among the more wealthy—all signs of denser population. But also at this time begins the general attack by the Germans along the whole line of the Rhine, the Roman wall and the Danube, from the North Sea to the Black Sea-direct proof of the continual growth and outward thrust of the population. For three centuries the fight went on, during which the whole main body of the Gothic peoples (with the exception of the Scandinavian Goths and the Burgundians) thrust south-east, forming the left wing on the long front of attack, while in the center the High Germans (Hermionians) pushed forward down the upper Danube, and on the right wing the Ischocvonians, now called Franks, advanced along the Rhine; the Ingoevonians carried out the conquest of Britain. By the end of the fifth century an exhausted and bleeding Roman Empire lay helpless before the invading Germans.

In earlier chapters we were standing at the cradle of ancient Greek and Roman civilization. Now we stand at its grave. Rome had driven the leveling plane of its world rule over all the countries of the Mediterranean basin, and that for centuries. Except when Greek offered resistance, all natural languages had been forced to yield to a debased Latin; there were no more national differences, no more Gauls, Iberians, Ligurians, Noricans; all had become Romans. Roman administration and Roman law had everywhere broken up the old kinship groups, and with them the last vestige of local and national independence. The half-baked culture of Rome provided no substitute; it expressed no nationality, only the lack of nationality. The elements of new nations were present everywhere; the Latin dialects of the various provinces were becoming increasingly differentiated; the natural boundaries which once had made Italy, Gaul, Spain, Africa independent territories, were still there and still made themselves felt. But the strength was not there to fuse these elements into new nations; there was no longer a sign anywhere of capacity for development, or power of resistance, to say nothing of creative energy. The enormous mass of humanity in the whole enormous territory was held together by one bond only: the Roman state; and the Roman state had become in the course of time their worst enemy and oppressor. The provinces had annihilated Rome; Rome itself had become a provincial town like the rest — privileged, but no longer the ruler, no longer the hub of the world empire, not even the seat of the emperors or sub-emperors, who now lived in Constantinople, Treves, Milan. The Roman state had become a huge, complicated machine, exclusively for bleeding its subjects, Taxes, state imposts and tributes of every kind pressed the mass of the people always deeper into poverty; the pressure was intensified until the exactions of governors, tax-collectors, and armies made it unbearable. That was what the Roman state had achieved with its world rule. It gave as the justification of its existence that it maintained order within the empire and protected it against the barbarians without. But its order was worse than the worst disorder, and the citizens whom it claimed to protect against the barbarians longed for the barbarians to deliver them.

Social conditions were no less desperate. Already in the last years of the republic the policy of Roman rule had been ruthlessly to exploit the provinces; the empire, far from abolishing this exploitation, had organized it. The more the empire declined, the higher rose the taxes and levies, the more shamelessly the officials robbed and extorted. The Romans had always been too occupied in ruling other nations to become proficient in trade and industry; it was only as usurers that they beat all who came before or after. What commerce had already existed and still survived was now ruined by official extortion; it struggled on only in the eastern, Greek part of the empire, which lies outside the present study. General impoverishment; decline of commerce, handicrafts and art; fall in the population; decay of the towns; relapse of agriculture to a lower level-such was the final result of Roman world rule.

Agriculture, always the decisive branch of production throughout the ancient world, was now more so than ever. In Italy, the enormous estates (latifundia) which, since the end of the republic, occupied 135 almost the whole country, had been exploited in two different ways. They had been used either as pastures, the population being displaced by sheep and cattle, which could be tended by a few slaves, or as country estates (villae), where large-scale horticulture was carried on with masses of slaves, partly as a luxury for the owner, partly for sale in the town markets. The great grazing farms had kept going and had probably even extended; the country estates and their gardens had been ruined through the impoverishment of their owners and the decay of the towns. The system of latifundia run by slave labor no longer paid; but at that time no other form of large-scale agriculture was possible. Small production had again become the only profitable form. One country estate after another was cut up into small lots, which were handed over either to tenants, who paid a fixed sum and had hereditary rights, or to *partiarii*, stewards rather than tenants, who received a sixth or even only a ninth of the year's product in return for their labor. For the most part, however, these small lots of land were given out to colon;, who paid for them a definite yearly amount, were tied to the soil and could be sold together with their lot. True, they were not slaves, but neither were they free; they could not marry free persons, and their marriages with one another were not regarded as full marriages, but, like those of slaves, as mere concubinage (*contubernium*). They were the forerunners of the medieval serfs.

The slavery of classical times had outlived itself. Whether employed on the land in large-scale agriculture or in manufacture in the towns, it no longer yielded any satisfactory return — the market for its products was no longer there. But the small-scale agriculture and the small handicraft production to which the enormous production of the empire in its prosperous days was now shrunk had no room for numbers of slaves. Only for the domestic and luxury slaves of the wealthy was there still a place in society. But though it was dying out, slavery was still common enough to make all productive labor appear to be work for slaves, unworthy of free Romans — and everybody was a free Roman now. Hence, on the one side, increasing manumissions of the superfluous slaves who were now a burden; on the other hand, a growth in some parts in the numbers of the coloni, and in other parts of the declassed freemen (like the "poor whites" in the ex-slave states of America). Christianity is completely innocent of the gradual dying out of ancient slavery; it was itself actively involved in the system for centuries under the Roman Empire, and never interfered later with slave-trading by Christians: not with the Germans in the north, or with the Venetians in the Mediterranean, or with the later trade in Negroes. Slavery no longer paid; it was for that reason it died out. But in dying it left behind its poisoned sting-the stigma attaching to the productive labor of freemen. This was the blind alley from which the Roman world had no way out: slavery was economically impossible, the labor of freemen was morally ostracized. The one could be the basic form of social production no longer; the other, not yet. Nothing could help here except a complete revolution.

Things were no better in the provinces. We have most material about Gaul. Here there was still a free small peasantry in addition to colon;. In order to be secured against oppression by officials, judges, and usurers, these peasants often placed themselves under the protection, the patronage, of a powerful person; and it was not only individuals who did so, but whole communities, so that in the fourth century the emperors frequently prohibited the practice. But what help was this protection to those who sought it? Their patron made it a condition that they should transfer to him the rights of ownership in their pieces of land, in return for which he guaranteed them the use of the land for their lifetime-a trick which the Holy Church took note of and in the ninth and tenth centuries lustily imitated, to the increase of God's glory and its own lands. At this time, it is true, about the year 475, Bishop Salvianus of Marseilles still inveighs indignantly against such theft. He relates that oppression by Roman officials and great landlords had become so heavy that many "Romans" fled into districts already occupied by the barbarians, and that the Roman citizens settled there feared nothing so much as a return to Roman rule. That parents owing to their poverty often sold their children into slavery at this time is proved by a decree prohibiting the practice.

In return for liberating the Romans from their own state, the German barbarians took from them two-thirds of all the land and divided it among themselves. The division was made according to the gentile constitution. The conquerors being relatively few in number, large tracts of land were left undivided, as the property partly of the whole people, partly of the individual tribes and gentes. Within each gens the arable and meadow land was distributed by lot in equal portions among the individual households. We do not know whether reallotments of the land were repeatedly carried out at this time, but in any event they were soon discontinued in the Roman provinces and the individual lots became alienable private property, allodium. Woods and pastures remained undivided for common use; the provisions regulating their common use, and the manner in which the divided land was to be cultivated, were settled in accordance with ancient custom and by the decision of the whole community. The longer the gens remained settled in its village and the more the Germans and the Romans gradually merged, the more the bond of union lost its character of kinship and became territorial. The gens was lost in the mark community, in which, however, traces of its origin in the kinship of its members are often enough still visible. Thus, at least in those countries where the mark community maintained itself - northern France, England, Germany and Scandinavia - the gentile constitution changed imperceptibly into a local constitution and thus became capable of incorporation into the state. But it nevertheless retained that primitive democratic character which distinguishes the whole gentile constitution, and thus even in its later enforced degeneration and up to the most recent times it kept something of the gentile constitution alive, to be a weapon in the hands of the oppressed.

This weakening of the bond of blood in the gens followed from the degeneration of the organs of kinship also in the tribe and in the entire people as a result of their conquests. As we know, rule over subjugated peoples is incompatible with the gentile constitution. Here we can see this on a large scale. The German peoples, now masters of the Roman provinces, had to organize what they had conquered. But they could neither absorb the mass of Romans into the gentile bodies nor govern them through these bodies. At the head of the Roman local governing bodies, many of which continued for the time being to function, had to be placed a substitute for the Roman state, and this substitute could only be another state. The organs of the gentile constitution had to be transformed into state organs, and that very idly, for the situation was urgent. But the immediate representative of the conquering people was their military leader. To secure the conquered territory against attack from within and without, it was necessary to strengthen his power. The moment had come to transform the military leadership into kinship: the transformation was made.

Let us take the country of the Franks. Here the victorious Salian people had come into complete possession, not only of the extensive Roman state domains, but also of the very large tracts of land which had not been distributed among the larger and smaller district and mark communities, in particular all the larger forest areas. On his transformation from a plain military chief into the real sovereign of a country, the first thing which the king of the Franks did was to transform this property of the people into crown lands, to steal it from the people and to give it, outright or in fief, to his retainers. This retinue, which originally consisted of his personal following of warriors and of the other lesser military leaders, was presently increased not only by Romans—Romanized Gauls, whose education, knowledge of writing, familiarity with the spoken Romance language of the country and the written Latin language, as well as with the country's laws, soon made them indispensable to him, but also by slaves, serfs and freedmen, who composed his court and from whom he chose his favorites. All these received their portions of the people's land, at first generally in the form of gifts, later of benefices, usually conferred, to begin with, for the king's lifetime. Thus, at the expense of the people the foundation of a new nobility was laid.

And that was not all. The wide extent of the kingdom could not be governed with the means provided by the old gentile constitution; the council of chiefs, even if it had not long since become obsolete, would have been unable to meet, and it was soon displaced by the permanent retinue of the king; the old assembly of the people continued to exist in name, but it also increasingly became a mere assembly of military leaders subordinate to the king, and of the new rising nobility. By the incessant civil wars and wars of conquest (the latter were particularly frequent under Charlemagne), the free land-owning peasants, the mass of the Frankish people, were reduced to the same state of exhaustion and penury as the Roman peasants in the last years of the Republic. Though they had originally constituted the whole army and still remained its backbone after the conquest of France, by the beginning of the ninth century they were so impoverished that hardly one man in five could go to the wars. The army of free peasants raised directly by the king was replaced by an army composed of the serving-men of the new nobles, including bondsmen, descendants of men who in earlier times had known no master save the king and still earlier no master at all, not even a king. The internal wars under Charlemagne's successors, the weakness of the authority of the crown, and the corresponding excesses of the nobles (including the counts instituted by Charlemagne, who were now striving to make their office hereditary), had already brought ruin on the Frankish peasantry, and the ruin was finally completed by the invasions of the Norsemen. Fifty years after the death of Charlemagne, the Empire of the Franks lay as defenseless at the feet of the Norsemen as the Roman Empire, four hundred years earlier, had lain at the feet of the Franks.

Not only was there the same impotence against enemies from without, but there was almost the same social order or rather disorder within. The free Frankish peasants were in a plight similar to their predecessors, the Roman coloni. Plundered, and ruined by wars, they had been forced to put themselves under the protection of the new nobles or of the Church, the crown being too weak to protect them. But they had to pay dearly for it. Like the Gallic peasants earlier, they had to transfer their rights of property in land to their protecting lord and received the land back from him in tenancies of various and changing forms, but always only in return for services and dues. Once in this position of dependence, they gradually lost their personal freedom also; after a few generations most of them were already serfs. How rapid was the disappearance of the free peasantry' is shown by Irminon's records of the monastic possessions of the Abbey of Saint Germain des Pris, at that time near, now in, Paris. On the huge holdings of this Abbey, which were scattered in the surrounding country, there lived in Charlemagne's time 2,788 households, whose members were almost without exception Franks with German names. They included 2,080 coloni, 35 lites, 220 slaves, and only eight freehold tenants! The godless practice, as Salvianus had called it, by which the protecting lord had the peasant's land transferred to himself as his own property, and only gave it back to the peasant for use during life, was now commonly employed by the Church against the peasants. The forced services now imposed with increasing frequency had had their prototype as much in the Roman angariae, compulsory labor for the state, as in the services provided by members of the German marks for bridge and road-making and other common purposes. To all appearances, therefore, after four hundred years, the mass of the people were back again where they had started.

But that only proved two things: first, that the social stratification and the distribution of property in the declining Roman Empire completely correspond to the level of agricultural and industrial production at that time, and had therefore been inevitable; secondly, that this level of production had neither risen nor fallen significantly during the following four centuries and had therefore with equal necessity again produced the same distribution of property and the same classes in the population. In the last centuries of the Roman Empire the town had lost its former supremacy over the country, and in the first centuries of German rule it had not regained it. This implies a low level of development both in agriculture and industry. This general situation necessarily produces big ruling landowners and a dependent small peasantry. How impossible it was to graft onto such a society either the Roman system of latifundia worked by slave-labor or the newer large-scale agriculture worked by forced services is proved by Charlemagne's experiments with the famous imperial country estates (*villae*). These experiments were gigantic in scope, but they left scarcely a trace. They were continued only by the monasteries, and only for them were they fruitful. But the monasteries were abnormal social bodies, founded on celibacy; they could produce exceptional results, but for that very reason necessarily continued to be exceptional themselves.

And yet progress was made during these four hundred years. Though at the end we find almost the same main classes as at the beginning, the human beings who formed these classes were different. Ancient slavery had gone, and so had the pauper freemen who despised work as only fit for slaves. Between the Roman colonus and the new bondsman had stood the free Frankish peasant. The "useless memories and aimless strife" of decadent Roman culture were dead and buried. The social classes of the ninth century had been formed, not in the rottenness of a decaying civilization, but in the birth-pangs of a new civilization. Compared with their Roman predecessors, the new breed, whether masters or servants, was a breed of men. The relation of powerful landowners and subject peasants which had meant for the ancient world the final ruin, from which there was no escape, was for them the starting-point of a new development. And, further, however unproductive these four centuries appear, one great product they did leave: the modern nationalities, the new forms and structures through which west European humanity was to make coming history. The Germans had, in fact, given Europe new life, and therefore the break-up of the states in the Germanic period ended, not in subjugation by the Norsemen and Saracens, but in the further development of the system of benefices and protection into feudalism, and in such an enormous increase of the population that scarcely two centuries later the severe blood-letting of the Crusades was borne without injury.

But what was the mysterious magic by which the Germans breathed new life into a dying Europe? Was it some miraculous power innate in the Germanic race, such as our chauvinist historians romance about? Not a bit of it. The Germans, especially at that time, were a highly gifted Aryan tribe, and in the full vigor of development. It was not, however, their specific national qualities which rejuvenated Europe, but simply their barbarism, their gentile constitution.

Their individual ability and courage, their sense of freedom, their democratic instinct which in everything of public concern felt itself concerned; in a word, all the qualities which had been lost to the Romans and were alone capable of forming new states and making new nationalities grow out of the slime of the Roman world-what else were they than the characteristics of the barbarian of the upper stage, fruits of his gentile constitution?

If they recast the ancient form of monogamy, moderated the supremacy of the man in the family, and gave the woman a higher position than the classical world had ever known, what made them capable of doing so if not their barbarism, their gentile customs, their living heritage from the time of mother-right?

If in at least three of the most important countries, Germany, northern France and England, they carried over into the feudal state a genuine piece of gentile constitution, in the form of mark communities, thus giving the oppressed class, the peasants, even under the harshest medieval serfdom, a local center of solidarity and a means of resistance such as neither the slaves of classical times nor the modern proletariat found ready to their hand - to what was this due, if not to their barbarism, their purely barbarian method of settlement in kinship groups?

Lastly: they were able to develop and make universal the milder form of servitude they had practiced in their own country, which even in the Roman Empire increasingly displaced slavery; a form of servitude which, as Fourier first stressed, gives to the bondsmen the means of their gradual liberation as a class (*"fournit aux cultivateurs des moyens d'affranchissement collectif et Progressif"*); a form of servitude which thus stands high above slavery, where the only possibility is the immediate release, without any transitional stage, of individual slaves (abolition of slavery by successful rebellion is unknown to antiquity), whereas the medieval serfs gradually won their liberation as a class. And to what do we owe this if not to their barbarism, thanks to which they had not yet reached the stage of fully developed slavery, neither the labor slavery of the classical world nor the domestic slavery of the Orient?

All the vigorous and creative life which the Germans infused into the Roman world was barbarism. Only barbarians are able to rejuvenate a world in the throes of collapsing civilization. And precisely the highest stage of barbarism, to which and in which the Germans worked their way upwards before the migrations, was the most favorable for this process. That explains everything.

Chapter IX: Barbarism and Civilization

We, have now traced the dissolution of the gentile constitution in the three great instances of the Greeks, the Romans, and the Germans. In conclusion, let us examine the general economic conditions which already undermined the gentile organization of society at the upper stage of barbarism and with the coming of civilization overthrew it completely. Here we shall need Marx's *Capital* as much as Morgan's book.

Arising in the middle stage of savagery, further developed during its upper stage, the gens reaches its most flourishing period, so far as our sources enable us to judge, during the lower stage of barbarism. We begin therefore with this stage.

Here - the American Indians must serve as our example - we find the gentile constitution fully formed. The tribe is now grouped in several gentes, generally two. With the increase in population, each of these original gentes splits up into several daughter gentes, their mother gens now appearing as the phratry. The tribe itself breaks up into several tribes, in each of which we find again, for the most part, the old gentes. The related tribes, at least in some cases, are united in a confederacy. This simple organization suffices completely for the social conditions out of which it sprang. It is nothing more than the grouping natural to those conditions, and it is capable of settling all conflicts that can arise within a society so organized. War settles external conflicts; it may end with the annihilation of the tribe, but never with its subjugation. It is the greatness, but also the limitation, of the gentile constitution that it has no place for ruler and ruled. Within the tribe there is as yet no difference between rights and duties; the question whether participation in public affairs, in blood revenge or atonement, is a right or a duty, does not exist for the Indian; it would seem to him just as absurd as the question whether it was a right or a duty to sleep, eat, or hunt. A division of the tribe or of the gens into different classes was equally impossible. And that brings us to the examination of the economic basis of these conditions.

The population is extremely sparse; it is dense only at the tribe's place of settlement, around which lie in a wide circle first the hunting grounds and then the protective belt of neutral forest, which separates the tribe from others. The division of labor is purely primitive, between the sexes only. The man fights in the wars, goes hunting and fishing, procures the raw materials of food and the tools necessary for doing so. The woman looks after the house and the preparation of food and clothing, cooks, weaves, sews. They are each master in their own sphere: the man in the forest, the woman in the house. Each is owner of the instruments which he or she makes and uses: the man of the weapons, the hunting and fishing implements, the woman of the household gear. The housekeeping is communal among several and often many families. What is made and used in common is common property - the house, the garden, the long-boat. Here therefore, and here alone, there still exists in actual fact that "property created by the owner's labor" which in civilized society is an ideal fiction of the jurists and economists, the last lying legal pretense by which modern capitalist property still bolsters itself up.

But humanity did not everywhere remain at this stage. In Asia they found animals which could be tamed and, when once tamed, bred. The wild buffalo-cow had to be hunted; the tame buffalo-cow gave a calf yearly and milk as well. A number of the most advanced tribes - the Aryans, Semites, perhaps already also the Turanians - now made their chief work first the taming of cattle, later their breeding and tending only. Pastoral tribes separated themselves from the mass of the rest of the barbarians: the first great social division of labor. The pastoral tribes produced not only more necessities of life than the other barbarians, but different ones. They possessed the advantage over them of having not only milk, milk products and greater supplies of meat, but also skins, wool, goat-hair, and spun and woven fabrics, which became more common as the amount of raw material increased. Thus for the first time regular exchange became possible. At the earlier stages only occasional exchanges can take place; particular skill in the making of weapons and tools may lead to a temporary division of labor. Thus in many places undoubted remains of workshops for the making of stone tools have been found, dating from the later Stone Age. The artists who here perfected their skill probably worked for the whole community, as each special handicraftsman still does in the gentile communities in India. In no case could exchange arise at this stage except within the tribe itself, and then only as an exceptional event. But now, with the differentiation of pastoral tribes, we find all the conditions ripe for exchange between branches of different tribes and its development into a regular established institution. Originally tribes exchanged with tribe through the respective chiefs of the gentes; but as the herds began to pass into private ownership, exchange between individuals became more common, and, finally, the only form. Now the chief article which the pastoral tribes exchanged with their neighbors was cattle; cattle became the commodity by which all other commodities were valued and which was everywhere willingly taken in exchange for them - in short, cattle acquired a money function and already at this stage did the work of money. With such necessity and speed, even at the very beginning of commodity exchange, did the need for a money commodity develop.

Horticulture, probably unknown to Asiatic barbarians of the lower stage, was being practiced by them in the middle stage at the latest, as the forerunner of agriculture. In the climate of the Turanian plateau, pastoral life is impossible without supplies of fodder for the long and severe winter. Here, therefore, it was essential that land should be put under grass and corn cultivated. The same is true of the steppes north of the Black Sea. But when once corn had been grown for the cattle, it also soon became food for men. The cultivated land still remained tribal property; at first it was allotted to the gens, later by the gens to the household communities and finally to individuals for use. The users may have had certain rights of possession, but nothing more.

Of the industrial achievements of this stage, two are particularly important. The first is the loom, the second the smelting of metal ores and the working of metals. Copper and tin and their alloy, bronze, were by far the most important. Bronze provided serviceable tools and weapons, though it could not displace stone tools; only iron could do that, and the method of obtaining iron was not yet understood. Gold and silver were beginning to be used for ornament and decoration, and must already have acquired a high value as compared with copper and bronze.

The increase of production in all branches - cattle-raising, agriculture, domestic handicrafts - gave human labor-power the capacity to produce a larger product than was necessary for its maintenance. At the same time it increased the daily amount of work to be done by each member of the gens, household community or single family. It was now desirable to bring in new labor forces. War provided them; prisoners of war were turned into slaves. With its increase of the productivity of labor, and therefore of wealth, and its extension of the field of production, the first great social division of labor was bound, in the general historical conditions prevailing, to bring slavery in its train. From the first great social division of labor arose the first great cleavage of society into two classes: masters and slaves, exploiters and exploited.

As to how and when the herds passed out of the common possession of the tribe or the gens into the ownership of individual heads of families, we know nothing at present. But in the main it must have occurred during this stage. With the herds and the other new riches, a revolution came over the family. To procure the necessities of life had always been the business of the man; he produced and owned the means of doing so. The herds were the new means of producing these necessities; the taming of the animals in the first instance and their later tending were the man's work. To him, therefore, belonged the cattle, and to him the commodities and the slaves received in exchange for cattle. All the surplus which the acquisition of the necessities of life now yielded fell to the man; the woman shared in its enjoyment, but had no part in its ownership. The "savage" warrior and hunter had been content to take second place in the house, after the woman; the "gentler" shepherd, in the arrogance of his wealth, pushed himself forward into the first place and the woman down into the second. And she could not complain. The division of labor within the family had regulated the division of property between the man and the woman. That division of labor had remained the same; and yet it now turned the previous domestic relation upside down, simply because the division of labor outside the family had changed. The same cause which had ensured to the woman her previous supremacy in the house - that her activity was confined to domestic labor - this same cause now ensured the man's supremacy in the house: the domestic labor of the woman no longer counted beside the acquisition of the necessities of life by the man; the latter was everything, the former an unimportant extra. We can already see from this that to emancipate woman and make her the equal of the man is and remains an impossibility so long as the woman is shut out from social productive labor and restricted to private domestic labor. The emancipation of woman will only be possible when woman can take part in production on a large, social scale, and domestic work no longer claims anything but an insignificant amount of her time. And only now has that become possible through modern large-scale industry, which does not merely permit of the employment of female labor over a wide range, but positively demands it, while it also tends towards ending private domestic labor by changing it more and more into a public industry.

The man now being actually supreme in the house, the last barrier to his absolute supremacy had fallen. This autocracy was confirmed and perpetuated by the overthrow of mother-right, the introduction of father-right, and the gradual transition of the pairing marriage into monogamy. But this tore a breach in the old gentile order; the single family became a power, and its rise was a menace to the gens.

The next step leads us to the upper stage of barbarism, the period when all civilized peoples have their Heroic Age: the age of the iron sword, but also of the iron plowshare and ax. Iron was now at the service of man, the last and most important of all the raw materials which played a historically revolutionary role - until the potato. Iron brought the tillage of large areas, the clearing of wide tracts of virgin forest; iron gave to the handicraftsman tools so hard and sharp that no stone, no other known metal could resist them. All this came gradually; the first iron was often even softer than bronze. Hence stone weapons only disappeared slowly; not merely in the Hildebrandslied, but even as late as Hastings in 1066, stone axes were still used for fighting. But progress could not now be stopped; it went forward with fewer checks and greater speed. The town, with its houses of stone or brick, encircled by stone walls, towers and ramparts, became the central seat of the tribe or the confederacy of tribes - an enormous architectural advance, but also a sign of growing danger and need for protection. Wealth increased rapidly, but as the wealth of individuals. The products of weaving, metal-work and the other handicrafts, which were becoming more and more differentiated, displayed growing variety and skill. In addition to corn, leguminous plants and fruit, agriculture now provided wine and oil, the preparation of which had been learned. Such manifold activities were no longer within the scope of one and the same individual; the second great division of labor took place: handicraft separated from agriculture. The continuous increase of production and simultaneously of the productivity of labor heightened the value of human labor-power. Slavery, which during the preceding period was still in its beginnings and sporadic, now becomes an essential constituent part of the social system; slaves no longer merely help with production - they are driven by dozens to work in the fields and the workshops. With the splitting up of production into the two great main branches, agriculture and handicrafts, arises production directly for exchange, commodity production; with it came commerce, not only in the interior and on the tribal boundaries, but also already overseas. All this, however, was still very undeveloped; the precious metals were beginning to be the predominant and general money commodity, but still uncoined, exchanging simply by their naked weight.

The distinction of rich and poor appears beside that of freemen and slaves - with the new division of labor, a new cleavage of society into classes. The inequalities of property among the individual heads of families break up the old communal household communities wherever they had still managed to survive, and with them the common cultivation of the soil by and for these communities. The cultivated land is allotted for use to single families, at first temporarily, later permanently. The transition to full private property is gradually accomplished, parallel with the transition of the pairing marriage into monogamy. The single family is becoming the economic unit of society.

The denser population necessitates closer consolidation both for internal and external action. The confederacy of related tribes becomes everywhere a necessity, and soon also their fusion, involving the fusion of the separate tribal territories into one territory of the nation. The military leader of the people, res, basileus, thiudans - becomes an indispensable, permanent official. The assembly of the people takes form, wherever it did not already exist. Military leader, council, assembly of the people are the organs of gentile society developed into military democracy - military, since war and organization for war have now become regular functions of national life. Their neighbors' wealth excites the greed of peoples who already see in the acquisition of wealth one of the main aims of life. They are barbarians: they think it more easy and in fact more honorable to get riches by pillage than by work. War, formerly waged only in revenge for injuries or to extend territory that had grown too small, is now waged simply for plunder and becomes a regular industry. Not without reason the bristling battlements stand menacingly about the new fortified towns; in the moat at their foot yawns the grave of the gentile constitution, and already they rear their towers into civilization. Similarly in the interior. The wars of plunder increase the power of the supreme military leader and the subordinate commanders; the customary election of their successors from the same families is gradually transformed, especially after the introduction of father-right, into a right of hereditary succession, first tolerated, then claimed, finally usurped; the foundation of the hereditary monarchy and the hereditary nobility is laid. Thus the organs of the gentile constitution gradually tear themselves loose from their roots in the people, in gens, phratry, tribe, and the whole gentile constitution changes into its opposite: from an organization of tribes for the free ordering of their own affairs it becomes an organization for the plundering and oppression of their neighbors; and correspondingly its organs change from instruments of the will of the people into independent organs for the domination and oppression of the people. That, however, would never have been possible if the greed for riches had not split the members of the gens into rich and poor, if "the property differences within one and the same gens had not transformed its unity of interest into antagonism between its members" (Marx), if the extension of slavery had not already begun to make working for a living seem fit only for slaves and more dishonorable than pillage.

We have now reached the threshold of civilization. Civilization opens with a new advance in the division of labor. At the lowest stage of barbarism men produced only directly for their own needs; any acts of exchange were isolated occurrences, the object of exchange merely some fortuitous surplus. In the middle stage of barbarism we already find among the pastoral peoples a possession in the form of cattle which, once the herd has attained a certain size, regularly produces a surplus over and above the tribe's own requirements, leading to a division of labor between pastoral peoples and backward tribes without herds, and hence to the existence of two different levels of production side by side with one another and the conditions necessary for regular exchange. The upper stage of barbarism brings us the further division of labor between agriculture and handicrafts, hence the production of a continually increasing portion of the products of labor directly for exchange, so that exchange between individual producers assumes the importance of a vital social function.

Civilization consolidates and intensifies all these existing divisions of labor, particularly by sharpening the opposition between town and country (the town may economically dominate the country, as in antiquity, or the country the town, as in the middle ages), and it adds a third division of labor, peculiar to itself and of decisive importance: it creates a class which no longer concerns itself with production, but only with the exchange of the products - the merchants. Hitherto whenever classes had begun to form, it had always been exclusively in the field of production; the persons engaged in production were separated into those who directed and those who executed, or else into large-scale and small-scale producers. Now for the first time a class appears which, without in any way participating in production, captures the direction of production as a whole and economically subjugates the producers; which makes itself into an indispensable middleman between any two producers and exploits them both. Under the pretext that they save the producers the trouble and risk of exchange, extend the sale of their products to distant markets and are therefore the most useful class of the population, a class of parasites comes into being, "genuine social ichneumons," who, as a reward for their actually very insignificant services, skim all the cream off production at home and abroad, rapidly amass enormous wealth and correspondingly social influence, and for that reason receive under civilization ever higher honors and ever greater control of production, until at last they also bring forth a product of their own - the periodical trade crises.

At our stage of development, however, the young merchants had not even begun to dream of the great destiny awaiting them. But they were growing and making themselves indispensable, which was quite sufficient. And with the formation of the merchant class came also the development of metallic money, the minted coin, a new instrument for the domination of the non-producer over the producer and his production. The commodity of commodities had been discovered, that which holds all other commodities hidden in itself, the magic power which can change at will into everything desirable and desired. The man who had it ruled the world of production - and who had more of it than anybody else? The merchant. The worship of money was safe in his hands. He took good care to make it clear that, in face of money, all commodities, and hence all producers of commodities, must prostrate themselves in adoration in the dust. He proved practically that all other forms of wealth fade into mere semblance beside this incarnation of wealth as such. Never again has the power of money shown itself in such primitive brutality and violence as during these days of its youth. After commodities had begun to sell for money, loans and advances in money came also, and with them interest and usury. No legislation of later times so utterly and ruthlessly delivers over the debtor to the usurious creditor as the legislation of ancient Athens and ancient Rome - and in both cities it arose spontaneously, as customary law, without any compulsion other than the economic.

Alongside wealth in commodities and slaves, alongside wealth in money, there now appeared wealth in land also. The individuals' rights of possession in the pieces of land originally allotted to them by gens or tribe had now become so established that the land was their hereditary property. Recently they had striven above all to secure their freedom against the rights of the gentile community over these lands, since these rights had become for them a fetter. They got rid of the fetter - but soon afterwards of their new landed property also. Full, free ownership of the land meant not only power, uncurtailed and unlimited, to possess the land; it meant also the power to alienate it. As long as the land belonged to the gens, no such power could exist. But when the new landed proprietor shook off once and for all the fetters laid upon him by the prior right of gens and tribe, he also cut the ties which had hitherto inseparably attached him to the land.

Money, invented at the same time as private property in land, showed him what that meant. Land could now become a commodity; it could be sold and pledged. Scarcely had private property in land been introduced than the mortgage was already invented (see Athens). As hetaerism and prostitution dog the heels of monogamy, so from now onwards mortgage dogs the heels of private land ownership. You asked for full, free alienable ownership of the land and now you have got it - "*tu l'as voulu*, Georges Dandin."

With trade expansion, money and usury, private property in land and mortgages, the concentration and centralization of wealth in the hands of a small class rapidly advanced, accompanied by an increasing impoverishment of the masses and an increasing mass of impoverishment. The new aristocracy of wealth, in so far as it had not been identical from the outset with the old hereditary aristocracy, pushed it permanently into the background (in Athens, in Rome, among the Germans). And simultaneous with this division of the citizens into classes according to wealth there was an enormous increase, particularly in Greece, in the number of slaves, whose forced labor was the foundation on which the superstructure of the entire society was reared.

Let us now see what had become of the gentile constitution in this social upheaval. Confronted by the new forces in whose growth it had had no share, the gentile constitution was helpless. The necessary condition for its existence was that the members of a gens or at least of a tribe were settled together in the same territory and were its sole inhabitants. That had long ceased to be the case. Every territory now had a heterogeneous population belonging to the most varied gentes and tribes; everywhere slaves, protected persons and aliens lived side by side with citizens. The settled conditions of life which had only been achieved towards the end of the middle stage of barbarism were broken up by the repeated shifting and changing of residence under the pressure of trade, alteration of occupation and changes in the ownership of the land. The members of the gentile bodies could no longer meet to look after their common concerns; only unimportant matters, like the religious festivals, were still perfunctorily attended to. In addition to the needs and interests with which the gentile bodies were intended and fitted to deal, the upheaval in productive relations and the resulting change in the social structure had given rise to new needs and interests, which were not only alien to the old gentile order, but ran directly counter to it at every point. The interests of the groups of handicraftsmen which had arisen with the division of labor, the special needs of the town as opposed to the country, called for new organs. But each of these groups was composed of people of the most diverse gentes, phratries, and tribes, and even included aliens. Such organs had therefore to be formed outside the gentile constitution, alongside of it, and hence in opposition to it. And this conflict of interests was at work within every gentile body, appearing in its most extreme form in the association of rich and poor, usurers and debtors, in the same gens and the same tribe. Further, there was the new mass of population outside the gentile bodies, which, as in Rome, was able to become a power in the land and at the same time was too numerous to be gradually absorbed into the kinship groups and tribes. In relation to this mass, the gentile bodies stood opposed as closed, privileged corporations; the primitive natural democracy had changed into a malign aristocracy. Lastly, the gentile constitution had grown out of a society which knew no internal contradictions, and it was only adapted to such a society. It possessed no means of coercion except public opinion. But here was a society which by all its economic conditions of life had been forced to split itself into freemen and slaves, into the exploiting rich and the exploited poor; a society which not only could never again reconcile these contradictions, but was compelled always to intensify them. Such a society could only exist either in the continuous open fight of these classes against one another, or else under the rule of a third power, which, apparently standing above the warring classes, suppressed their open conflict and allowed the class struggle to be fought out at most in the economic field, in so-called legal form. The gentile constitution was finished. It had been shattered by the division of labor and its result, the cleavage of society into classes. It was replaced by the state.

The three main forms in which the state arises on the ruins of the gentile constitution have been examined in detail above. Athens provides the purest, classic form; here the state springs directly and mainly out of the class oppositions which develop within gentile society itself. In Rome, gentile society becomes a closed aristocracy in the midst of the numerous plebs who stand outside it, and have duties but no rights; the victory of plebs breaks up the old constitution based on kinship, and erects on its ruins the state, into which both the gentile aristocracy and the plebs are soon completely absorbed. Lastly, in the case of the German conquerors of the Roman

Empire, the state springs directly out of the conquest of large foreign territories, which the gentile constitution provides no means of governing. But because this conquest involves neither a serious struggle with the original population nor a more advanced division of labor; because conquerors and conquered are almost on the same level of economic development, and the economic basis of society remains therefore as before - for these reasons the gentile constitution is able to survive for many centuries in the altered, territorial form of the mark constitution and even for a time to rejuvenate itself in a feebler shape in the later noble and patrician families, and indeed in peasant families, as in Ditmarschen.

The state is therefore by no means a power imposed on society from without; just as little is it "the reality of the moral idea," "the image and the reality of reason," as Hegel maintains. Rather, it is a product of society at a particular stage of development; it is the admission that this society has involved itself in insoluble self-contradiction and is cleft into irreconcilable antagonisms which it is powerless to exorcise. But in order that these antagonisms, classes with conflicting economic interests, shall not consume themselves and society in fruitless struggle, a power, apparently standing above society, has become necessary to moderate the conflict and keep it within the bounds of "order"; and this power, arisen out of society, but placing itself above it and increasingly alienating itself from it, is the state.

In contrast to the old gentile organization, the state is distinguished firstly by the grouping of its members on a territorial basis. The old gentile bodies, formed and held together by ties of blood, had, as we have seen, become inadequate largely because they presupposed that the gentile members were bound to one particular locality, whereas this had long ago ceased to be the case. The territory was still there, but the people had become mobile. The territorial division was therefore taken as the starting point and the system introduced by which citizens exercised their public rights and duties where they took up residence, without regard to gens or tribe. This organization of the citizens of the state according to domicile is common to all states. To us, therefore, this organization seems natural; but, as we have seen, hard and protracted struggles were necessary before it was able in Athens and Rome to displace the old organization founded on kinship.

The second distinguishing characteristic is the institution of a public force which is no longer immediately identical with the people's own organization of themselves as an armed power. This special public force is needed because a self-acting armed organization of the people has become impossible since their cleavage into classes. The slaves also belong to the population: as against the 365,000 slaves, the 90,000 Athenian citizens constitute only a privileged class. The people's army of the Athenian democracy confronted the slaves as an aristocratic public force, and kept them in check; but to keep the citizens in check as well, a police-force was needed, as described above. This public force exists in every state; it consists not merely of armed men, but also of material appendages, prisons and coercive institutions of all kinds, of which gentile society knew nothing. It may be very insignificant, practically negligible, in societies with still undeveloped class antagonisms and living in remote areas, as at times and in places in the United States of America. But it becomes stronger in proportion as the class antagonisms within the state become sharper and as adjoining states grow larger and more populous. It is enough to look at Europe today, where class struggle and rivalry in conquest have brought the public power to a pitch that it threatens to devour the whole of society and even the state itself.

In order to maintain this public power, contributions from the state citizens are necessary - taxes. These were completely unknown to gentile society. We know more than enough about them today. With advancing civilization, even taxes are not sufficient; the state draws drafts on the future, contracts loans, state debts. Our old Europe can tell a tale about these, too.

In possession of the public power and the right of taxation, the officials now present themselves as organs of society standing above society. The free, willing respect accorded to the organs of the gentile constitution is not enough for them, even if they could have it. Representatives of a power which estranges them from society, they have to be given prestige by means of special decrees, which invest them with a peculiar sanctity and inviolability. The lowest police officer of the civilized state has more "authority" than all the organs of gentile society put together; but the mightiest prince and the greatest statesman or general of civilization might envy the humblest of the gentile chiefs the unforced and unquestioned respect accorded to him. For the one stands in the midst of society; the other is forced to pose as something outside and above it.

As the state arose from the need to keep class antagonisms in check, but also arose in the thick of the fight between the classes, it is normally the state of the most powerful, economically ruling class, which by its means becomes also the politically ruling class, and so acquires new means of holding down and exploiting the oppressed class. The ancient state was, above all, the state of the slave-owners for holding down the slaves, just as the feudal state was the organ of the nobility for holding down the peasant serfs and bondsmen, and the modern representative state is the instrument for exploiting wage-labor by capital. Exceptional periods, however, occur when the warring classes are so nearly equal in forces that the state power, as apparent mediator, acquires for the moment a certain independence in relation to both. This applies to the absolute monarchy of the seventeenth and eighteenth centuries, which balances the nobility and the bourgeoisie against one another; and to the Bonapartism of the First and particularly of the Second French Empire, which played off the proletariat against the bourgeoisie and the bourgeoisie against the proletariat. The latest achievement in this line, in which ruler and ruled look equally comic, is the new German Empire of the Bismarckian nation; here the capitalists and the workers are balanced against one another and both of them fleeced for the benefit of the decayed Prussian cabbage Junkers.

Further, in most historical states the rights conceded to citizens are graded on a property basis, whereby it is directly admitted that the state is an organization for the protection of the possessing class against the non-possessing class. This is already the case in the Athenian and Roman property classes. Similarly in the medieval feudal state, in which the extent of political power was determined by the extent of landownership. Similarly, also, in the electoral qualifications in modern parliamentary states. This political recognition of property differences is, however, by no means essential. On the contrary, it marks a low stage in the development of the state. The highest form of the state, the democratic republic, which in our modern social conditions becomes more and more an unavoidable necessity and is the form of state in which alone the last decisive battle between proletariat and bourgeoisie can be fought out - the democratic republic no longer officially recognizes differences of property. Wealth here employs its power indirectly, but all the more surely. It does this in two ways: by plain corruption of officials, of which America is the classic example, and by an alliance between the government and the stock exchange, which is effected all the more easily the higher the state debt mounts and the more the joint-stock companies concentrate in their hands not only transport but also production itself, and themselves have their own center in the stock exchange. In addition to America, the latest French republic illustrates this strikingly, and honest little Switzerland has also given a creditable performance in this field. But that a democratic republic is not essential to this brotherly bond between government and stock exchange is proved not only by England, but also by the new German Empire, where it is difficult to say who scored most by the introduction of universal suffrage, Bismarck or the Bleichroder bank. And lastly the possessing class rules directly by means of universal suffrage. As long as the oppressed class - in our case, therefore, the proletariat - is not yet ripe for its self-liberation, so long will it, in its majority, recognize the existing order of society as the only possible one and remain politically the tall of the capitalist class, its extreme left wing. But in the measure in which it matures towards its self-emancipation, in the same measure it constitutes itself as its own party and votes for its own representatives, not those of the capitalists. Universal suffrage is thus the gauge of the maturity of the working class. It cannot and never will be anything more in the modern state; but that is enough. On the day when the thermometer of universal suffrage shows boiling-point among the workers, they as well as the capitalists will know where they stand.

The state, therefore, has not existed from all eternity. There have been societies which have managed without it, which had no notion of the state or state power. At a definite stage of economic development, which necessarily involved the cleavage of society into classes, the state became a necessity because of this cleavage. We are now rapidly approaching a stage in the development of production at which the existence of these classes has not only ceased to be a necessity, but becomes a positive hindrance to production. They will fall as inevitably as they once arose. The state inevitably falls with them. The society which organizes production anew on the basis of free and equal association of the producers will put the whole state machinery where it will then belong - into the museum of antiquities, next to the spinning wheel and the bronze ax.

Civilization is, therefore, according to the above analysis, the stage of development in society at which the division of labor, the exchange between individuals arising from it, and the commodity production which combines them both, come to their full growth and revolutionizes the whole of previous society.

At all earlier stages of society production was essentially collective, just as consumption proceeded by direct distribution of the products within larger or smaller communistic communities. This collective production was very limited; but inherent in it was the producers' control over their process of production and their product. They knew what became of their product: they consumed it; it did not leave their hands. And so long as production remains on this basis, it cannot grow above the heads of the producers nor raise up incorporeal alien powers against them, as in civilization is always and inevitably the case.

But the division of labor slowly insinuates itself into this process of production. It undermines the collectivity of production and appropriation, elevates appropriation by individuals into the general rule, and thus creates exchange between individuals - how it does so, we have examined above. Gradually commodity production becomes the dominating form.

With commodity production, production no longer for use by the producers but for exchange, the products necessarily change hands. In exchanging his product, the producer surrenders it; he no longer knows what becomes of it. When money, and with money the merchant, steps in as intermediary between the producers, the process of exchange becomes still more complicated, the final fate of the products still more uncertain. The merchants are numerous, and none of them knows what the other is doing. The commodities already pass not only from hand to hand; they also pass from market to market; the producers have lost control over the total production within their own spheres, and the merchants have not gained it. Products and production become subjects of chance.

But chance is only the one pole of a relation whose other pole is named "necessity." In the world of nature, where chance also seems to rule, we have long since demonstrated in each separate field the inner necessity and law asserting itself in this chance. But what is true of the natural world is true also of society. The more a social activity, a series of social processes, becomes too powerful for men's conscious control and grows above their heads, and the more it appears a matter of pure chance, then all the more surely within this chance the laws peculiar to it and inherent in it assert themselves as if by natural necessity. Such laws also govern the chances of commodity production and exchange. To the individuals producing or exchanging, they appear as alien, at first often unrecognized, powers, whose nature Must first be laboriously investigated and established. These economic laws of commodity production are modified with the various stages of this form of production; but in general the whole period of civilization is dominated by them. And still to this day the product rules the producer; still to this day the total production of society is regulated, not by a jointly devised plan, but by blind laws, which manifest themselves with elemental violence, in the final instance in the storms of the periodical trade crises.

We saw above how at a fairly early stage in the development of production, human labor-power obtains the capacity of producing a considerably greater product than is required for the maintenance of the producers, and how this stage of development was in the main the same as that in which division of labor and exchange between individuals arise. It was not long then before the great "truth" was discovered that man also can be a commodity; that human energy can be exchanged and put to use by making a man into a slave. Hardly had men begun to exchange than already they themselves were being exchanged. The active became the passive, whether the men liked it or not.

With slavery, which attained its fullest development under civilization, came the first great cleavage of society into an exploiting and an exploited class. This cleavage persisted during the whole civilized period. Slavery is the first form of exploitation, the form peculiar to the ancient world; it is succeeded by serfdom in the middle ages, and wage-labor in the more recent period. These are the three great forms of servitude, characteristic of the three great epochs of civilization; open, and in recent times disguised, slavery always accompanies them.

The stage of commodity production with which civilization begins is distinguished economically by the introduction of (1) metal money, and with it money capital, interest and usury; (2) merchants, as the class of intermediaries between the producers; (3) private ownership of land, and the mortgage system; (4) slave labor as the dominant form of production The form of family corresponding to civilization and coming to definite supremacy with it is monogamy, the domination of the man over the woman, and the single family as the economic unit of society. The central link in civilized society is the state, which in all typical periods is without exception the state of the ruling class, and in all cases continues to be essentially a machine for holding down the oppressed, exploited class. Also characteristic of civilization is the establishment of a permanent opposition between town and country as basis of the whole social division of labor; and, further, the introduction of wills, whereby the owner of property is still able to dispose over it even when he is dead. This institution, which is a direct affront to the old gentile constitution, was unknown in Athens until the time of Solon; in Rome it was introduced early, though we do not know the date; among the Germans it was the clerics who introduced it, in order that there might be nothing to stop the pious German from leaving his legacy to the Church.

With this as its basic constitution, civilization achieved things of which gentile society was not even remotely capable. But it achieved them by setting in motion the lowest instincts and passions in man and developing them at the expense of all his other abilities. From its first day to this, sheer greed was the driving spirit of civilization; wealth and again wealth and once more wealth, wealth, not of society, but of the single scurvy individual - here was its one and final aim. If at the same time the progressive development of science and a repeated flowering of supreme art dropped into its lap, it was only because without them modern wealth could not have completely realized its achievements.

Since civilization is founded on the exploitation of one class by another class, its whole development proceeds in a constant contradiction. Every step forward in production is at the same time a step backwards in the position of the oppressed class, that is, of the great majority. Whatever benefits some necessarily injures the others; every fresh emancipation of one class is necessarily a new oppression for another class. The most striking proof of this is provided by the introduction of machinery, the effects of which are now known to the whole world. And if among the barbarians, as we saw, the distinction between rights and duties could hardly be drawn, civilization makes the difference and antagonism between them clear even to the dullest intelligence by giving one class practically all the rights and the other class practically all the duties.

But that should not be: what is good for the ruling class must also be good for the whole of society, with which the ruling-class identifies itself. Therefore the more civilization advances, the more it is compelled to cover the evils it necessarily creates with the cloak of love and charity, to palliate them or to deny them - in short, to introduce a conventional hypocrisy which was unknown to earlier forms of society and even to the first stages of civilization, and which culminates in the pronouncement: the exploitation of the oppressed class is carried on by the exploiting class simply and solely in the interests of the exploited class itself; and if the exploited class cannot see it and even grows rebellious, that is the basest ingratitude to its benefactors, the exploiters.

And now, in conclusion, Morgan's judgment of civilization:

"Since the advent of civilization, the outgrowth of property has been so immense, its forms so diversified, its uses so expanding and its management so intelligent in the interests of its owners, that it has become, on the part of the people, an unmanageable power. The human mind stands bewildered in the presence of its own creation. The time will come, nevertheless, when human intelligence will rise to the mastery over property, and define the relations of the state to the property it protects, as well as the obligations and the limits of the rights of its owners. The interests of society are paramount to individual interests, and the two must be brought into just and harmonious relations. A mere property career is not the final destiny of mankind, if progress is to be the law of the future as it has been of the past. The time which has passed away since civilization began is but a fragment of the past duration of man's existence; and but a fragment of the ages yet to come. The dissolution of society bids fair to become the termination of a career of which property is the end and aim; because such a career contains the elements of self-destruction. Democracy in government, brotherhood in society, equality in rights and privileges, and universal education, foreshadow the next higher plane of society to which experience, intelligence and knowledge are steadily tending. It will be a revival, in a higher form, of the liberty, equality and fraternity of the ancient gentes."

Appendix. A Recently Discovered Case of Group Marriage
1892 From *Die Neue Zeit* Vol. XI, No. I, pp. 373-75 Since it has recently become fashionable among certain rationalistic ethnographers to deny the existence of group marriage, the following report is of interest; I

translate it from the *Russkiye Vyedomosti*, Moscow, October 14, 1892 (Old Style). Not only group marriage, i.e., the right of mutual sexual intercourse between a number of men and a number of women, is expressly affirmed to be in full force, but a form of group marriage which closely follows the punaluan marriage of the Hawaiians, the most developed and classic phase of group marriage. While the typical punaluan family consists of a number of brothers (own and collateral), who are married to a number of own and collateral sisters, we here find on the island of Sakhalin that a man is married to all the wives of his brothers and to all the sisters of his wife, which means, seen from the woman's side, that his wife may freely practice sexual intercourse with the brothers of her husband and the husbands of her sisters. It therefore differs from the typical form of punaluan marriage only in the fact that the brothers of the husband and the husbands of the sisters are not necessarily the same persons.

It should further be observed that this report again confirms what I said in *The Origin of the Family*, 4th edition, pp. 28-29: that group marriage does not look at all like what our brother-obsessed philistine imagines; that the partners in group marriage do not lead in public the same kind of lascivious life as he practices in secret, but that this form of marriage, at least in the instances still known to occur today, differs in practice from a loose pairing marriage or from polygamy only in the fact that custom permits sexual intercourse in a number of cases where otherwise it would be severely punished. That the actual exercise of these rights is gradually dying out only proves that this form of marriage is itself destined to die out, which is further confirmed by its infrequency.

The whole description, moreover, is interesting because it again demonstrates the similarity, even the identity in their main characteristics, of the social institutions of primitive peoples at approximately the same stage of development. Most of what the report states about these Mongoloids on the island of Sakhalin also holds for the Dravidian tribes of India, the South Sea Islanders at the time of their discovery, and the American Indians. The report runs:

"At the session of October 10 (Old Style; October 22, New Style) of the Anthropological Section of the Society of the Friends of Natural Science, N. A. Yanchuk read an interesting communication from Mr. Sternberg on the Gilyaks, a little-studied tribe on the island of Sakhalin, who are at the cultural level of savagery. The Gilyaks are acquainted neither with agriculture nor with pottery; they procure their food chiefly by hunting and fishing; they warm water in wooden vessels by throwing in heated stones, etc. Of particular interest are their institutions relating to the family and to the gens. The Gilyak addresses as father, not only his own natural father, but also all the brothers of his father; all the wives of these brothers, as well as all the sisters of his mother, he addresses as his mothers; the children of all these 'fathers' and 'mothers' he addresses as his brothers and sisters. This system of address also exists, as is well known, among the Iroquois and other Indian tribes of North America, as also among some tribes of India. But whereas in these cases it has long since ceased to correspond to the actual conditions, among the Gilyaks it serves to designate a state still valid today. To this day every Gilyak has the rights of a husband in regard to the wives of his brothers and to the sisters of his wife; at any rate, the exercise of these rights is not regarded as impermissible. These survivals of group marriage on the basis of the gens are reminiscent of the well-known punaluan marriage, which still existed in the Sandwich Islands in the first half of this century. Family and gens relations of this type form the basis of the whole gentile order and social constitution of the Gilyaks.

"The gens of a Gilyak consists of all-nearer and more remote, real and nominal-brothers of his father, of their fathers and mothers of the children of his brothers, and of his own children.

One can readily understand that a gens so constituted may comprise an enormous number of people. Life within the gens proceeds according to the following principles. Marriage within the gens is unconditionally prohibited. When a Gilyak dies, his wife passes by decision of the gens to one of his brothers, own or nominal. The gens provides for the maintenance of all of its members who are unable to work. 'We have no poor,' said a Gilyak to the writer. 'Whoever is in need, is fed by the khal (gens).' The members of the gens are further united by common sacrificial ceremonies and festivals, a common burial place, etc.

"The gens guarantees the life and security of its members against attacks by non-gentiles; the means of repression used is blood-revenge, though under Russian rule the practice has very much declined. Women are completely excepted from gentile blood-revenge. In some very rare cases the gens adopts members of other gentes. It is a general rule that the property of a deceased member may not pass out of the gens; in this respect the famous provision of the Twelve Tables holds literally among the Gilyaks: *si suos heredes non habet, gentiles familiam habento* — if he has no heirs of his own, the members of the gens shall inherit. No important event takes place in the life of a Gilyak without participation by the gens. Not very long ago, about one or two generations, the oldest gentile member was the head of the community, the starosta of the gens; today the functions of the chief elder of the gens are restricted almost solely to presiding over religious ceremonies. The gentes are often dispersed among widely distant places, but even when separated the members of a gens still remember one another and continue to give one another hospitality, and to provide mutual assistance and protection, etc. Except under the most extreme necessity, the Gilyak never leaves the fellow-members of his gens or the graves of his gens. Gentile society has impressed a very definite stamp on the whole mental life of the Gilyaks, on their character, their customs and institutions. The habit of common discussion and decision on all matters, the necessity of continually taking an active part in all questions affecting the members of the gens, the solidarity of blood-revenge, the fact of being compelled and accustomed to live together with ten or more like himself in great tents (yurtas), and to be, in short, always with other people-all this has given the Gilyak a sociable and open character. The Gilyak is extraordinarily hospitable; he loves to entertain guests and to come himself as a guest. This admirable habit of hospitality is especially prominent in times of distress. In a bad year, when a Gilyak has nothing for himself or for his dogs to eat, he does not stretch out his hand for alms, but confidently seeks hospitality, and is fed, often for a considerable time.

"Among the Gilyaks of Sakhalin crimes from motives of personal gain practically never occur. The Gilyak keeps his valuables in a storehouse, which is never locked. He has such a keen sense of shame that if he is convicted of a disgraceful act, he immediately goes into the forest and hangs himself. Murder is very rare, and is hardly ever committed except in anger, never from intentions of gain. In his dealings with other people, the Gilyak shows himself honest, reliable, and conscientious.

"Despite their long subjection to the Manchurians, now become Chinese, and despite the corrupting influence of the settlement of the Amur district, the Gilyaks still preserve in their moral character many of the virtues of a primitive tribe. But the fate awaiting their social order cannot be averted. One or two more generations, and the Gilyaks on the mainland will have been completely Russianized, and together with the benefits of culture they will also acquire its defects. The Gilyaks on the island of Sakhalin, being more or less remote from the centers of Russian settlement, have some prospect of preserving their way of life unspoiled rather longer. But among them, too, the influence of their Russian neighbors is beginning to make itself felt. The Gilyaks come into the villages to trade, they go to Nikolaievsk to look for work; and every Gilyak who returns from such work to his home brings with him the same atmosphere which the Russian worker takes back from the town into his village. And at the same time, working in the town, with its chances and changes of fortune, destroys more and more that primitive equality which is such a prominent feature of the artlessly simple economic life of these peoples.

"Mr. Sternberg's article, which also contains information about their religious views and customs and their legal institutions, will appear unabridged in the *Etnografitcheskoye Obozrenic* (Ethnographical Review).